The Pregnancy Herbal

The Pregnancy Herbal

Holistic Remedies,

Nutritional Therapies,

and Soothing Treatments

from Nature's Pharmacy

for the Mother-to-Be

Jaqulene Harper-Roth

 THREE RIVERS PRESS
NEW YORK

For Zak, Josh–Posh, and Tamara, my family and my inspiration.

Copyright © 2001 by Jaqulene Annha Harper-Roth

Published by Three Rivers Press, New York, New York. Member of the Crown Publishing Group.

Random House, Inc. New York, Toronto, London, Sydney, Auckland
www.randomhouse.com

THREE RIVERS PRESS is a registered trademark and the Three Rivers Press colophon is a trademark of Random House, Inc.

Printed in the United States of America

Design by Cynthia Dunne

LIBRARY OF CONGRESS CATALOGING-IN-PUBLICATION DATA

Harper-Roth, Jaqulene.
    The pregnancy herbal : holistic remedies, nutritional therapies, and soothing treatments from nature's pharmacy for the mother-to-be / Jaqulene Harper-Roth.—1st ed.
    Includes bibliographical references and index.
    1. Pregnancy. 2. Herbs—Therapeutic use.
3. Pregnancy—Nutritional aspects. 4. Infants—Care.
I. Title.
RG525 .H267 2001
618.2'4—dc21   00-063281

ISBN 0-609-80437-5

10 9 8 7 6 5 4 3 2 1

First Edition

Acknowledgments

Neither I—nor this book—would be here today if it weren't for the following:

My mom, who always gave me love, encouragement, and nurturing.

Stefanie and Candice, who brought culture, laughter, and fun times to my children, especially when Mom was distracted with writing (see, kids, I didn't fall into the computer!) and being a working mom at home.

Gustavo, who with his outstanding computer skills saved more than a few files from being erased during my crash course of computer know-how.

My three wee tots, who helped lay the foundations for this book (thanks for not fussing—too much—with the recipes and remedies).

Kathy Sigmon, who taught me to be kind and patient with my healing body. I haven't quite reclaimed my pre-motherhood figure, but I have learned to respect and love all the physical changes that my body performed in giving me my young family.

Gil, and our cats, who helped sustain my sanity.

My agent, Noah Lukeman.

Three Rivers Press, who took a chance with my ideas: a very special thank-you to Carrie Thornton, Deborah Kops, and Dave Stern.

And to all the natural herbalists and nutritionists, who over the decades have written down a wealth of information: Thanks for showing me an avenue to experience and adapt, living within those natural laws, throughout my pregnancies and growth into motherhood.

Contents

The introduction discusses the kinds of ingredients you'll need to have on hand and the different types of preparations you can make at home, both remedies and pampering treatments.

Chapter 1 explains the physical and emotional transitions you'll go through during your pregnancy. This section provides simple herbal remedies for the most common discomforts associated with pregnancy, as well as preventative treatments for those ailments.

Chapter 2 explores the benefits of herbal nutrition. The chapter outlines a natural diet for your pregnancy full of active, easily assimilated digestive enzymes, vitamins, minerals, and essential-for-your-skin fatty acids. You will learn about the influence of maternal diet on your baby, and how birth marks, beauty spots, and other newborn physical features are determined. In here, you'll also find dozens of recipes to use every day.

In Chapter 3 you'll learn how simple it is to include herbal lore in your lifestyle to help you cope with the inevitable stresses of pregnancy. You'll learn how to plant an herbal first-aid garden inside or outside your home. Specific hazards harmful to your baby's growth and normal development, such as teratogens, maternal smoking, drug use, over-the-counter medications, and artificial additives and stimulants are also discussed.

Foreword

The Pregnancy Herbal, in my opinion, invites all women to evolve with nature and the many changes of pregnancy, offering an understanding of the age-old relationship between herbalism and women.

So often through my nursing career I have been struck by the lack of nurturing that pregnant women give themselves and their unborn children. As a working mother I can relate to the many stresses of rearing infants and older children in a culture that is antagonistic toward families, which are a precious institution and our last hope in a technological world. *The Pregnancy Herbal* is a refreshing alternative that invites us into a world of functional and achievable simplicity, where self-celebration and indulgent nurturing are recognized and recommended.

I chose a career in prenatal and family care because I, too, believe that the most important time in a child's life is when he or she is in the womb, and being part of preventing illness and enhancing the good health of an unborn child and pregnant mother promotes a sense of positive well-being. As a family and marriage counselor and obstetric nurse, I view the increase in the number of women requesting an alternative to the clinical approach to childbirth as an integral part of pregnancy, motherhood, and childcare.

Jaqulene Harper-Roth brings into focus many aspects of herbalism in the home—with well-balanced nutrition—offering food preparation that excites the appetite, fulfills the cravings, calms moods, and even promotes beauty and good health throughout pregnancy and early motherhood. She openly and frankly offers her own experiences, sharing the pleasures, challenges, and rewards of pregnancy, which I believe will offer other women the self-rewarding and fulfilling transitional experience through a way of life—which, in itself, is a healing alternative.

I am very impressed with the emphasis on whole health and the earthly connection between the mother and her unborn child, with the "lighter" welcoming approach to cesarean birth *The Pregnancy Herbal* offers women safe, inexpensive, historically proven, and body-enhancing herbal remedies and recipes that encourage the natural healing and regenerative processes of life, within the mother and her unborn child, using the medical philosophy of "Let plants be your medicine," and emphasizing "Let foods nourish and heal you, while inducing a natural inside-out beauty."

After reading and recognizing this responsible and caring approach to pregnancy and the health and well-being of the mother on all levels of reception, I feel very good about recommending *The Pregnancy Herbal* to my clients as a valuable contribution to self-care, bringing the knowledge and application of herbal medicine, beauty enhancement, and baby health back into the family home. I am sure that many present and future pregnant women and new mothers of all ages will use the gifts and treatments offered in *The Pregnancy Herbal* again and again, throughout their nine months and counting transition into motherhood and beyond.

A timely and wonderful book, *The Pregnancy Herbal* is a "manual" I wish I had had thirty-six years ago.

Ingrid Peake, M.A., R.N., wellness woman family and marriage counselor, obstetric nurse
June 1999

Thyme
for an
Introduction

Why another book on pregnancy?

Even more to the point, why a book about herbal pregnancy—
a book that equates the health and well-being of you and your
growing baby with a reliance on naturally occurring foods, medicinal remedies, and beauty treatments?

Well . . . you are a reflection of what you eat.

That old saying is doubly true when you are pregnant: you and
your baby are both what you eat. I believe your skin, general

appearance, and health all reflect the food you give your body on a daily basis. When I became pregnant with my first child and realized I would soon be giving life to another growing person, I decided to seek out the purest foods available. To find those foods, I turned to nature.

I'd originally become a vegetarian at the age of nineteen to cure a skin condition that I had suffered since I was a teenager. Simply changing my diet brought that chronic condition under control, and I began immersing myself in the fascinating field of alternative medicine and disease prevention and became a dedicated student of herbal healing.

During those years I was living in the English countryside, where I could easily forage for wild edible foods and native herbs. I soon discovered that regardless of what ailed me, the cure was available for the taking in the fields and hedgerows near my home. The herbs and flowers I used were plentiful in the spring and summer months: soon I learned techniques for preserving their living essences, and I was able to continue using their potent botanical extracts through autumn and winter, as well. I kept abundant supplies of green life in my kitchen and bathroom—trays, jars, and bottles full of sprouting seeds, nuts, beans, and legumes.

The next logical step was using these same foods as my primary source of nutrition. I took a good long look at the things I had stored in my kitchen cabinets and refrigerator—and got rid of them. The more I experimented, the more I realized that I needed only the herbs, fruits, flowers, seeds, nuts, and other natural resources growing outside my door to maintain the healthy lifestyle I sought. Soon my grocery bill for the week was less than twenty dollars. I ate with the seasons: I grew what I could and foraged for the rest.

Nature's pantry provided not only nutrition and health remedies but beauty treatments as well. When I ate fresh fruit, I used the skin or peel for a quick active-enzyme facial. I ground nuts and seeds into fine meal and mixed them with cold-pressed plant oils to make a soothing scrub or hand-washing paste. I stopped washing with commercial soaps (of any brand); instead, I splashed my skin each morning with sparkling mineral water, infused with essential oils rich in nutrients. For a change of pace, I used flower-infused oils and fresh coconut milk to keep my skin supple and lock in moisture.

This simple lifestyle was not only healthy and pleasurable for mind and body but also affordable, even on the very low income I had then. Bringing nature and herbal lore into my life gave me an innate youthfulness, radiant health, and a strong sense of well-being.

And then I got pregnant.

Naturally, I wanted to know more about the experience I was about to have. At local bookstores, I discovered many volumes explaining in great detail what to expect emotionally and physically during pregnancy, and what dietary supplements were required to maintain and promote my health and that of my growing baby, month by month, trimester by trimester. I found books that monitored, informed, and reassured the expectant mother at every turning point. Some talked about what to expect during labor and childbirth, others about how to care for the newborn. Still others talked about finding and/or keeping a loving companionship during pregnancy. I read many of these informative books from cover to cover.

I found almost nothing about nature and herbal lore in any of these books.

To me this was a glaring oversight. I knew that, developmentally, the most important time in my child's life was while he or she was within the womb. I also knew that living naturally had brought me to an optimum state of health: could it do any less for my child?

In the volumes I read, I also found relatively little about the importance of feeling good about yourself and the way you look throughout the nine (plus) months of your pregnancy. I knew how important a positive attitude was toward my own mental well-being: there were times during each of my three pregnancies when I would stare in the mirror and feel a tinge of indignation toward the child growing within me for changing my body.

My children were born a year apart from each other. Throughout each of those pregnancies and birth experiences, I turned to nature and herbal lore for both nutritional and medicinal remedies for minor ailments and discomforts. I created a green pharmacy using homegrown and wild herbs, compresses, poultices, and tinctures. My medicinal garden grew in the bathroom, my herbal tea garden in the kitchen; in planters along the kitchen and bedroom window sills, I grew edible weeds and flowers. What I couldn't grow, I found in my local supermarket and health-food store.

Each of my pregnancies furthered my journey into the realm of an herbal lifestyle. I studied macrobiotics, herbalism, vegetarianism, color energy, and sprout nutrition. I was developing the philosophy that forms the core of this book—a unique combination of diet, exercise, spa treatments, and aromatherapy that not only relaxed and invigorated me but also made me feel good about myself at every stage of pregnancy. After my children were born, the importance of bathing rituals, massage, and safe, nontoxic earth remedies was self-evident and something I encouraged for the whole family.

In 1992 I received three higher national diplomas (HNDs) in nutritional medicine (a therapy that adapts a person's diet in order to improve both mental and physical health), chromopsychology and healing (the study and application of colored-light energy to heal diseases of the mind and body), naturopathy (a system of therapy that depends on the healing powers of sleep, exercise, and food), herbalism (also known as medical pharmacology, the use of plants to prevent or cure disease), and homeopathy (a system of care that uses minerals and herbs to treat a wide variety of acute health problems brought about by stress). I then went to work spreading the word about the benefits of living within nature and her laws.

The book you now hold in your hands, *The Pregnancy Herbal*, is the culmination of those many years of experimentation and study. The recipes and techniques contained herein constitute a holistic approach to pregnancy, an approach that focuses on healing with nutrition and herbal remedies, an approach that also provides techniques for pampering, relaxing, and boosting the self-confidence of the expectant mother.

With *The Pregnancy Herbal* as your guide, you will discover how to nourish your own body (and thus, your growing baby's), and how to satisfy your desires, needs, and passions on a daily basis. You will begin feeling revitalized and full of energy, with a refreshed complexion and elastic, toned skin all over your body.

You will be delighted to discover that there is a natural way of being an expectant mother that brings with it the potential for a united body, mind, and spirit. It is a world of sensual wonders where the mother to be is the center of attention—a world full of delicious, appetizing menus to delight the senses of the most exacting gourmands and to satisfy the concerns of the most experienced nutritionists. It is a world of aromatherapy and massage, where you can learn how to make and use earth-herbal body treatments for your complexion and your growing, stretching body suit; where you can learn to prepare and cook herbal feasts for your yourself and your family.

The Pregnancy Herbal provides you with easy-to-follow instructions for making herbal preparations for your own use and the care and health of your newborn. The book also offers a quick-reference herbal pharmacy with living remedies from the countryside and from your own garden.

To use this book, you need only the most basic cooking and gardening skills. (I am not a gourmet chef—my children will vouch for that! And I am an impatient gardener, too.) The herbs you will use require no maintenance (they are easy to grow and they take care of themselves), and the recipes and remedies contained herein call for only a few flowers or leaves, a handful of berries or fruit, and the ability to stir, mash, chop or grind. Simple. If you have a garden, great: you are in for a wonderful adventure of planting, harvesting, eating, and applying. If you don't have a garden or an outdoor space to plant, make an indoor greenhouse using the instructions provided in this book. If gardening is simply not to your taste, all the ingredients can easily be purchased from your local grocery or health-food store, or through mail-order sources. (See Resources, page 301.) In addition to this volume, you should have a trusted botanical reference book on herbs. *The Little Herb Encyclopedia*, by Jack Ritchason, M.D. (Woodland Publishing Inc.), and *The New Age Herbalist*, by Richard Mabey (Fireside Books), are two great guides, in case some of the herbs I suggest are unfamiliar to you.

The homemade recipes contained herein for whole body pampering—earth-herbal remedies for yourself and your new-born—are 100 percent pure, natural, and living. They can be tailor-made to suit individual tastes and needs. Fragrances and colors that are included in some recipes for aesthetic purposes can be omitted. There are no preservatives. Either the ingredients are naturally preserving, or a recipe will yield only enough for one application.

Aside from the obvious monetary savings to be gained by making your own beauty and health preparations, there are other advantages to using only pure, living, natural ingredients that are safe for you and your baby. You make choices, you are persuaded by your instincts, you take control. You understand your bodily needs and begin caring for your skin as it changes throughout this remarkable journey of bodily transition: conception, pregnancy, birth, motherhood—the development and growth of two people in less than ten months.

The Pregnancy Herbal is not just a reference manual: it is a total experience, offering an exciting, rewarding new approach to life from preconception to birth—and beyond. With the simple instructions and guidelines offered in this book, you, too, can master natural, herbal health, develop a lasting inner and outer beauty, and celebrate your body throughout your pregnancy and afterward.

An important point: I think it is fair to say that not every woman embarks on the journey to motherhood with a compassionate, loving partner who shares her feelings of fear and excitement. You must make it your own responsibility to know your body from the inside out and the outside in; know how to take advantage of the many pleasures and rewards that are part of bringing a new human life into your world.

The responsibility of pregnancy and motherhood goes far beyond becoming a parent. Women are the guardians of the human race: with that powerful responsibility we must make it second nature to do the very best for our unborn baby.

HOW TO USE THIS BOOK 🐾

The Pregnancy Herbal is a new approach to nutrition, beauty, and holistic living that will guide you through a healthful and beautiful birth experience. It's a reference book, not a novel: you don't need to read it from cover to cover. The best way to become familiar with this volume is to simply start flipping through the pages.

The information and guidance offered in *The Pregnancy Herbal* represents years of my own experience, as well as information gathered from herbalists, midwives, and ordinary people who have been using herbs and living a holistic lifestyle for generations. In some cultures, an unbroken tradition of herbal medicine and nutrition, guided by the same nutritional principles and philosophies you'll find within these pages, has produced healthy mothers and babies for thousands of years.

Pregnancy is a challenging time—a time of change and opportunity for inner growth and understanding. Throughout each month and each trimester of your pregnancy you'll face new challenges, new feelings, new desires, new instincts. Honor each of these openly. Celebrate your changing form with love, nurture, and increased self-worth.

Pregnancy should be an enchanting time, but the stress of other commitments—work, relationships, compromises, the demands of day-to-day life—leaves most women unable to enjoy it to the fullest. I want you to know that there is always time to make changes and choices in your lifestyle, to add the benefits of natural herbal living, seasonal eating, and self-pampering. You will be grateful, and so will your child.

STOCKING YOUR HERBAL PANTRY 🌿

Before we begin talking about specific remedies, recipes, and procedures, it's worth taking a moment to discuss what you'll need to have on hand to use this book. Generally speaking, the ingredients on the following pages will be available at your local supermarket (some may already be on your weekly shopping list).

Following is a list of the basic building blocks and general formulas you'll need to make your own herbal preparations. As you go through the book, you'll find which specific herbs, oils, tinctures, etc., you want to stock in your cupboard and refrigerator. All of the exercises and techniques offered in *The Pregnancy Herbal* are intended to fall within everyone's budget and abilities. If you absolutely cannot find an ingredient, make do with what you have or can inexpensively obtain: making herbs a part of your life should be an easy and stress-free experience. All you need is enthusiasm and effort, and you, too, can enjoy an herbal pregnancy that nurtures the health of your mind, body, and spirit.

Herbs

Most herbs are very low-maintenance plants; they grow and thrive near rivers and lakes and atop hard-to-reach cliffs throughout the wastelands of America. If you are buying from mail-order companies, look for smaller, family-run, community-oriented sources—organic growers who exhibit a love for growing, harvesting, and drying their crops. The herbal preparations in this book require the best organically grown or wild herbs for optimal texture, aroma, flavor, consistency, and potency. When your herbs arrive, make sure they're brightly colored, with a life force you should be able to "feel." Touch them, inhale them. If they have no scent, or worse, smell of chemicals or mold, send them back (with a few chosen words), demand a full refund, and reorder from another supplier. The quality of your herbal remedies depends on the quality of the plants you harvest, preserve, or order, as well as the quality of the water (always use freshly boiled, distilled water, available at pharmacies).

When purchasing live plants for first-aid or tea-garden projects, make sure that you purchase well-established, two-year-old plants, so that the pickings for a recipe won't strip your young plant bare.

Oils

The recipes and treatments in this book call for several different kinds of oils.

Volatile essential oils, such as chamomile and frankincense, are very difficult to make at home (to make just a few drops involves a large quantity of raw materials and a difficult distillation process), so you should buy your essential oils by the bottle. You can purchase amounts ranging from fifty drops to one and a half fluid ounces.

Cold-pressed plant oils contain live extracts derived from the raw plant matter. These special extracts are destroyed through heat and chemical extraction. I use them only in my herbal preparations. While they are a little more expensive than refined oils, they are free from the petroleum residues used in the refining process. These easily absorbed, nutrient-rich oils make ideal bases for massage and spa treatments. Grapeseed, jojoba, sesame, and almond cold-pressed oils are included often in both mother and baby skin treatments throughout this book.

Flower- and leaf-infused oils, such as calendula and rosemary, are easier to prepare yourself, although they do need about two to four weeks of exposure to the sun before you can use them. Delicate herbal flowers and leaves are packed in oil rather than water, so that their volatile essential oils and other botanical extracts are preserved in suspension. This type of oil is called an extracted oil.

Macerated oils and glycerin can also be made at home, using a cold or stove-top method, but they do require a great deal of advance preparation—six to eight weeks. This may seem like a lot of bother, but the end product will last for up to two years. My recipes call for only a few drops at a time, so once a macerated oil or glycerin is made, you'll have enough of this very potent skin-rejuvenating ingredient at your fingertips for every conceivable usage.

Clays, Powders, Resins and Gels

Ingredients such as Rhassoul mud, Fuller's earth, myrrh and benzoin gum may be available at your supermarket, but they're more commonly available in health-food stores or through herbal and soap-making suppliers. My brother is a potter by hobby, and so he always has a variety of clays, powders, and mud in his shed. Before ordering from suppliers, take a good look around your home (and maybe your mother's!). Check the laundry cabinets, garden, and even under the kitchen sink: you may be pleasantly surprised by your hoard. Those boxes full of "things I might need one day" could turn out to be a gold mine, full of beautifying ingredients such as castor oil and borax, which can be used to make carpet refresher or therapeutic massage oils.

Fresh Organic Produce and Wild Edibles

Domestic, organically grown fresh fruits and vegetables and wild edibles are active and living ingredients with their own special life force. They make at-home beauty and healing recipes simple and enjoyable. For example, wild fruits and berries, nuts, and seeds make wonderful facial scrubs, steams, enzyme peels, and penetrating packs. Spring tree or flower buds can be collected and macerated in glycerin to preserve their skin-rejuvenating properties. Overripe wild berries can be mashed and applied to your expanding pregnant belly and breasts, or juiced and mixed with glycerin and fresh milk for an unusual skin- and spirit-refreshing body splash. An added benefit of making beauty and healing preparations at home: nothing goes to waste, and because you make only enough for one application, there's no "storage waste" either.

Equipment

The great thing about making home beauty and healing remedies is that you can make do with what you have. If you don't have a blender, you can use a fork and a whisk. No juicer? Most grasses and fibrous vegetables will yield fresh juice when pushed through a manual meat grinder. You don't need fancy: when I started making these recipes, I went out and bought an old blender that lasted me through two pregnancies (and I still use the type of old-fashioned meat grinder my mother had to juice my sprouted grasses and leafy herbs). Nuts and seeds can be ground into powders with a blender or coffee bean grinder.

Make sure the utensils you use are reserved for your herbal

recipes. Store them in a sealed box or container and wash them separately from your other cooking equipment. The oils and other concentrated substances used in your remedies can permeate the equipment, causing it to "taste" or smell—not so good for a dessert. If a recipe calls for heating ingredients, use only Pyrex dishes or nonreactive saucepans. If you're using plastic pitchers or bowls for making infusions or steams, make sure they're heatproof. Use stainless-steel cutlery for measuring, mixing, and ladling. And always use a sharp vegetable knife for chopping fresh produce. Blunt knives cut more knuckles than they do fruit or herbs.

AN HERBAL HOME

Herbs and plants used throughout this book:

Herbal Remedies Ingredients
- A: alfalfa, aloe, alum, angelica, arame, arrowroot
- B: barley, basil, bee balm, birth root, blackberry, black elder, blueberry, borage, burdock
- C: calendula, camphor, caraway, catnip, cayenne, celery, chickweed, chicory, clary sage, cloves, comfrey, corn flowers, currants
- D: dandelion, dill, dulse
- E: echinacea, elecampane, eucalyptus, eyebright
- F: feverfew, flax seed
- G: garlic, geranium, ginger, ginseng, goldenseal
- H: henna, honeysuckle, horseradish, horsetail, hyssop
- I: ivy
- J: juniper berries
- K: kelp

L: lavender, lemon balm, licorice, linden, linseed, lobelia, luffa

M: marjoram, marsh mallow, mints, motherwort, mugwort, mullein

N: nasturtium, nettle, nutmeg

O: oak bark, oats, onion, orange blossom, orange peel, orris root

P: parsley, pennyroyal, peppermint, plantain

R: red-raspberry leaves, red clover, rice, rose hips, rosemary

S: safflower, sage seed and leaves, slippery-elm bark, soapwort, St. John's wort, strawberry, sunflower

T: tansy, tobacco

V: violet

W: wakame, watercress, white-willow bark, wintergreen, witch hazel

Y: yarrow, yucca

Clays, Ground Herbs, and Powders

Arrowroot, baking soda, burdock root, citrus peel, comfrey root, cornstarch, Fuller's earth, gingerroot, green clay, kaolin clay, oatmeal, Rhassoul mud, roce, sea salt, slippery elm bark

Oils

ESSENTIAL OILS
Bergamot, catnip, citrus, clary sage, geranium, jasmine, lavender, melissa, neroli, peppermint, rose, spearmint, ylang-ylang

INFUSED OILS
Calendula, chamomile, comfrey leaf, lavender, marjoram, plantain, rose, rosemary, thyme, wintergreen

COLD-PRESSED OILS

Avocado, castor, corn, grape seed, jojoba, sesame, sunflower, sweet almond, virgin olive, wheat germ

Fresh Fruits and Veggies

Apples, apricots, avocados, bananas, beets, blackberries, broccoli, cabbage, carrots, cherries, cucumber, dandelion, fennel, figs, grapes, kiwifruit, lemons, lettuce, mangoes, melon, onions, orange, peaches, pears, plums, potatoes, strawberries, tomatoes, watermelon

BASIC HERBAL PREPARATIONS

Here is an introduction to creating many of the most helpful herbal remedies, which can be used for a wide variety of wonderful and healthful treatments. You will find these easy to prepare, but they will become the backbone of your herbal lifestyle.

Herb-Infused Oil

A mixture produced when an herb has infused a vegetable or seed oil mixed with a small amount of wine or vinegar over a number of weeks. This type of oil can be used in baths and for therapeutic massage.

Herbal Ointment

A salve or paste prepared for topical application. It is produced by adding crushed herbs to melted beeswax and oils and simmering the mixture for a short period of time.

Herbal Poultice

A hot, macerated mixture of herbs. The herbs are briefly steamed in hot water and then applied externally.

Herbal Syrup

A liquid produced by adding sugar, molasses, or honey to an herbal infusion or decoction (similar to an infusion, but more potent), and simmering the mixture until it is thick and syrupy. These preparations are ideal for children because of the sweet taste.

Bud-Macerated Glycerin

This specialized technique (actually quite simple to make at home) extracts valuable ingredients from the young buds of trees, shrubs, and bushes, which are then preserved in glycerin. Like seeds, the bud of a plant contains a high concentration of active youth-nutrients. Pol Henry, a leader in the developing field of herbal healing, pioneered this technique, basing his work on the theory that the growth tissues of plants contain special substances that have powerful therapeutic and cosmetic properties.

Collect the buds during late winter or early spring, before they begin to open. Select a few young branches, full of new buds, and snip off the branches with clippers. (Do not snap or twist off a branch as this will cause the plant to bleed, and it will eventually lose the part of the branch that you left on the plant.)

Gently cut off the buds and wash them with a spray bottle. Let them air-dry, discarding any imperfect ones and any showing signs of frost damage.

Here's an example of a great recipe using bud-macerated glycerin:

Black Currant Skin-Rejuvenating Glycerin

A soothing moisturizer that improves the texture and appearance of the delicate tissues surrounding the eyes.

2 tablespoons freshly pruned black currant buds
2 cups vegetable glycerin
1 cup 100 proof vodka

Put the buds, vodka, and glycerin in a blender. Blend on a low speed for 30 seconds, then 30 seconds on a high one. Pour the mixture into a 1-pint amber jar with a screw cap. Leave the jar in a warm, sunny spot for 3 weeks, agitating it daily.

Strain the glycerine mixture through a fine-mesh strainer or cheesecloth. Gently squeeze out all the valuable oil. Fill small amber or cobalt 1½-ounce bottles with the mixture all the way to the top to prevent oxidation, and seal. Clearly print the name of the bud and the date on a label and store the black currant glycerin away from sunlight.

MAKES 2 CUPS

All of the following skin-rejuvenating and tissue- and cell-rebuilding buds can be macerated using the same technique. I use them in my facials, bathing recipes, and in some healing salves. Here are a few of my favorite buds for making macerated glycerins.

Apple buds	Good for dry skin conditions.
Black currant buds	Excellent for facial and upper body packs and scrubs.
Cherry buds	Good for balancing the pH of oily skin.
Hazelnut buds	Good for balancing the pH of combination skin.
Lime and lemon buds	Antiseptic and deep-tissue cleansing.
Orange buds	Aromatic and detoxifying.
Red-raspberry and white currant buds	Improve skin texture.
Rose buds	Reduce fine facial lines.

Cellular Herbal Juice Extraction

Nothing added, nothing taken away—that is the theory behind the use of cellular herb juices, which are pure juices extracted from the cellular pulp of plants. They offer a simple, effective way to benefit from the healing powers of herbs throughout pregnancy. Herbal juices are a safe alternative to standard medications for the prevention and treatment of common ailments, from anemia to zinc deficiency. With a pulp juicer (see Note), liquid nectar can be produced from what looks like dry, fibrous material. It can be expensive and it's not easy, so unless you have a pulp juicer, buy the juice.

NOTE: A PULP JUICER SPINS THE JUICE OUT OF THE PLANT. IT EXTRACTS THE JUICE WITHOUT YOUR HAVING TO STOP THE MACHINE TO REMOVE THE ACCUMULATED PULP. THERE'S NO CENTRIFUGAL ACTION; IT HAS MAGNETIC ROLLERS, WHICH DELAY THE OXIDATION OF THE JUICE. THE GREEN POWER JUICER, MADE IN JAPAN, IS THE ULTIMATE PREGNANCY KITCHEN MATE.

Basic Recipe for Cellular Herbal Juice Extraction

2 tablespoons freshly extracted herbal juice
1 cup water, or 1 cup vegetable or fruit juice

MAKES 1 CUP

Here is an example of a great herbal remedy that is ideal for a common pregnancy discomfort:

Stomach Gas Formula

Flatulence is a common complaint during pregnancy, especially during the last trimester, when all your organs are pushed up toward your chest to allow room for your growing baby. The following gentle herbal juice remedy neutralizes stomach acids and activity, increases the metabolism and is antispasmodic (relieves cramps), too. Drink this with apple or pear juice and a few crushed ice cubes three times a day before meals and at bedtime for three weeks once this problem begins to appear.

3 tablespoons potato juice
2 tablespoons yarrow juice
2 tablespoons black radish juice
½ teaspoon ground slippery-elm bark
1 cup fresh apple juice

In a glass, mix the potato, yarrow, and black radish juices with the apple juice. Sprinkle with the slippery-elm bark and stir.

Drink in small mouthfuls, swishing the juice around in your mouth 5 times before swallowing.

MAKES 1 CUP

Here is a list of herbal juices I made use of for various problems during pregnancy:

Bleeding gums	Chamomile, sage
Constipation	Sauerkraut
Cough	Fennel, plantain, thyme
Fever	Acerola, red beet, yarrow
Flatulence	Black radish, fennel, yarrow
Heartburn	Potato
Superficial wound	Echinacea, horsetail

Freshly extracted cellular juices are a concentrated form of a complex whole, and because they are so complete in structure, they are far superior than any drug prescribed for the same purpose. Cellular freshly pressed herbal juices bottled by Walther Schoenenberger are available throughout the world. They are sold in drug stores and health-food stores. Some naturopathic practitioners will supply them to you on request. See Resources (page 301).

Fresh Herb–Macerated Oil

Maceration is a fancy word for the process that is used to extract volatile botanical oils from fresh aromatic herbs. The process takes a period of 3 weeks, but it can be speeded up if the jar is exposed to a gentle heat of approximately 95°F.

You can also use dried herbs to make macerated oils. Just remember to hydrate the herb in a bowl filled with 2 to 3 inches of cold water and let it soak for 30 minutes. Strain and shake the herb; then macerate as with the fresh herbs.

The amber or cobalt glass jars you will need come in a variety of sizes, from ⅛ ounce to 2 liters. They can be purchased from herbal or soap-making suppliers, or even from your local pharmacy. Ask around; if you tell people what you need them for, they are often more than happy to help you find a supplier with discount prices.

Basic Recipe for Fresh Herb–Macerated Oil

---

1 cup fresh herbs
½ cup dry white wine
½ cup cold-pressed seed, nut, or vegetable oil

Place all the ingredients into a blender. Blend on a low speed for 30 seconds. Stop and stir; then blend on a high speed for about 30 seconds.

Pour the herbal mixture into a 1-pint, wide-mouth canning jar. Make sure you fill the jar to the very top to prevent oxidation from occurring. If necessary, add more oil. Screw on the top, label the contents, including the date; then place on a sunny shelf or on a shelf over a radiator. Make sure the jar is placed out of the reach of children. Agitate the jar daily for 3 weeks.

After the maceration period, pour the mixture into a small heatproof ceramic bowl. Place the bowl in a saucepan half-filled with warm water. Bring the water in the saucepan to a simmer over low heat and continue simmering until the wine in the bowl has evaporated, about 5 minutes. Remove saucepan from the heat. Carefully remove bowl and set aside to cool.

Press the mixture through a cheesecloth-lined strainer set over a bowl. Using a funnel, pour the precious macerated oil into 1½-ounce amber or cobalt bottles with dropper caps and seal. Label the contents, including the date, and store in a cool dark place.

MAKES 2 CUPS

Here's another sample recipe; there are many more in Chapter 4.

Calendula Antiseptic Lotion

A soothing skin lotion that clears up spots, pimples, and blemishes.

> *1 cup chopped fresh calendula flowers*
> *½ cup dry white wine*
> *½ cup cold-pressed olive oil*

See the basic recipe for fresh herb-macerated oil on page 21. Use this lotion on cuts, bruises, and skin rashes.

MAKES 2 CUPS

Floral Mist

This is probably the most simple herbal preparation you can make. To speed up the process, use ready-made herbal tea bag combinations or loose dried herbs. I like to use fresh flowers and leaves from my garden. It has always been a pleasure to be surrounded by my blooming herbs during April and May, and now it's fun for my children to help select the brightly colored blooming flowers and sweet-smelling leaves that make up our floral body mists and fabric-deodorizing sprays.

Floral mists make wonderful additions to any herbal body treatment, especially for midday facial misters, moisturizers, and massaging lotions. See below for an example of this easy-to-make preparation.

Violet Mist

This is one of my favorite fresh-flower remedies. Our lawn is carpeted with white and purple violets from late March to early April, and it is so enchanting to sit amongst these delicate, happy flowers and carefully pick a small basket. Tiny bags containing drying violet sprigs line my kitchen window each spring.

Always apply a floral mist to your face after using a deep-cleansing facial or scrub, or any topical remedy that requires the skin to be undressed, sloughed, cleansed, or exfoliated. After misting, air dry and repeat as necessary. If you're in a hot or humid climate, you'll love spraying these floral mists all over to keep you feeling moisturized, sensually cool, and feminine.

2 tablespoons fresh violet flowers, or 1 tablespoon dried
3 cups freshly boiled distilled water

Put the flowers in a medium bowl. Cover with the freshly boiled distilled water, and let steep for 3 hours. Strain carefully through a fine-mesh strainer set over a bowl. Pour the infusion into a spray bottle and refrigerate at least 15 minutes before use.

You can also use this mist to clear blurred vision and refresh your eyes after they have become strained through reading and close computer work: Look up, spray the mist into open eyes, blink a few times, and leave for 3 to 5 minutes. Close your eyes and rest for 5 to 10 minutes. Repeat as necessary. There's no need to wash out the solution.

Floral Waters

Most aromatic herbs can be used to make floral waters. Here are some of the more effective ones, grouped by the skin type they are generally used to balance.

Calendula, lemon balm, spearmint   Normal skin
Comfrey, lavender, rose, rose hip   Dry skin
Dandelion, ginseng, rosemary, sage   Oily skin

The best time to make a floral water is when you are already working in your kitchen. This way, you can keep a watchful eye on the procedure, which can take 2 to 3 hours.

Basic Recipe for Floral Water

2 pounds fresh herbs, such as rose petals
Distilled water to cover the herbs (about 2½ cups)
1 large block of ice (see Note)

Put a large (16- to 19-quart) stockpot on top of the stove. Put a clean flat stone or brick in the center of the pot. Place the herbs around the stone. Add enough distilled water to completely cover the stone and herbs. Place a stainless-steel bowl in the pot so that it is suspended from the pot and the bottom does not touch the stone. Put the block of ice in the bowl.

Turn on the heat and bring the water in the pot to a simmer. Continue simmering for 3 hours. *Make sure that there is always enough ice in the bowl.* Remove the stainless-steel bowl. (The aromatic steam will waft throughout your home.)

Collect the floral water in a glass bowl and then pour into amber or cobalt bottles. Label each bottle with the date of distillation and the name of the herb used.

MAKES I CUP

NOTE: YOU CAN EITHER PURCHASE A LARGE ICE BLOCK, OR MAKE YOUR OWN BY FREEZING BOTTLES OF WATER AND THEN BREAKING OPEN THE PLASTIC. ICE CUBES DO WORK, BUT BECAUSE THEY MELT QUICKLY, THE PROCEDURE WILL REQUIRE MORE OF YOUR ATTENTION.

Growing Your Own Luffas

Make your own herbal scrub mitts straight from the garden, with no expense and no waste! Contrary to popular belief, luffas are plants, not sponges. They are related to the cucumber and are easy to grow.

You can obtain luffa seeds by purchasing a whole luffa from a health-food store; the small, flat seeds are attached to the inner skeletal structure. Alternatively, you can buy luffa seeds at most organic garden centers. They need tender loving care as they germinate, so plant them in small flats and keep them inside until you have healthy shoots. Transplant them to a sunny spot outside and let the seedlings climb a trellis or bean pole for support.

It will take about 2 months for the plant to produce gourds. When their skins turn a golden brown, they are ready to be picked. Remove from the plant and place in a warm, well-ventilated room, shed, or greenhouse until completely dry, usually 7 to 10 days. Soak the gourds in cold water until the outer skin loosens, peel them off, and—voila! Luffas abound.

Herbal Decoctions

A decoction is a stronger, more potent remedy than an infusion. Its purpose is to pull out the essential mineral salts and bitter principles of the plant. This method is often used on roots, barks, seeds, and pods for medicinal and cosmetic preparations, but it can also be used to boil down an herbal mixture to make a concentrated remedy.

Basic Recipe for Herbal Decoction

½ cup fresh herb leaves, such as witch hazel or comfrey
2 cups distilled water

Bring to a boil, then simmer for 10 minutes. For remedies that are to be consumed, add a little molasses or vegetable seasoning for taste.

Here is an herbal remedy for baby using an herbal decoction.

Cradle Cap Lotion

Good for baby, or a mom with excessively oily hair, this sweet-smelling lotion dries and lifts the crusty specks of dried oil secretions on the scalp or tangled within the hair.

½ cup chopped burdock root
1 pint distilled water

Place the burdock root in a 1-quart saucepan and add the water. Cover and bring to a boil. Lower the heat and simmer the mixture, partially covered, for 20 minutes, stirring continuously. Turn off the heat and cover the saucepan tightly.

Leave burdock decoction to steep for 5 minutes. Strain through a fine-mesh sieve set over a bowl. Pour the brownish-colored liquid into a long-neck bottle and put aside to cool.

Carefully pour the liquid over the scalp, and massage it over the affected areas. Wait for 10 minutes, then rinse with warm water. Repeat daily for 1 week.

Make decoctions fresh each day, as they will not keep.

MAKES APPROXIMATELY ½ CUP

Herbal Infusion or Tea Tonic

This is one of the simplest methods for preparing herbal material for use in nutritive, cosmetic, or medicinal remedies. Infusions are useful when you want to use the active ingredients of a plant that is rich with aromatic oils.

Basic Recipe for Herbal Infusion or Tea Tonic

This basic recipe is only a guideline. A sample recipe follows.

2 tablespoons dried herbs or flowers, or 1 tablespoon fresh herbs or flowers

3 cups freshly boiled distilled water (for medicinal purpose), or 3 cups freshly boiled spring water (for tea)

The infusion should be made in a glass or china teapot and allowed to steep for 15 minutes before drinking as a remedy. For a stronger tonic, let it steep between 1 and 8 hours, depending on the herb and its required use.

MAKES 3 CUPS

Here is a tea that I often drank during my pregnancies to increase energy:

Anti-Anemia Tea

A light, minty tea tonic full of energy-giving herbs to give you an extra boost, especially during the first three months of pregnancy.

> ½ teaspoon dried nettle leaves
> ½ teaspoon dried comfrey leaves
> ½ teaspoon dried parsley leaves
> ½ teaspoon dried chickweed
> ½ teaspoon dried yellow dock
> ½ teaspoon dried mullein
> ¼ teaspoon dried spearmint leaves
> 2 quarts freshly boiled distilled water

Measure the herbs and place them in a 2-quart glass jar. Add the water, filling the jar to the top; then cover tightly. Allow the tea to steep for 8 hours, or overnight.

Strain the tea through a fine-mesh sieve set over a large bowl. Rinse out the glass jar. Discard the herbs, return the infusion to the glass jar, and store in the refrigerator.

Drink up to 5 cups a day for 1 week during each month of pregnancy. There are five excellent sources of iron in this brew, which also provides folic acid and vitamin B_{12}. All the green herbs contain some vitamin C, which helps iron absorption, while the spearmint makes it taste good, too.

MAKES 1½ QUARTS

Herbal and Spice Tinctures

These are extracts preserved in alcohol, which will keep indefinitely. Herbal and spice tinctures are some of the most common herbal medications prescribed by medical herbalists. Making tinctures at home is very easy; most herbs can be used either fresh or dried. These mixtures of alcohol, water, and herbs are very concentrated, so the dosage needed for a remedy will be in drops.

Basic Recipe for Tincture

¾ cup minced or ground herbs or spices
4 cups 100 proof alcohol, such as vodka

Place the herbs or spices into a wide-mouth jar. Add the alcohol and close tightly. Shake the jar daily for a minimum of 15 days. The more the tincture is agitated, the better chance it has to macerate and disperse the botanicals into the spirit base. After 15 days, wearing rubber gloves to protect your hands from the alcohol, pour the mixture through a cheesecloth-lined strainer set over a bowl and squeeze out the cheesecloth gently. If you need to make a stronger tincture, wash the jar, pour the liquid back in, and add more fresh herbs or spices. Macerate the mixture for another 14 days, agitating it daily. Strain through coffee filter paper and pour the liquid into small cobalt or amber dropper-cap bottles. Label the contents of the bottles, date, and store them in a cool, dark place until needed.

All tincture storage bottles and their dropper caps should be glass, and not plastic, which may react with the alcohol.

MAKES 2 TO 4 TABLESPOONS

Labor Tincture

Make up this tincture during the early months of pregnancy so that it is ready to use when you're in labor. The herb blue cohosh stimulates the uterine muscles, thereby advancing a delayed delivery, and it also reduces inflammation of the uterus. Black cohosh calms after-birth pains. Birth root speeds the action of the ginger and cohoshes to energize the uterus and bring about a swift birthing experience.

> *1 ounce blue cohosh root*
> *¼ ounce gingerroot, minced*
> *¼ ounce birth root*
> *¼ ounce black cohosh root*
> *2 cups 100 proof vodka*

Place the herbs in a 1-pint glass canning jar, and cover with the vodka. Label the contents and seal tightly with a nonreactive lid. Allow the mixture to steep for 6 weeks, agitating daily. Pour the mixture through a cheesecloth-lined strainer set over a bowl and squeeze out the cheesecloth carefully. (Protect your hands with rubber gloves.) Strain again through a coffee-filter paper; then funnel into small amber or cobalt dropper-cap bottles.

Label and date the contents; then store in a cool, dark place until needed.

MAKES 1½ CUPS

Herbal-Vinegar Tinctures

I make vinegar tinctures for cosmetic purposes, such as for the hair rinse that follows. August is the best time to make herbal-vinegar tinctures, when almost all herbal flowers are fair game. These tinctures aren't as potent as those with alcohol bases, but they're quick, simple, and aromatic enough to make a pregnant woman feel feminine and refreshed after cleansing. Herbal-vinegar tinctures made with lavender, rose, violet, carnation, and elder were very popular during the nineteenth century. For the best results, use freshly picked flowers.

Basic Recipe for Herbal-Vinegar Tincture

¾ cup fresh herbal flowers and leaves, or ½ cup dried
3 cups cider, wine, or rice vinegar (not distilled white vinegar)

Place the herbs in a 1-pint glass canning jar and cover with the vinegar. Cover tightly with a nonreactive lid, such as glass. Shake the contents daily for 4 weeks. The more the mixture is agitated, the stronger the resulting tincture will be, and the sooner it will be ready. After 1 month, remove the contents from the jar, and strain through a fine-mesh sieve into a bowl. Line the sieve with a double layer of cheesecloth and strain again. Funnel the final, aromatic liquid into small amber or cobalt glass bottles with glass dropper caps. Seal, and label and date the contents. Store in a dark cupboard until needed.

MAKES 2 TO 4 TABLESPOONS

This is a wonderful recipe for a flower-vinegar tincture to maintain healthy hair during pregnancy.

Rosemary and Thyme Hair Rescue

A delightful hair restorative rinse to nourish the roots and strengthen each strand throughout the visible stresses of pregnancy.

2 cups red wine vinegar
1 tablespoon fresh rosemary leaves
1 tablespoon fresh thyme leaves

Pour the vinegar into a blender; then add the herbs. Blend on a high speed for 15 seconds; then pour the macerated mixture into a 1-pint glass canning jar with a nonreactive lid. Secure the lid tightly. Agitate daily for 4 weeks. Strain through a fine-mesh sieve and then through coffee-filter paper. Funnel the remaining tincture into a long-neck glass bottle, and store in the refrigerator for up to 5 days. Use as an after-shampoo, leave-in rinse every evening for 1 week, rinsing it out with warm water the following morning. This mixture will strengthen and deeply nourish the hair roots, restoring pH balance and promoting a lustrous shine. Repeat as necessary.

MAKES 5 TREATMENTS

Herbal Compresses

Another simple way of using the healing benefits of herbs throughout pregnancy is with a compress, also called a fomentation. These preparations are either decoctions or strong infusions in which a cloth is soaked and then applied to an area of the body needing therapy. They can be applied either hot or cold.

A hot compress is made by placing a cotton diaper or thick wad of cotton in the hot infusion or decoction and letting it soak for I minute. The cloth is then wrung out and aired for a few seconds (so that it does not scald the skin), and then applied to the affected area and covered with a warm towel to retain the heat. After the cloth begins to cool, it is placed back into the solution to soak; then reapplied once more. The herbal liquid is covered during the treatment so that it stays warm.

A cold compress is an excellent method of reducing swelling or fevers. The cold herbal preparation stimulates the production of white and red blood cells and reduces the pulse rate. The easiest way to make a cold compress is to prepare a strong infusion or decoction and allow it to cool.

Basic Recipe for Hot Compress

½ *cup herbs*
4 cups distilled water

Pour the water in a medium saucepan and sprinkle with the herbs. Cover the saucepan and bring mixture to a boil. Lower the heat and simmer for 10 minutes. Remove from the heat and let it stand for 5 minutes, covered.

Place a thick cotton wad or cotton diaper into the solution and let it soak for 1 minute.

MAKES ENOUGH FOR 1 TREATMENT

Mastitis Compress

Inflamed breasts are quickly relieved and soothed with this sweet-smelling compress.

> ½ cup ground marsh-mallow root
> 4 cups distilled water

See the basic recipe for hot compress on page 33. Place the compress (which should be as hot as you can stand) over the infected breast. Cover with plastic wrap to prevent the mucilage from escaping. Mucilage is a substance in plants made up of soft and slippery sugar molecules. It protects mucous membranes and inflamed tissues. Cover with a warmed towel to retain the heat. Leave on for 5 minutes; then repeat 3 times on the affected breast.

MAKES ENOUGH FOR 1 TREATMENT

Sty Compress

Here is an effective treatment for painful eye irritations.

> 2 teaspoons freshly ground comfrey root
> 2 teaspoons freshly ground goldenseal root
> 2 cups distilled water
> 1 tablespoon eyebright flowers and leaves

1 teaspoon fresh chamomile flowers
1 teaspoon red-raspberry leaves

Put the comfrey and goldenseal in a medium saucepan and add the water. Cover and bring to a boil. Lower the heat and simmer for 10 minutes. Remove from the heat; then add the eyebright, chamomile, and raspberry leaves. Cover and allow the herbs to steep for 15 minutes.

Strain the mixture through a fine-mesh sieve; then divide between two bowls. Add ice cubes to one bowl to cool it quickly, and leave the other one hot. Place a cotton wad in the hot mixture and another wad in the cold one. Remove the hot compress carefully, and wring out the excess liquid. Then place over the infected eye. Leave in place for a few minutes. Remove the warm compress. Wring out the cold compress and leave it on the eye for a few minutes.

Repeat the alternating hot and cold compresses 3 times, twice a day, until the sty has healed. The Sty Compress should be made fresh for each treatment, as it does not store well.

MAKES ENOUGH FOR 1 COMPRESS

Herbal Powders

The use of powdered herbs, rather than liquid preparations, is merely for convenience. They're quick to prepare and easy to carry around, especially while traveling. An herbal powder can be prepared in several ways. I like to dry herbs, grind them finely with a mortar and pestle, and sift them through a mesh strainer. When my children were infants, I made tooth powders and diapering powders daily by grinding the herbs as needed so that they were fresh and active.

Horsetail Tooth Powder

High in silicon, horsetail helps calcium absorption and has a mild
scouring effect on the enamel, thus whitening your teeth, too.

> *1 tablespoon horsetail stem*
> *1 tablespoon sage*
> *1 tablespoon myrrh gum*
> *1 tablespoon yucca root*
> *¼ teaspoon ginger root*
> *¼ teaspoon crushed fennel seeds*

Powder the herbs in a grinder, pestle and mortar, or ice
crusher. Sift through a fine-mesh strainer. The resulting
powder should be very fine (like dust). Store in a jar with a
mouth wide enough for a small spoon.

Measure the herbs required. Combine in a small bowl,
then resift. Store tooth powder in a small jar. Dip a
moistened toothbrush into the mixture and brush
thoroughly after meals.

THIS RECIPE WILL MAKE ENOUGH TOOTH POWDER FOR A
WHOLE WEEK'S BRUSHING.

A Note About Packaging

Many of the recipes in this book yield only enough for one
application, thus preventing spoilage of active, living ingredients.
Some of the moisturizers, herbal dusting powders, massage oils,
and splash lotions, however, yield about 5 to 6 applications, and
can be saved for further use. Small baby food jars, condiment
bottles, ice-cream tubs, plastic containers with screw-cap lids, old
lipstick holders, and the many cosmetic and body-cleansing con-

tainers you throw away every day all make first-class packaging for your natural, living, home-created preparations and remedies. With babies in my home, I'm never short of small jars.

Body powders	Sugar shakers
Lip salves	Bottle caps, old lipstick holders
Packs and scrubs	Spreadable margarine tubs
Conditioners, shampoo	Dish-detergent bottles
Tooth powders	Baby food jars

Not everything can be stored, or needs to be. Some preparations must be freshly made and active. But busy moms will tell you that while cooking for the family, you can save time and money by making a few of your herbal treatments and storing them in the refrigerator for use within a few days. Nothing goes to waste, and the best thing is that you are helping to save our planet by recycling. And your baby will benefit from your carefully made herbal preparations.

1

Thyme
for an Herbal
Pregnancy

CONGRATULATIONS, YOU'RE PREGNANT!

So it's finally happened: you have another life growing inside you. Yet once the delight of being pregnant yields to the horror of feeling nauseated morning, noon, and night, your pending motherhood seems very distant. And the discomforts don't stop with morning sickness: every stage of your pregnancy will occasion some moans and groans.

Cheer up: pregnancy needn't be discomforting (all the time!). And it needn't mean repeated trips to your medicine cabinet for a pill for this, a syrup for that, a powder, a capsule, a cream. Your doctor may recommend a drug for your symptoms that is supposedly safe, but is any drug really safe while you are transfusing its effects to your baby's fragile body? Thankfully, there are many simple, wonderful, and noninvasive herbal remedies that will alleviate the symptoms and conditions associated with pregnancy.

This chapter discusses, in alphabetical order, the discomforts of pregnancy and the herbal remedies that will help you cope with them.

PREGNANCY DISCOMFORTS AND NATURAL REMEDIES

As you read this chapter, look back to the basic herbal preparation recipes in Chapter 2. Simply include the recommended herbs in this basic recipe, and you'll have a wonderful and effective treatment for all of your pregnancy discomforts.

NOTE: ALWAYS CONSULT WITH YOUR DOCTOR BEFORE SELF-DIAGNOSING OR TREATING A CONDITION WITH HERBAL REMEDIES. ALL OF THE FOLLOWING TREATMENTS AND PROCEDURES ARE SAFE FOR USE DURING PREGNANCY, BUT SINCE WE ARE ALL DIFFERENT, OUR TOLERANCE OF AND RESISTANCE TO CERTAIN NATURAL SUBSTANCES WILL BE DIFFERENT, TOO.

Abdominal Pain

Abdominal pain, experienced as cramps or sharp stabbing pains, is usually caused by the stretching of the muscles and ligaments supporting the uterus. These pains can be momentary or last for a few hours.

REMEDY

• *Red-Raspberry-Leaf and Nettle Tea Tonic (infusion) (see basic recipe, page 27).* Red raspberry contains fragine, an alkaloid that tones the muscles of the uterus and strengthens the power of the vitamins and minerals naturally found in this plant. There is a rich concentration of vitamins A, C, E, and B complex, as well as a rich supply of calcium, iron, phosphorus, and potassium.

Nettle contains every known vitamin and mineral needed for healthy human growth. Vitamins A, C, D, and K are particularly abundant, as are the essential minerals calcium, potassium, sulfur, phosphorus, and iron. Nettle tea tonic eases cramping and pain of the abdomen and legs during pregnancy and labor and after birth.

Both of these native garden herbs are abundant in the springtime, and can be harvested and dried for use during the winter. Drink this nutrient-rich tonic 3 times a day to relieve symptoms.

Backache

Back pain in the early stages of pregnancy is generally indicative of a diet that is out of balance. Too many fruits and fruit juices, too much milk and too many other dairy products, too many sodas, black tea, honey—too much liquid overall, which puts stress on your kidneys. A lack of essential minerals and complex sugars can also contribute to a backache during pregnancy.

Backache in the later stages of pregnancy can also be attributed to the increasing weight of your growing baby, and the resultant shift in your center of gravity. This is what makes sitting and standing so difficult.

There are no safe medications to take during pregnancy for back-pain relief. The condition can be treated with proper exercise and nutrition and the judicious use of herbal remedies.

REMEDIES

• *Diet.* Eat a rich supply of seaweeds (especially kelp and wakame), root vegetables (especially burdock), fibrous greens (especially chickweed, kale, beet tops, and turnip leaves), beans, miso (and other mineral-rich condiments), wheat-grass sprouts or juice, and dandelion flowers and leaves.

• *Exercise.* Cat-flex stretching can ease backache pain: On a firm surface, rest on your hands and knees. Inhale deeply and let your head hang loosely. Then exhale and arch your back, like a cat stretching, lifting your head all the way up and flexing your spine. Repeat, rhythmically flexing your spine up and down with deep inhale, exhale breaths for 5 minutes.

• *Herbal Compress.* Apply a hot, gingerroot-infused compress to the painful area (see basic recipe, page 33). Keep in place, covered with a warm, dry towel, for 5 minutes; then replace with another hot compress. Repeat procedure for 15 minutes, keeping the warm dry towel in place over the compress to trap body heat. (Don't use this herbal compress on your abdomen or the front of your body during pregnancy, as it is too stimulating).

• *Herbal Beverage.* Have a daily drink of nettle and comfrey tea blended with freshly extracted wheat-grass juice. The fresh juice from sprouted-wheat grass is full of concentrated nutrients needed to strengthen the back muscles, keep the spine flexible, and calm the nerves. Nettle tones and aids the kidneys, while the comfrey provides all the vitamins and minerals required to prevent backache.

• *Herbal Liniments.* Soak in a warm to hot bath for 10 minutes. Put 2 tablespoons of a light, cold-pressed vegetable oil in a small dish and mix in 5 drops of either Olbas, Zheng Gu Shui, or Tiger Balm oil. While your skin is still warm and moist, massage the potent, muscle-penetrating liniment over the affected area to relieve pain and discomfort.

• *Tinctures (see basic recipe, page 29).* St. John's wort is excellent for relieving backache and muscle spasms. Mix 20 drops of tincture with 8 ounces of water or pear juice. Take 1 glass every 2 hours until the pain subsides.

• *Cellular Herbal Juice (see basic recipe, page 19).* Use celery, horsetail, and yarrow. Horsetail and yarrow cellular herbal juices strengthen the back muscles and underlying tissues, while the celery acts as a natural diuretic.

Bladder Infections

Urinary-tract infections are common during the last trimester. Preventive treatment is the best course of action: failing that, prompt treatment of symptoms is important. Always wear cotton underwear, or even better, wear no underwear, as harmful bacteria thrive in moist, warm conditions. Increase your consumption of pure water, and use the toilet as soon as you feel the urge to urinate. Always wipe from front to back, and pee after sexual intercourse. Strengthen your kidneys by drinking at least 7 cups a week of red-raspberry-leaf and nettle tea (see basic recipe, page 27) during the last trimester.

REMEDIES
• *Diet.* Drink plenty of unsweetened cranberry juice. Eliminate sugar-saturated foods and reduce your consumption of dairy

products. Get your calcium from other sources, such as broccoli, cauliflower, and sprouted-seed beverages.

• *Tea Tonics (see basic recipe, page 27).* Uva ursi kills bacteria in the bladder. It is a very strong diuretic and should be used with caution during pregnancy. In the form of a leaf infusion or tea tonic, the dose is 1 cup every 12 hours for 2 days; then 1 cup, once a day, for another 3 days. Continue treatment for 5 days, even if the symptoms clear up sooner. Do not use this treatment for more than 7 days.

Yarrow-flower tea is antibacterial and astringent, and will clear up a severe bout if the previous remedy is insufficient.

Constipation

Pregnancy slows down digestive-tract functions, resulting in large, infrequent stools. Poor dietary habits (a lack of unhulled grains and raw fruits and vegetables), sleep deprivation, not drinking enough fresh water, and psychological distress can also contribute to the problem. Commercial or herbal laxatives should not be used during pregnancy.

REMEDIES
• *Diet.* Cut down or eliminate red meat consumption, especially cured or smoked meats. Reduce your intake of dairy products. Drink at least 6 to 8 glasses of water daily. Increase your consumption of fibrous foods, especially seasonal vegetables, which restore the elasticity and natural regularity of intestinal function. Sauerkraut has a high lactic-acid content, and is an excellent herbal remedy for constipation. A small glass of pure prune juice each morning will soften stools and keep you regular (the old favorite for constipation is safe for pregnancy, too). To make prune juice, soak 6 dried prunes in 2 cups of water and steep overnight.

Whatever you eat, make sure that you chew each small mouthful at least 30 times before swallowing (see Basic Rules for a Healthy Pregnancy, page 46).

• *Massage.* On the back of the hands there is a point between the base of the thumb and first finger called the large-intestine reflex. Press deeply, then rub in circular, massaging movements for about 5 minutes on each hand to stimulate the intestines.

Shoulder massage is useful for decongesting the intestines, since both the large- and small-intestine meridians run along the shoulders. Massage, beginning at the nape of the neck and working toward the shoulders for 10 minutes. This will relax and soften the muscles.

• *Exercise.* Yoga, swimming and brisk walking all prevent constipation.

• *Tea Tonics (see basic recipe, page 27).* Drink warm violet and amaranth tea twice daily. Soak umeboshi plums in hot bacha tea (or eat them with boiled rice). Eaten alone, they are very sour. They can be purchased from any good health-food store.

Depression and Emotional Fatigue

Many women experience bouts of depression throughout pregnancy: symptoms include insomnia, loss of appetite, lack of sexual desire, and feelings of melancholy and discouragement. Fatigue is most pronounced during the early stages of pregnancy, when your body is devoting so much energy to the development of the placenta. Insufficient iron or protein intake can also contribute to the problem. Common signs of fatigue include irritability, poor concentration, and impatience.

Basic Rules for a Healthy Pregnancy

Over the years, I've drawn from many different philosophies and nutritional principles—macrobiotics, herbalism, vegetarianism, color energy, sprout nutrition—to develop the guidelines laid out in this book. Here's a handy summary of thirteen of my most important recommendations for a healthy pregnancy.

1. *Keep the air in your home fresh and oxygenated*. Have large green plants, medicinal herbs, and soothing tea herbs and flowers throughout your house. Open a window daily (even in cold weather) to allow fresh air to circulate.

2. *Take daily baths that are nutritional for your skin*. I like to use herbal-infusion washes and mists to nourish and refresh my skin and promote healing. Use an herbal bathing mitt and a natural luffa to exfoliate, or clean away dead, flaky skin on the skin's surface. Sprinkle rolled or ground oats in running bath water to heal skin irritations and lock in moisture. Limit the use of bathing products that leach essential minerals from the skin, especially commercial or homemade soaps made with beef tallow.

3. *Exfoliate your skin by dry brushing it with a natural bristle, handheld body brush before showering and air-drying*. Take short, warm showers, finishing off with a few seconds of cold water; then air-dry outside in the fresh air or in a well-ventilated, warm room, near an open window; and, finally, brush your body, paying special attention to the stretching skin around your breasts, legs, and belly. For best results, perform twice daily.

4. *Become aware of the colors you wear.* This is especially important on days when you feel overwhelmed, sad, angry, despondent, depressed, or lonely. Use positive, and thus healing, color energies, such as yellow for happiness, green for generosity, blue for inspiration, and purple for

creativity. Consider the colors you choose for drinks, foods, furnishings, and lighting as well as clothing. Color energies are a form of inner healing and outer expression.

5. *Be active in your daily life.* Perform systematic exercise programs such as yoga, calisthenics, and the gentler sports; do not allow yourself to become exhausted. Take frequent water breaks and don't do more than 20 to 30 minutes of exercise per day.

6. *Walk barefoot around your home as much as possible.* If you have a garden or access to a park or beach, exercise and aerate your feet first thing in the morning. This very pleasurable, toe-exercising activity promotes whole-body well-being through stimulation of the foot-reflex points.

7. *When possible, cook with a gas or wood-burning stove.* These are preferable because the sometimes invisible tetrogens generated by electrical and microwave appliances can cause birth defects.

8. *Scrub your feet and hands daily, including each toe and finger.* Use herbal skin washes and soaks to revitalize and refresh, then air-dry. Expose your feet and hands to sunlight daily, not to tan them, but to energize your body and stimulate circulation.

9. *Be early to bed, and early to rise.* Go to sleep before 10 P.M., and wake with the dawn and the morning songbirds. Upon waking, stand by an open window and breathe in deeply 20 times through the nostrils, and then out through the mouth. Open and close your day with a short affirmation (words that trigger action or emotional response) and visualization (pictures that promote emotional well-being), recognizing and celebrating your pregnancy.

10. *Keep your home orderly and clean.* Make sure that all kitchen counter tops are sterilized with vinegar or fresh lemon juice to prevent bacterial and fungal infestations where food is prepared.

11. *Eat your meals with an earned appetite.* Eat when you're hungry, not according to tradition or out of habit. Eat in a peaceful, soothing environment, using the subtle energies of color and aroma to stimulate appetite

and digestion. Let variety be your guide: eat with the seasons, and complement your meals with wild edible flowers, herbs, greens, and home-grown sprouted foods and drinks.

12. *Chew your food thoroughly before swallowing.* Make a conscious effort to chew each small mouthful 30 times before swallowing. Swish each liquid meal (protein shakes, juices, beverages, and even water) around in your mouth before swallowing.

13. *Drink 2 to 3 cups of any liquid an hour before eating a full solid food meal.* After eating, wait at least 1½ hours before drinking a protein or yogurt shake, juices, or herbal teas. Don't drink during a meal (it disrupts digestion), and eat your meals warm, not hot.

14. *Leave your meal feeling satisfied, not full.* Spend between 30 minutes and 1 hour enjoying all the benefits of your food.

REMEDIES

• *Diet.* Eat generous supplies of root vegetables and their leafy greens. Minimize or eliminate sweet foods, exotic fruit juices (like mango or papaya), dairy products, and pastries, as these foods leach essential minerals from your tissues. Although they cause an immediate feeling of satisfaction, these types of foods increase your thirst, decrease your energy reserves, slow down your metabolism, and increase the production of fatty deposits. Eat dried fruits for a more satisfying and healthy sweet-tooth alternative.

• *Exercise.* Get involved with nature. Go for long walks. Walk barefoot in the morning dew. Run, skip, and dance in the rain. Physical activity in any form is an excellent way to combat depression.

• *Relaxation.* Deep relaxation is a powerful tool for soothing frazzled nerves. Before going to sleep or upon rising, give yourself 5 or 10 minutes of total-body relaxation. Make a tape of a relaxation technique, or recite it in your mind as you command your body to let go of all tension.

• *Affirmations.* First thing in the morning and last thing at night, recite a short, self-fulfilling affirmation about your pregnancy and the new life forming within. Here's one that I used to prepare myself for my day:

> Today I extend my evolutionary history, as mother,
> Creating a new life that nourishes and understands me;
> I love every changing part of me; as we grow in strength,
> I can feel movements of expression inside my
>   changing image;
> Our baby is a duality of our relationship and love for
>   each other;
> Today is a another new chapter of our commitment to
>   this new life.

• *Tinctures (see basic recipe, page 29).* Motherwort and skullcap tinctures are excellent mood calmers. Motherwort gives you peace of mind without drowsiness, making it an ideal treatment to use while working, whenever you feel stressed. (Warning: this herb can be psychologically habit-forming. If you begin to feel that you can't get through the day without it, discontinue its use.) The dose is 5 drops in a small glass (about 3 ounces) of water or pear juice. It takes about 20 minutes for the herb to take effect. Repeat the dose every 2 hours during a particularly bad anxious spell. Skullcap provides deep, peaceful sleep so that you awaken refreshed and alert. The dose is 5 to 10 drops in a small glass of water or pear juice at least 30 minutes before going to bed. (The tincture should be made from fresh leaves.)

• *Herbal Infusions (see basic recipe, page 27).* Red-raspberry-leaf and spearmint tea will calm and lift your spirits and increase your energy levels. Sarsaparilla is a bitter herb that, with occasional use, will calm you and diminish those ever-present mood swings.

• *Cellular Herbal Juices (see basic recipe, page 19).* Mix I teaspoon each of rosemary leaves and oats in a small glass (about 3 ounces) of water or pear juice and drink 3 times a day. Oats restore the glandular and nervous systems, while rosemary is a restorative and a circulatory stimulant.

Edema (swelling of the tissues)

Swelling of the tissues is caused by retention of fluid and is very common during pregnancy. During the last trimester, many women experience edema in the ankles, especially during long periods of standing. Fluid retention is related to the functioning of the kidneys.

REMEDIES

• *Diet.* Eliminate baked goods made with flour from your diet, as these make the kidneys constrict more. Stimulate them to flush out excess fluid by eating daikon (a large white radish) and kombu (seaweed) with a little miso or tamari soy sauce once a day until the condition subsides. Daikon tea is a stronger treatment, which has traditionally been used throughout Asia. It is especially beneficial for treating edema in the hands and fingers.

• *Exercise.* Physical exercise throughout pregnancy alleviates swelling.

• *Massage.* Rubbing the body with a hot towel in the morning and evening (especially the fingers, toes, arms, and legs) stimulates circulation.

Folic-Acid Deficiency and Anemia

An essential B-complex vitamin, folic acid works better when consumed with vitamin C, and it is rapidly destroyed by heat and light. Folic acid can be taken in herbal form throughout pregnancy to prevent a deficiency. Folic-acid anemia is caused by a deficiency of this vitamin, which is essential for blood formation and the regeneration of new cells in the body.

REMEDIES

• *Diet.* The best vegetarian food sources of folic acid are broccoli, peanuts, asparagus, and leafy green root tops, such as beet greens.

• *Herbs.* The best herbal sources of folic acid are amaranth, chicory, dandelion, parsley, and watercress. All can be eaten raw in salads, or drunk as an infusion.

Headaches

These are common during the first and last trimesters. Whether they are mild annoyances or severe migraines, they are often indicative of dietary imbalance and/or physical inactivity. The location of the pain dictates the treatment.

Headaches that originate at the front of the head result from an excessive intake of sweet foods, mango and other exotic fruits and their juices, chocolate, and pasteurized honey.

Headaches that originate at the side of the head are caused by excessive consumption of greasy and oily foods, such as fries, potato chips; sodium-dusted dried fruits; and beer and spirits.

Headaches that begin at the back of the head are usually due to the
overconsumption of fish, poultry, salty foods, and eggs.

REMEDIES
Correct diet, and a combination of massage and compresses will
bring quick relief from even the most severe migraine.
• *Diet.* Eliminate the foods that cause front, side, and back
headaches. Eat plenty of whole grains; fresh fruits and vegetables; fermented and sprouted foods, such as whole wheats and
apples; and seasonal herbal mixtures.
• *Herbal Compress (see basic recipe, page 33).* Periwinkle, thyme, and
wood-betony hot- or cold-infusion compresses.

  Frontal headaches   Apply a cold compress to forehead.
  Side headaches   Apply a cold compress to the side of the
      head, especially where the pain is.
  Back headaches   Apply a hot compress to the painful area.

• *Meridian Massage.*

  Frontal headaches   Massage second and third toe for
      2 minutes; then massage both toes together. First do the
      right foot, then the left. Before completing, pull the toes
      outward vigorously for another minute.
  Side headaches   Massage the fourth toe of both feet in the
      same fashion.
  Back headaches   Massage and pull the fifth toe of both feet.

Heartburn

The burning sensation usually referred to as indigestion or
heartburn has nothing to do with the heart. During pregnancy, it

occurs when the enlarging uterus pushes against part of the stomach or the diaphragm and the digestive juices in the stomach back up, irritating the esophagus.

Foods that are highly acidic, such as animal proteins, coffee, exotic fruits, and cooked spices, aggravate an already acidic stomach. Most over-the-counter remedies for heartburn are contraindicated during pregnancy, but there are many herbal remedies that are safe and very effective.

REMEDIES

• *Diet.* Avoid all greasy and spicy foods. Eat small meals frequently and chew each small mouthful thoroughly before swallowing. Be conscious of chewing each mouthful at least 30 times, so that it enters the stomach predigested and in near-liquid form. Snack on nuts and sprouted seeds when away from home. Do not drink while eating a meal, but do drink plenty of fluids between meals. Observe which foods cause you heartburn; then eliminate them. Avoid lying down after eating; go for a short, brisk walk in the fresh open air instead, leaving at least 30 minutes between eating and resting. Eating raw almonds when you travel can also ease the condition.

• *Herbs.* Slippery-elm bark, mixed with a little maple syrup (1 teaspoon slippery elm and ¾ teaspoon maple syrup) relieves acid stomach, soothes the stomach lining, and absorbs intestinal gas. Most good health-food stores sell slippery-elm lozenges, which can be sucked to relieve heartburn while traveling or away from home.

Fennel-seed tea sipped after meals aids digestion. Chew on fresh orange or apple peel or pineapple or papaya skin after a meal: they all contain enzymes that aid digestion and relieve heartburn.

Hemorrhoids (varicosis)

Hemorrhoids are commonplace during pregnancy, and after birth as well. Commercial hemorrhoid preparations should not be used during pregnancy because they contain local anesthetics and mercury, both of which are absorbed through the skin and blood and can be harmful to the growing fetus. There are safe herbal remedies that with regular exercises can safely treat varicosis of the rectum or vagina throughout pregnancy and beyond.

Varicosis in the rectum, legs, groin, or vulva is often inherited. For prevention, take care not to stand for long periods of time and control constipation through diet.

REMEDIES
- *Exercise.* Swimming and brisk walking are ideal exercises to boost the circulatory system. Both keep the bowels functioning well, thus preventing constipation and aiding digestion.
- *Diet.* Eat foods such as dandelions, chickweed, and sprouted wheat, which nourish and strengthen the circulatory system and help veins to maintain and regain elasticity. Avoid cayenne and black pepper and hot spices and sauces, which cause congestion of the veins in the rectum and bleeding.
- *Herbs.* Apply a fresh plantain-leaf poultice to the swollen veins and leave on for 15 minutes. Applying a witch-hazel solution or fresh lemon juice will sting at first, but will also stop the bleeding. Raw grated potato, applied in a gauze poultice, will ease swelling and relieve the stinging pain.
- *Bath.* An herbal sitz bath will eliminate severely swollen, bleeding, and protruding hemorrhoids. A sitz bath is a shallow tub in which you can soak your nether regions to heal hemorrhoids or a

vaginal yeast infection. The best healing herb for this is witch hazel, although plantain leaves, comfrey root, or white-oak bark make good substitutes.

To prepare the bath, make an 8-cup infusion of the astringent herb by covering ½ cup of the herb with 8 cups of freshly boiled, distilled water and leave it to steep 8 hours or overnight. Strain the liquid, discard the herb, and pour the infusion into a warm, shallow bath. Sit in it for 15 minutes. This remedy is absorbed through the skin and heals without direct contact to each hemorrhoid. Pain relief is felt within minutes, and the swollen veins shrink and even disappear within a few days. The same liquid can be used again and again until healing has occurred.

• *Suppository.* Insert an oiled clove of raw garlic, lightly wrapped in gauze, into the rectum and leave it overnight to ease swelling and shrink the hemorrhoids.

Miscarriage

Most miscarriages occur in the early stages of pregnancy, between the first and third months. Poor diet can be a cause: the capillaries and blood vessels that line the uterus can become overexpanded, causing bleeding. As these blood vessels rupture, the placenta and enclosed embryo separate from the lining of the uterus and are expelled from the body. More often, early miscarriage is due to natural selection; an abnormal embryo is discarded because it would be incapable of survival or is defective.

The most common causes of miscarriage are radiation, pesticide and herbicide exposure, a loose or incomplete cervix, and hormonal imbalances. Previous abortions and fibroid tumors can also be contributing factors. Of these, herbal remedies can prevent hormonal imbalances: correct vegetarian, macrobiotic, and other plant-derived diets can help prevent an early miscarriage if the embryo is normal and has a good chance of survival. Miscarriage is not preventable once bright red blood begins to flow.

The symptoms of a miscarriage vary; they include lower-back pain and pressure felt over the lower body, cramps and bleeding, a heavy pinkish-brown vaginal discharge, and blood flow that is heavier than during menstruation.

Use one of the remedies for miscarriage described below only if you had a previous miscarriage or if any women in your family had a history of miscarriages.

PREVENTIVE REMEDIES

• *Herbs.* False unicorn root is recommended in tincture form (see basic recipe, page 29) for women who have had repeated miscarriages. It is considered a powerful pregnancy tonic.

The dose is: 3 drops of tincture in a small glass (about 3 ounces) of water or pear juice 3 to 5 times a day 1 month before conception; then each day of pregnancy during the first trimester.

Black hawthorn–root-bark infusion should be consumed in half cupfuls as soon as you become pregnant. Drink daily throughout your pregnancy.

A threatened miscarriage can be prevented by drinking an infusion of wild yam root, which contains glycosides, from which the body is able to manufacture the hormones progesterone and cortisone, both of which are needed to maintain pregnancy.

Indian tobacco, also known as lobelia, will prevent miscarriage if the growing fetus is healthy and strong. Drink lobelia leaf or seed tea in small mouthfuls over a period of 1 hour and repeat 2 hours later.

Lobelia tincture is less likely to cause nausea. The dose is 10 drops in a small glass (about 3 ounces) of water every 15 to 20 minutes for 2 days.

Itchy Abdomen

As the pregnant body begins to stretch, the skins starts itching and becomes dry.

REMEDIES

The best way to prevent this itching is to lightly dry brush your skin daily, being especially gentle with your expanding abdomen. Lightly oil the area with sweet-almond or grapeseed oil, infused with chamomile essential oil. Sweet-almond oil is quickly absorbed, and the chamomile is skin nourishing and cell regenerating. Both of these simple natural remedies also reduce the risk of stretch marks after birth.

Morning Sickness

Although very common throughout the first trimester (and a common indicator of an unsuspected pregnancy), morning sickness can also be caused by eating too many oversweetened foods, tropical fruits, milk, or other dairy products. Eating too much salt can also be a causative factor.

The recognized symptoms include nausea, lack of desire for certain foods, and vomiting. Most women experience morning sickness upon awakening, but there are a few who experience it midmorning or even throughout the day. In general, this condition is not considered serious and will often disappear after the third month of pregnancy.

REMEDIES

• *Diet.* Avoid all spicy, greasy, or peppered foods. Limit fresh exotic fruits and their juices, as well as sugary foods and dairy products. Cooked soft rice, barley, and millet soothe the stomach. Make a point of discovering foods that appeal to your appetite. This is a good opportunity to broaden your cooking horizons by discovering the variety of different tastes, textures, colors, and combinations of a well-balanced vegetarian diet.

• *Herbs.* Red-raspberry-leaf infusion (see basic recipe, page 27) gives gentle relief from nausea and stomach distress. Anise infusion makes a great morning tea that also curtails morning sickness. Dried peach-leaf tea relieves nausea and morning sickness as well, while a peppermint or spearmint infusion first thing in the morning lifts the spirit and acts as an effective antinausea remedy. Spearmint infusion also soothes evening sickness due to hormonal imbalances. Drink 2 cups every 3 hours.

One of the best herbal remedies for nausea is fresh gingerroot tea, although due to its powerful uterine stimulative properties it should be avoided during the first eight weeks of pregnancy. Wild-yam-root infusion or decoction is slower acting, but far safer, than any over-the-counter medications for severe or persistent morning sickness.

Nosebleeds

Many pregnant women experience nasal and sinus congestion. Too many fluids, fats, and sugars lead to the accumulation of mucus and excess fluid throughout the body, especially in the inner ear and sinuses. In some cases, the capillaries in the nose expand and burst, causing bleeding.

REMEDIES

• *Diet.* During a nosebleed, chew on an umeboshi plum to heal the ruptured capillaries, enabling them to contract. Umeboshi plums are extremely sour, as they are sun dried and salt pickled. The longer they remain soaking in brine, the more valuable they are medicinally. Chew a small bit of the plum every 15 minutes, swallowing the juice (spit out the flesh if you do not want to swallow).

• *Compress.* Dip a small piece of saliva-moistened tissue into a pinch of finely ground sea salt; then place it gently into the affected nostril. Leave for 2 to 3 minutes; then remove. The salt will cause the ruptured capillaries within the nostril to contract, stopping the bleeding and beginning the natural healing process.

"Pins and Needles" in Fingers and Toes

Tingling sensations in the fingers (especially the index and middle finger) and toes are common during the last few months of pregnancy. Overconsumption of dairy products and stimulants (such as the tannins in black tea and caffeine in coffee—forbidden during pregnancy—and complex sugars in sweets) cause the heart and circulatory system to overwork, resulting in the expansion and overactivity of the large intestine and lungs. This action diminishes the flow of electromagnetic energy along the lungs and heart meridians, leading to a tingling sensation, tightness, and sometimes throbbing pain in the arm, fingers, and hand. When these hand tissues become expanded through incorrect diet, the nerves on the inside of the wrists become compressed.

REMEDIES
- *Diet.* Eliminate foods and drinks that aggravate this condition. Eat plenty of onions, leeks, carrots, oats, barley, and olives, which have opposing effects.
- *Rest.* Relief can be obtained by raising the affected arm or foot on a pillow and resting.
- *Massage.* Rubbing the hands, fingers, and wrists (or toes and ankles) with a hot moist towel twice daily will increase blood circulation to the area and bring some relief. Clapping your hands together a few times, then rubbing your fingers, can also curtail the problem. You can also use this method on your feet, combined with wiggling your toes when the problem occurs.

Placenta Previa

Implantation of the placenta usually occurs in the upper end of the uterus. Sometimes, the placenta will implant in the lower part of the uterus, even as far down as the cervix. About 1 in every 100 pregnancies will develop this way; this condition is due to a poor diet of mostly meats prior to conception.

The condition causes bleeding during the last few weeks of pregnancy, when the cervix begins to dilate in preparation for labor. In severe cases, hemorrhage can result. Premature separation of the placenta during the latter stages of pregnancy can also cause bleeding.

Either condition requires immediate medical treatment.

Preeclampsia (toxemia of pregnancy)

The most serious, and yet most preventable, complication of pregnancy is referred to as metabolic toxemia, or preeclampsia. The symptoms, which usually appear after the twenty-eighth week, are edema, protein in the urine, and hypertension. Evidence suggests that preeclampsia is the result of maternal malnutrition during pregnancy, and therefore completely preventable. The condition results from the overconsumption of refined, processed, and artificially sweetened foods and dairy products. These foods weaken the excretory and circulatory systems, causing swelling and the progressive buildup of fatty acids and mucus in the heart, kidneys, and major blood vessels. Women who suffer from hypertension, inflammation of the kidneys, or diabetes are more likely to develop preeclampsia than those who do not.

Once the condition has become severe, medical intervention usually terminates the pregnancy before convulsions begin. Herbal remedies for treating the condition should only be taken under the supervision of a skilled professional, as self-diagnosis and treatment can result in irreversible liver damage, or even death.

PREVENTIVE REMEDIES
• *Diet.* Consume at least 2,400 calories daily.

Limit salt intake. Too much salt causes edema, while a lack of salt causes preeclampsia. Use salt as a condiment only.

Increase the intake of potassium-rich foods. Help lower the potassium : sodium ratio in your blood by drinking freshly extracted beetroot juice, up to ½ cup daily, and/or I tablespoon of powdered spirulina or chorella in your daily diet.

Tone and nourish the uterus and placenta with daily infusions of dandelion, nettle, and red-raspberry leaf.

Eat plenty of calcium-rich foods (especially hijiki seaweed, which has ten times as much calcium as milk)—at least 1,000 grams daily.

Maintain your daily protein quota. Protein is an essential building block for the growth of the uterus, placenta, and fetus throughout pregnancy.

An ideal dietary treatment for preeclampsia is the consumption of fresh young dandelion leaves, either in a raw salad daily, or infusions 3 times a day.

Skin Blemishes

Cloasma are brownish patches of skin (sometimes called melasma, and, more colloquially, the masks of pregnancy) that may appear on the forehead, upper lip, or cheeks. This pregnancy discoloration usually disappears after delivery, but in a few cases it continues for years after childbirth. There is a hormonal and dietary link between these patches and a deficiency of folic acid.

REMEDIES
• *Herbal Infusions.* Increase your vitamin C intake with an herbal infusion rich in this infection-fighting, immune-boosting nutrient, such as rose hip and elderberry herbal tea tonic: put ½ cup elderberries and 6 crushed rose hips in a small bowl. Cover with 2 cups of freshly boiled, distilled water and steep for 15 minutes. Strain through a fine-mesh sieve into a tea cup. Drink 1 cup 3 times a day.
• *Skin Brushing.* Dry brush the skin to accelerate the sloughing of dead skin cells from the surface and aerate it with gentle friction.
• *Diet.* Focus on keeping pregnancy weight gain steady, gradual, and moderate.

Stretch Marks

As pregnancy progresses into the sixth, seventh, and eighth months, the stretching of the skin can cause pink or reddish, lightly indented, itchy streaks on breasts, hips, and abdomen. These marks are frequently referred to as "stretch marks."

REMEDIES

• *Skin Brushing.* There are many creams, lotions, and salves available to diminish this legacy of pregnancy, but the treatment I recommend most is regular dry brushing of the skin throughout your pregnancy. Start your day with a brisk, whole-body skin brush, followed by a warm shower and a wet-skin oil or glycerin massage. Then air-dry your skin in the sun. Once you get into the habit, you'll want to be kind to your skin, and your skin will start demanding this treatment, too.

Vaginal Infections

Like many other disorders of the female sex organs, vaginal infections are a result of poor diet, and they are very common during pregnancy. Many of these infections result from an over-consumption of animal fats. Even health-conscious women are susceptible to vaginal infections if they consume too many oily foods.

The color of vaginal discharge can be indicative of the kind of infection:

A thick white discharge (consisting of clumps of yeast) is caused by a fungus organism called monilla. This infection causes the labia to become swollen and red, resulting in a stinging pain during urination.

If the discharge is greenish in color, this usually points to an acute infection deep within the vagina wall, and may indicate cancer.

Yellow discharge indicates fibroid formation.

White discharge indicates a soft cyst formation.

Clear discharge results from excessive mucus in the cervix and vagina and is not considered serious.

REMEDY

• *Hip bath.* Mix 1 cup of cider vinegar with 8 cups of water and pour the solution into a warm bath. Soak for 10 minutes twice a day until the stinging pain subsides. Never use distilled white vinegar for soaking or douching, as it will burn the fragile mucous membranes lining the inside of the vagina and external labia.

Anxiety About Weight Gain

Gaining enough, but not too much, weight during pregnancy is a major concern (and a distraction) for women during pregnancy.

REMEDY

The remedy for this anxiety is knowledge: once you understand where all the calories go and what the essential nutrients are for, it lessens the burden of feeling overweight.

If you maintain a healthy herbal, macrobiotic, or vegetarian diet (without too many dairy products) and receive your micronutrients in the form of seaweed and wild edible foods, infusions, juices, and powders, you can eat lots of good-tasting, body-fueling, and fetus-growing foods throughout pregnancy and while nursing, without guilt. Much of the pregnancy weight you will have gained (about 40 percent) will be a healthy baby.

Where does the rest of the weight go? About 22 percent is a blood-volume increase, 10 percent is uterus enlargement, 10 percent is amniotic fluid, 10 percent is the placenta, and 8 percent is breast enlargement. The minimum weight gain is between 20 and 35 pounds.

Here's a recap of some of the most useful herbal remedies for this time:

Remedies for General Well-Being During Pregnancy

Blackberry tincture	An old home remedy for diarrhea.
Comfrey, yarrow, and mullein poultice	Eases achiness of tightened veins.
Dandelion tincture	Excellent for relieving a variety of stomach upsets.
Freshly extracted (or unsweetened bottled) cranberry juice	Prevents bladder infections.
Freshly extracted cucumber juice	Reduces high blood pressure.
Grated raw potato compress	Eases swelling and pain of hemorrhoids.
Melissa infusion	Helps reduce postpartum depression.
Oatstraw tea	Strengthens capillaries.
Raw almonds	Chew to relieve heartburn.
Raw beet juice	Balances sodium:potassium ratio in blood.
Siberian gingseng	Helps body adjust to changing condition; also good for jet lag.
Skullcap infusion	Reduces high blood pressure.
Slippery-elm-bark and honey paste	Neutralizes stomach acids; soothes digestion.
Witch-hazel compress	Soothes swollen varicose veins.
Witch-hazel sitz bath	Eliminates severely swollen and bleeding hemorrhoids.

LABOR THYME 🌾

A word about your birth experience:

For this experience to be as personalized as possible, be in control. You have rights and choices. Ask lots of questions, and make sure your needs are known to your health caregiver before going into the hospital or birthing clinic. Be open and friendly. If you know what you want and how you would like things to go during labor and birth, make up a birthing plan and discuss it with your husband, doctor, or midwife, so that the room can be set up accordingly.

During the first stage of labor, when contractions begin to come at a steady pace, stay at home as long as possible. Cope with the contractions by using breathing exercises. This is also a wonderful time to take an herbal labor bath or to apply herb-soaked compress pads on your lower back and abdomen to relieve the stress and pain of contractions and ease the tension. Herbal compresses can be a soothing and healing skin refresher and pain reliever. But if your water breaks, call your doctor and go straight to the hospital. Do not attempt a self-examination or take a bath.

During my first labor experience, my water broke before I went into labor, and I was unable to take a planned labor bath before being rushed to the hospital. I quickly made up a few pure essential oil- and water-infused compress pads and had my husband place them on my abdomen and lower back when the contractions began to get stronger and longer. This felt so good, so relieving. I was sure that I could get through labor and birth without painkillers.

Unfortunately, I had an emergency cesarean in a very sterile environment. I was unable to use any natural relaxants or bring my baby into a natural, welcoming environment. (Although I was a little upset and felt a sense of defeat, my thoughts were directed toward the health and safety of my baby.)

For the birth of my second baby, I had a planned cesarean. I took an herbal labor bath daily and massaged with calming, sweet-smelling oils that refreshed and unwound me. I massaged my swollen abdomen with wheat-germ oil and warmed shea butter daily. I dry brushed my abdomen, thighs, and breasts from month four of my pregnancy. I applied daily herbal skin mists. During the last two months, I welcomed each day with early-morning sunbaths and air-drying after bathing. This resulted in a comforting and comfortable pregnancy that made my cesarean easier to accept and recover from.

My herbal lifestyle made each day of pregnancy inspiring. Herbs have delighted me for over twenty-five years, and my adaptation to motherhood has evolved and matured. Once I allowed myself to become curious about the uses of herbs, I discovered so many different avenues of pleasure, and got to thinking about how I wanted to live my life.

Pregnancy brought me a great responsibility—I was in charge of two developing bodies. It was up to me to use all my learning tools from nature to care for each and give them the nourishment, medicine, and skin care required for each developmental stage. Looking back, I know it was a difficult challenge for mind, body, and spirit, but my deep-rooted herbal background gave me the inner strength to seek, experiment, and find healthy alternatives using all nature's pharmacy had to offer.

An Herbal Labor Bath

This is an ideal prehospital experience no matter what type of labor you think you're going to have. Because I was scheduled for a cesarean birth, I made this prebirth ritual as relaxing and harmonizing as possible.

The Botanicals

1 teaspoon fresh jasmine flowers

1 teaspoon fresh clary sage leaves

1 teaspoon lavender flowers and a few leaves

2 teaspoons fragrant rose petals

1 heaping tablespoon chamomile flowers

2 cups very hot water

2 tablespoons coarse sea salt

Measure out ½ teaspoon of each herb and flower, place inside a square of muslin cloth, and secure with a rubber band. Or use a resealable 4-by-6-inch tea bag. Place in your hospital overnight bag so that your clothing and personal items will be scented by the same aromas that filled your home the day you bid farewell to your "bump" and welcomed your baby into the world.

Place the remaining herbs into a large heat-resistant plastic or Pyrex pitcher and cover with 2 cups of hot, not boiling, water. Boiling water deadens the active ingredients of the herbs and nullifies their healing powers. Let steep for 15 minutes.

Strain through a fine-mesh sieve, reserving the herbs and flowers for another use. (They can be placed inside a washcloth or piece of muslin and used as a skin wash during bathing.) Pour the infusion into a running hot bath. Add the sea salt.

When the bath is half full, turn off the faucet and close the bathroom door. Let the aroma of the botanicals and the hot steam fill the room. After 10 to 15 minutes, step into the bath, slowly immersing your body. Close your eyes and relax for 15 to 20 minutes, adding more warm water if necessary.

Air-dry in the warm sunshine or in a warm, well-ventilated room.

If you are taking this bath the night before a scheduled morning surgery, wrap yourself in a warm wool blanket and snuggle into bed. If your surgery is after lunch and you take a bath in late morning, wrap yourself in a wool blanket and sit outside in the fresh air or near an open window.

Take 10 minutes to perform a short visualization to welcome your baby into the world.

THE VISUALIZATION

This is my own personal birthing visualization:

Close your eyes, take a few deep breaths, and breathe out slowly and calmly. Relax your body: feel at peace with your thoughts and choice.

You are bathing in a clear turquoise-colored ocean. Your boat is anchored 100 feet from where you are drifting. The sun is warm on your skin. The sky is clear blue; there are no clouds.

You lie on your back, paddling your feet to keep afloat. Your pregnant body feels weightless. You feel free-spirited and joyful.

As you lie back and absorb the beauty of your tranquil surroundings, you hear a distant song. The song does comes not from birds; it is a haunting and provocative echo that resonates within your whole being. You feel it vibrate in your womb.

You start swimming toward the echo, as though it were a magnet pulling you closer. You submerge: the song is louder beneath the surface of the water. Like a mermaid, you dive.

Your nudity feels refreshing as you swim. Looking around, you see a wondrous sight: nursing whales just below you. They encircle and protect you. Their senses connect with yours: they acknowledge you as one of them, and allow their young to lift you back up to the surface and your boat.

You climb aboard, and as you begin sailing, the whales swim by your side. Dolphins leap and dive across your path.

You turn toward the shore, and a brilliant light forms from the ocean surface, collecting life force from the whale families. It showers on you like a soft rainfall of golden light. You are at peace from the inside out and outside in. You feel a special bond with Mother Earth and her many gifts of life.

Open your eyes. Breath in deeply, wiggle your toes, stretch your arms and legs. Slowly get to your feet. Your visualization is complete.

WHEN TO CALL THE MIDWIFE OR DOCTOR

While herbal remedies may be sufficient to ensure a healthful pregnancy, there are times when calling a doctor is absolutely necessary. For the symptoms listed below, medical intervention or attention is definitely required.

Symptom	Possible Cause
Blisters or sores in or around the vaginal area, with itching and discharge	Vaginal infection or sexually transmitted disease
Absence of fetal movement after thirtieth week of pregnancy or beyond	Fetal death

Symptom	Possible Cause
Chill and fever over 100°F (unaccompanied by cold or sinus infection)	Infection
Dizziness, fainting, or light-headedness	Preeclampsia (toxemia)
Hot, painful, and reddened area behind the knee	Phlebitis (blood clot)
Leaking or gushing fluid with clots from the vagina before thirty-sixth week	Premature rupture of membranes (water break)
Pain or burning during urination	UTI (urinary tract infection) or sexually transmitted disease
Severe vomiting or nausea more than three times in one hour over a few days	Hyperemesis gravidarum, a rare complication of pregnancy, which can be controlled only with antiemetic drugs; or it could be an infection
Sudden swelling of the eyes, cheeks, fingers and/or toes, especially during late pregnancy	Preeclampsia (toxemia)
Severe abdominal pain anytime during pregnancy	Ectopic pregnancy (wherein gestation occurs elsewhere than in the uterus), premature labor or placental abruption (partial or complete detachment of the placenta from the uterine wall before the baby is born)

Symptom	*Possible Cause*
Uterine contraction before week thirty (with more than five in an hour)	Threatened miscarriage

Remedies Especially for Womb Health and Labor

RED-RASPBERRY-LEAF INFUSION (see basic recipe, page 27). An infusion made from "the Pregnancy Herb" tones your uterus, eases morning sickness, reduces pain during labor, helps bring down the placenta, and increases the production of milk while you are breast-feeding.

EVENING-PRIMROSE OIL. Helps soften the cervix prior to labor. Take orally. Purchase the oil from a drug store.

SLIPPERY-ELM-BARK PASTE. Soothes pain and binds torn tissues together after perineal tears. If comfrey-root powder is added to the mixture, it will speed up the healing. Make the paste by spreading 1 teaspoon of slippery-elm-bark powder on a sterile cotton wad, then adding 1 teaspoon of honey. Spread the mixture evenly over the wad and dust with ½ teaspoon comfrey-root bark. To apply, tuck the paste side of the pad close to the torn skin (much like a menstruation pad, between your skin and your panties), and leave in place between baths.

FRESH ALOE VERA GEL. Soothes pain, seals burn, and cools perineal tears. Remove the gel from a fresh leaf or purchase from a pharmacy.

PURE VITAMIN E OIL. Excellent for healing closed wounds without scarring.

CAYENNE POWDER. An effective styptic, it will sting a bit but stops bleeding from small external wounds.

2

Thyme for an Herbal Pregnancy Diet

GUIDELINES FOR HEALTHY EATING

Throughout your pregnancy, your body changes dramatically. Your nutritional needs change as well.

During the first three months of pregnancy, it is normal for a woman to crave acidic foods, rather than healthier, more alkaline foods. The rapidly growing fetus requires a great deal of energy.

The expectant mother wants to feed this demand with candies, chocolates, and other foods she either hasn't had before or hasn't eaten for a long time. Don't worry: little indulgences are natural and healthy, as long as they don't become a habit.

Changes in your body, especially those as profound as the ones brought on by pregnancy, require adjustments in your daily routine. But with a little thought, preparation, and effort, you can find nutritious, natural food alternatives that will enhance your pregnancy.

There is no one diet that is suitable for every pregnant woman: we are all different. You will also need to continually adapt your pregnancy diet to fit your ever-changing condition. My intention here is to provide you with a diet that not only satisfies the body's needs for fuel but also provides an alternative to the junk food our commercially driven society tempts you with every day. Realize that the cost of these foods isn't as much in the cash you hand over as in your health. Now that you're pregnant, you're responsible for the health and well-being of two people—yourself and your baby. It's your responsibility to eat well for both of you, even if you're not vegetarian.

Eating a healthy, well-balanced diet, as outlined on the following pages, will ensure you lots of good-tasting, body-fueling, and baby-growing foods throughout pregnancy and nursing. If you avoid the temptation to binge, and stay away from high-fat, high-sugar junk foods, you will have the advantage of knowing that much of the weight you gain (about 40 percent) will be your baby.

If you want to get started on eating healthy, turn to the recipes beginning on page 108. Or read on for more information.

Avoid

✦ When possible, foods that are refined, processed, or canned, especially those that fall into the category of junk food.

+ All consumption of alcohol, even wine.

+ All sodas—they're packed with artificial sweeteners and nutritionally empty calories.

+ When possible, over-the-counter pain relief and sleep medications and dietary supplements. If you have a medical condition, discuss using natural alternatives (herbs, nutrients, homeopathic treatments) with your doctor.

+ All fasting and dieting. If you feel you are putting on too much weight during your pregnancy, wait until after you've given birth and ceased nursing to begin a weight-loss program.

+ All caffeine-rich beverages—including that first thing pick-me-up cup of coffee.

+ All curried, peppered, or highly spiced meals. These increase your chances of painful heartburn and indigestion, and can cause much discomfort for both you and your baby.

+ All smoking. Avoid inhaling second-hand, passive smoke as well. Your chances of miscarriage or a low-birth-weight baby are three times greater if you're a smoker, and your baby has a 30 percent higher risk of mortality. While you are nursing, your milk carries small amounts of nicotine, which will make your baby prone to chronic respiratory conditions throughout his or her life.

+ All dairy products, including hard cheese, milk, butter, sour cream, and ice cream. According to many allergists, alternative health-care specialists, naturopaths, and even a few orthodox practitioners, cow's milk products are extremely difficult to digest for humans, and have a deleterious effect on human-growth potential, health, and well-being. Many digestive disorders cease, PMS effects are reduced, and allergies of all kinds are eliminated when milk and dairy products are eliminated from your diet.

Minimize

+   All red meats, poultry, and fish.
+   Potatoes, yams, tomatoes, avocados, mayonnaise, ketchup, hot sauces.
+   Sugar, tropical-fruit-juice blends, cashew nuts, chocolate, black tea.

Include

+   Seaweeds of all varieties, outer green leafy vegetables (outer dark green leaves are more rich in vitamins than the pale inner leaves) and mineral-rich wild edibles.
+   All varieties of melon. They are great skin and tissue flushers and taste great chilled on a summer day. For optimal benefit to both you and your baby, make an effort to chew melon chunks thoroughly, especially the seeds and inner skin. Digestion can be slow and painful if you swallow half-chewed melon chunks. If you have any left over, mash it up and mix it with a little yogurt or honey for a refreshing facial.
+   Easy-to-digest foods, like steamed vegetables, whole grains, pasta, raw vegetables, sprouted beans, stir-fry vegetables, and cooked seasonal fruits. By doing this you are gradually eradicating the gas-forming foods from your diet, making both you and your baby more comfortable.
+   Plenty of whole grains, raw seeds (sesame, pumpkin, sunflower), sprouted nuts, seeds and grains, fermented foods (yogurt, nut cheeses, savory and sweet spreads), sprouted nut and grain foods such as sun-dried breads, nut and seed milks.
+   Super-green foods, such as spirulina, alfalfa, chlorella, and wheat and barley grasses carefully grown and harvested to maximize their micronutrient content.

+ 8 to 12 glasses (10 to 17 ounces each) of pure water every day. This helps flush your system and keep your bodily fluids flowing. Remember, humans are 75 percent water. While you're pregnant, you are two "water bodies," which need this vital fluid source cleansed and replenished daily.

+ Plenty of folic-acid-rich foods, such as spinach and asparagus.

+ Plenty of zinc-rich foods, such as raw or sprouted pumpkin and sesame seeds.

+ Plenty of vitamin-C-rich foods. Your requirements for this nutrient increase during pregnancy. Because your body is better able to assimilate vitamins from natural food sources than from supplements, include plenty of broccoli, green bell peppers, rose-hip tea or jelly, and lots of fresh apples and seasonal berries to meet your daily needs for this vitamin.

+ Remember to eat only when you're hungry. That could be more (or less) often than tradition or habit dictates.

+ A pregnancy diet that consists of at least 50 percent whole-grain cereals, 25 percent vegetables, 15 percent beans and sea vegetables, and 10 percent strained or puréed vegetable broth optimizes the health, happiness, and growth potential of your baby.

NUTRITIONAL BENEFITS OF HERBS

Orthomolecular medicine is a new branch of science that deals with the use of nutrients in the treatment of disease. Conditions acute and chronic, such as heart disease, arthritis, obesity, and diabetes are being treated with mineral and vitamin supplements and wholesome foods.

New research has revealed that certain chemicals in herbs and other natural foods promote good health (something those of us who have lived a vegetarian, macrobiotic lifestyle already knew).

Nutritive herbs are classified according to the nutritional value they add to a person's diet. They may also display some mild medicinal effects, but more important, they provide large quantities of easily assimilated proteins, fats, carbohydrates, vitamins, and minerals.

Vital Pregnancy Nutrients Available from Herbs

CALCIUM

This is the main constituent of bones and teeth. It is essential to muscle, heart, and nerve development as well as blood clotting and enzyme activity for both baby and mother. If a growing fetus is unable to draw enough calcium indirectly from the foods eaten by the mother, it will draw upon the calcium deposits in her bones.

Recommended intake: 4 servings daily.
• *Ten Herbal Sources of Calcium:* kelp, nettle leaf, senna leaf, thyme, grapevine, damiana leaf, white-oak bark, cabbage, plantain, horsetail.

FATS

These are classified by their chemical structure. There are saturated fats, polyunsaturated fats, phospholipids, unsaturated fats, sterols, oils, waxes, and fixed fats. They are a major portion of our daily nutritional intake and provide the most concentrated form of energy, yielding approximately nine calories per gram of fat.

Eliminating fat from your pregnancy diet is dangerous: it is a vital nutrient for your growing baby. Nonetheless, do not overdo your consumption of saturated fats. Keep a careful watch on the high-fat foods you eat on a daily basis; no more than 30 percent of your daily caloric intake should come from fat.

Recommended intake: 4 servings daily
• *Ten Herbal Sources of Fats:* plantain, sage leaf, fennel seed, celery seed, gota kola, thyme, gingerroot, passion flower, fenugreek, pumpkin seed (the highest quality).

FIBER

Fiber is a substance that contains indigestible carbohydrates, such as cellulose, hemicellulose, lignin, pectin, and various gums and mucilages. Fiber in the diet increases stool frequency and decreases the time food pulp takes to pass through the large intestine. Fiber reduces cholesterol by preventing absorption of dietary cholesterol. It also speeds the elimination of bile acids and the removal of hepatic synthesized cholesterol (the bad cholesterol). Cellulose is the most abundant dietary fiber source.

Recommended intake: 2 servings daily.
• *Ten Herbal Sources of Fiber:* rose hips, alfalfa, thyme, sage leaf, milk-thistle seed, red-raspberry leaf, dandelion leaf and root, pennyroyal leaves, blue-cohosh root.

PROTEINS

These are primarily composed of amino acids. Certain amino acids are essential to the diet because they cannot be synthesized by the body. Proteins are the building blocks of human cells and are particularly important in building the new cells of your baby.

Recommended intake: 4 servings daily.
• *Ten Herbal Sources of Protein:* spirulina, pollen, feverfew, cauliflower, broccoli, nettle leaf, parsley, alfalfa, pumpkin seeds, plantain.

VITAMIN A AND BETA-CAROTENE

These are best known for aiding night vision and being actively anti-infective. Both the vitamin and the precursor (which turns the substance into vitamin A so that the body can utilize it) are used by the epithelium skin layer to protect the body from infections and harmful radiation rays from the sun. Vitamin A and carotenes are antioxidants that react with potential carcinogens, forming harmless reaction products. Since your baby's cells multiply at such a rapid rate, you need to ensure that your daily intake of these vital nutrients is adequate for your own body and your baby's also.

Recommended intake: 3 or more servings of the following herbs per day.
• *Ten Herbal Sources of Vitamin A and Beta-carotene:* spirulina, violets, parsley, alfalfa, nettle leaf, broccoli, gotu-kola, barley grass, blessed-thistle herb, red-raspberry leaf.

VITAMIN C

Both you and your growing baby need this vital micronutrient for tissue repair, wound healing, and other metabolic processes. Normal growth potential is ensured if an ample supply of this vitamin is consumed by the mother from food or herbal sources throughout the baby's gestation. Since the body is unable to store vitamin C, fresh supplies have to be absorbed from food sources daily. Look further than the humble orange for your vitamin C sources; the plant world has a varied and plentiful supply.

Recommended intake: 2 servings daily.
• *Ten Herbal Sources of Vitamin C:* horsetail root, broccoli, rose hips, aloe juice, red-raspberry leaf, spirulina, pumpkin seeds, onion bulb, red-clover tops, yellow-dock root.

CHROMIUM

Essential for the production of GTF (glucose-tolerance factor). Minor deficiencies raise blood-sugar levels and thus the levels of insulin required to metabolize it. Chromium is also used in metabolizing carbohydrates, especially sugars.

Recommended intake: 1 cup tea or 3 drops of tincture diluted in 1 cup water or juice daily
• *Five Herbal Sources of Chromium:* spirulina, barley grass, red-clover flowers, oat-straw herb, hibiscus flower

MAGNESIUM

Adequate levels are essential for the synthesis of RNA and DNA molecules and proteins. More than 300 enzymes require the presence of magnesium, which is more than any other enzyme cofactor. Magnesium is often referred to as the "circulatory mineral," due to its ability to regulate muscle contractions. The best sources of magnesium come from the plant world, especially the chlorophyll-rich greens. Magnesium deficiency plays a key role in diseases of the heart, such as angina, stroke, hypertension, high LDL cholesterol levels, migraine headaches, and epilepsy.

Recommended intake: 1 cup of tea or 3 drops of tincture in 1 cup of water or juice daily
• *Five Herbal Sources of Magnesium:* oat-straw, licorice root, kelp, elecampane root, dulse.

PHOSPHORUS

This is one of the major nonmetals in the body, and thus combines well with many of the metals or organic acids to perform a great variety of chemical reactions. Herbs, seeds, and flowers contain large quantities of phosphorous—especially caraway seeds, watercress, nettles, and chicory—because the reproductive organs of plants must store great amounts of energy in the form of plant oils and fats. A dietary deficiency of this mineral is unlikely but can be caused by a high-fat diet, sugar, and mental stress.

Recommended intake: I cup of tea or 3 drops of tincture in I cup of water or juice daily
• *Five Herbal Sources of Phosphorous:* blue-cohosh root, bilberry, soybean, horseradish root, Siberian ginseng root.

POTASSIUM

This is the second-most abundant mineral in plants. In the human body, it plays a crucial role in isomotics (the process by which the cells are nourished and cleansed) and assists in carbohydrate metabolism and protein synthesis. Raw foods are the best source of potassium, since cooking and processing leaches this mineral from them. Potassium deficiency is quite widespread, causing high blood pressure, which is a common pregnancy ailment.

Recommended intake: I cup of tea or 3 drops of tincture in I cup of water or juice daily
• *Five Herbal Sources of Potassium:* parsley, barley grass, catnip, cauliflower, asparagus.

SELENIUM

This is an extremely beneficial antioxidant, protecting DNA structures from damage. Selenium is an essential building block for your body's powerful antioxidant glutathione. It enhances the immune system of both mother and baby. It is highly concentrated in the pancreas, liver, and pituitary gland. Supplements of this mineral can strengthen the immune system by increasing antibody production but exceeding a dose of 200 micrograms daily can be toxic. The best sources of selenium are grains and herbs.

Recommended intake: 1 cup of tea or 3 drops of tincture in 1 cup of water or juice daily
• *Herbal Sources of Selenium:* hibiscus flowers, lemongrass, yarrow flower, dulse, pumpkin seeds.

ZINC

Zinc is essential for proper immune function. It helps to rejuvenate the thymus gland, and with its antioxidant properties it helps in the maintenance of healthy skin and nails and the sense of taste. It promotes healing and full-term, successful pregnancies. Zinc deficiency in a pregnant woman can impair the development of her baby's immune system.

Recommended intake: 1 cup of tea or 3 drops of tincture in 1 cup of water or juice daily
• *Five Herbal Sources of Zinc:* bilberry, wild-yam root, echinacea root, chickweed herb, spirulina.

The best way to ensure that you get all these essential minerals is to do what I did: make a combined herbal tincture and take 10 drops in water or juice daily.

HERBAL JUICES

Treating disease and promoting cellular regeneration with herbal juices is a long-standing holistic therapy dating back 2,000 years. Today there is an explosion of interest in this natural method of disease control and health promotion. This enthusiasm is welcomed by the many herbal practitioners who have been working under the guise of "alternative medicine" for long enough.

You get the same vitamins and minerals from 3 teaspoons of concentrated herbal juice as you do from 2 full meals of raw herbs. Since there are many times during pregnancy, maybe due to nausea or bloating, when you just don't feel like eating a full meal of green vegetables for your mineral and vitamin intake, why not drink these essentials in the form of a concentrated herbal juice? These potent juices flood the body with nutrients to build healthy cells, transmuting disease into wellness.

I discovered these herbal wonders a few years ago: now, using a juicer for my daily nutritional needs is as automatic as relying on a dishwasher or ice maker. You can either juice the herbal plants yourself or purchase freshly pressed cellular juices (see Resources, page 301).

The following recipes are my own delicious flower and juice combinations. The more comfortable you become using herbs and their flowers in drinks, such as cooling or warming teas, the more skilled you will become at creating tasty juices that are beneficial to your changing moods and the progress of your pregnancy.

Gil's Healing Tisane

A delicious, light, sweet-smelling tea to lift your spirits.

2 cups chamomile-flower infusion (see basic recipe, page 27)
3 tablespoons pineapple juice
1 teaspoon fresh lemon juice
1 cup dandelion-flower infusion (see basic recipe)
Dandelion and chamomile flower petals for garnish

Mix the chamomile infusion, pineapple juice, lemon juice, and dandelion infusion in a pitcher. Chill for 20 minutes. Serve, garnished with flower petals.

MAKES 3 TO 4 CUPS

My Morning Pick-Me-Up Beverage

A refreshing tea to start you up for the day.

2 cups lemon-balm flower infusion
1 cup apple juice
Bee balm petals for garnish

Mix the lemon infusion and apple juice in a pitcher. Serve cool, garnished with petals.

MAKES 3 CUPS

High-Energy Tea

A sweet-smelling tea that makes you feel energized.

2 cups red-raspberry-leaf infusion (see basic recipe, page 27)
1 cup kiwi purée

½ cup green grape juice
Dandelion and lavender petals for garnish

Mix the raspberry infusion, kiwi purée, and grape juice in a pitcher. Chill for 20 minutes. Serve, garnished with petals.

MAKES 3 TO 4 CUPS

My Nerves-Soothing Tea

A light flower tea to soothe frazzled nerves.

1 cup honeysuckle-flower infusion (see basic recipe, page 27)
1 cup chamomile-flower infusion (see basic recipe)
½ cup fresh apple juice
Dill-and-fennel-seeds infusion made with 6 seeds of each
  (see basic recipe)
Dill and chamomile flower petals for garnish

Mix the honeysuckle infusion, chamomile infusion, apple juice, and dill-and-fennel infusion in a pitcher. Serve warm, garnished with flower petals.

MAKES 3 CUPS

Appetite-Pleasing Tea

For all those days when food is not so appealing to your palate, drink a few cups of this fruity mint tea.

2 cups spearmint-flower infusion (see basic recipe, page 27)
1 cup fresh apple juice
½ cup fresh grape juice
½ cup pineapple juice
Spearmint and bee balm petals for garnish

Mix the spearmint infusion, apple juice, grape juice, and pineapple juice in a pitcher. Chill for 20 minutes. Serve, garnished with petals.

MAKES 4 CUPS

Midsummer's Night Bedtime Tea

Watch the stars twinkle while sipping this aromatic floral blend—you won't need to count sheep tonight!

>   *1 cup chamomile-flower infusion*
>   *1 cup lavender-flower infusion*
>   *1 cup fresh pear juice*

Mix the chamomile infusion, lavender infusion, and pear juice in a pitcher. Serve warm.

MAKES 3 CUPS

GETTING YOUR NUTRITION FROM NATURE

Eating organically doesn't mean limiting yourself to a few leafy green vegetables at every meal. Nature offers you a wide variety of foods for your pregnancy diet, including those noted in this chapter. Using wild edibles in your meals lets you create menus that are not only nutritious and health giving but colorful, textured, aromatic, and naturally flavored. There are a wide variety of edible flowers, herbs, spices, leafy vegetables, sea vegetation, and fungi available to you. Introduce these new foods a little at a time, adding a few leaves of a wild vegetable into a garden salad, some scattered flower petals in juices and teas, and sea vegetables as condiments.

No matter what time of year you are pregnant, there's a plentiful supply of fresh organic vegetables, fruit, and herbs to include in your daily diet. Look into the far reaches of your garden. Beyond the tailored flower borders, you'll find a variety of wild edible offerings from nature's pastures. They may look like bothersome weeds to you, but before wrenching them out to make space for yet another annual, take a few minutes and look through the pages of a botanical dictionary. Identify the species: more often than not, you'll discover a highly nutritious food source. There's nothing more pleasing to the palate—and the eye—than a colorful garden salad of flower petals, leaves, and roots, with their distinctive aromas and flavors.

If the idea of foraging in a damp woodland for your supper seems daunting, relax: don't forget that almost every garden vegetable in your supermarket has a wild ancestor flourishing in the open countryside. There's a whole world of pure, unadulterated nutrition out there for you to explore. Wild edibles are free for the taking, readily available, and tolerant of diseases and growing conditions that would decimate cultivated plants. They are invaluable during times of famine, poverty, and crisis.

Picking from the wild, open countryside has an ecological impact, so take sparingly from nature's pastures. Remember that these special plants provide a habitat and diet for many wild birds, insects, and animals.

Some of my most delicious meals and snacks came from the wonders of my garden, and especially my "weed patch," where I have tenderly reared and cared for generations of dandelions, comfrey, chickweed, burdock, alfalfa, wild violets, and stinging nettles. Wild edibles have made a home for themselves (which they are most adamant about not leaving!) in my garden, and they are a welcomed guest at my table, whether I am preparing a meal for myself or my family or entertaining friends.

Rules for Foraging

There are a few rules to follow regarding the gathering and harvesting of wild edibles that will help guarantee the quality of your pickings and the health and survival of the remaining plant.

1. Always carry an illustrated botanical field guide to identify edible species. Never rely on illustrations alone, however. Always double-check the plant against the description in the guide. Many poisonous and safe edible herbs and flowers look remarkably alike. So check, identify, and check again. If you are unsure about the safety of a food, don't eat it. Your health and the health of your unborn child are under your care, and it is important to pay attention to details.

2. Even though it is essential to know what you are picking, do not become too worried about the possible dangers of poisonous plants. In comparison with edible species, they are few and far between. To put the danger into perspective, consider these facts: Most cultivated foods purchased in supermarkets are sprayed with fertilizers and pesticides, which leave residues. When eaten in excess, many cultivated, genetically manipulated foods can bring on chronic and acute degenerative conditions, and almost any food substance can provoke an allergic reaction, but all these effects are rare. The point is, they are all a part of the hazards of eating and don't pertain to a particular food category. After considering your own survival in light of having eaten these nutritious, health-promoting, and beauty-enhancing foods, ponder the continued survival of the plant species.

3. Take only a few leaves, flowers, berries, seeds, or nuts from a group of plants of the same species, instead of stripping bare one plant.

4. Always cut the plant part with a sharp knife or pair of scissors.
5. Take your harvest home in an open basket so as not to squash it; then wash it well in cold, running water, sort out any dead or decaying parts, and let dry.

Roots

Of all the wild edibles available, roots are probably the least used. Few species form thick, fleshy roots, and those few that do are used mainly for flavoring other dishes. (In Britain, it is illegal to dig up the roots of a wild plant unless it is in your own garden.) Of the roots that are available, many are versatile enough to be included in soups, vegetable stews, salads, and drinks. Gingerroot, burdock, dandelion, and chicory roots cook quickly and are palatable when prepared with other tasty herbs and vegetables.

Green Leafy Vegetables

Most wild greens are smaller than their cultivated cousins. Picking enough for a family meal can be time-consuming, but worth the effort: their nutritional content is as much as 50 percent higher. The optimum picking time for these plants is while they are in flower and easily identified. They can be used in salads, soups, garnishes, blended sauces, and stews. Dandelions, sea beet, chickweed, and nettle can be cooked like spinach, or added raw to salads for a refreshing, palatable change from iceberg lettuce.

Herbs and Spices

These leafy plants and seeds are used mainly as seasonings for other foods. Their textures and aromas can enhance a salad or garnish an entree with their vibrant colors and delicate flavors. All herbs can be used to flavor vinegars, oils, and drinks.

Flowers

A word of caution: not all flowers are edible. Some are highly poisonous and can be fatal. If you cannot positively identify a flower as being edible, do not eat it. Do not garnish plates or bowls of food with nonedible flowers at picnics or parties. It is especially important when foraging for flowers to have your field guide with you, even when you're only going to the far reaches of your own garden!

Edible Flowers
  Anise hyssop (*Agastache foeniculum*)
  Apple (*Malus—rose family*)
  Basil (*Ocimum basilicum*)
  Bee balm (*Monarda didyma*)
  Borage (*Borago officinalis*)
  Chamomile, English (*Anthemis nobilis*)
  Chicory (*Cichorium intybus*)
  Dandelion (*Taraxacum officinale*)
  Dill (*Anethum graveolens*)
  Elder flower (*Sambucus careulea*)
  Honeysuckle (*Lonicera japonica*)
  Hyssop (*Hyssopus officinalis*)
  Johnny-jump-up (*Viola tricolor*)
  Lavender (*Lavandula angustifolia*)
  Marjoram (*Origanum marjorana*)
  Mustard (*Brassica*)
  Nasturtium (*Tropaeolum majus*)
  Pansy (*Viola*)
  Pea (*Pisum sativum*)
  Radish (*Raphanus sativus*)

Rose (*Rosa*)
Sage (*Salvia officinalis*)
Signet marigold (*Tagetes signata*)
Squash blossoms (*Cucurbita pepo*)

Toxic Flowers (Do Not Eat!)

Azalea (*Azalea*)
Boxwood (*Buxus*)
Buttercup (*Ranunculus*)
Cherry laurel (*Prunus carolinia*)
Clematis (*Clematis*)
Daffodil (*Narcissus*)
Delphinium (*Delphinium*)
Foxglove (*Digitalis purpurea*)
Goldenrod (*Solidago virgaurea*)
Hyacinth (*Hyacinthus orientalis*)
Hydrangea (*Hydrangea*)
Iris (*Iris*)
Jack-in-the-pulpit (*Arisaema triphyllum*)
Jimsonweed (*Datura stramonium*)
Lily of the valley (*Convallaria majalis*)
Lobelia (*Lobelia*)
Marsh marigold (*Caltha palustris*)
Mistletoe (*Phoradendron*)
Mountain laurel (*Kalmia latifolia*)
Nightshade (*Solanum*)
Oleander (*Nerium oleander*)
Pennyroyal (*Hedeoma pulegioides*)
Poppy (*Papaver somniferum*)
Rhododendron (*Rhododendron*)
Spurge (*Euphorbia*)

Sweet pea (*Lathyrus odoratus*)
Wisteria (*Wisteria*)
Yellow allamanda (*Allamanda cathartica*)

If you are allergic to pollen or are prone to contact dermatitis, do not eat edible flowers. You should eat only flowers that have been grown organically. If you don't spray your own garden with pesticides or weed killers, the wild edibles will be naturally organic for generations and thus safe to eat. Do not be tempted to eat edible flowers grown in nurseries or garden centers. Do not pick flowers grown on the roadside, even those way out in the countryside. Generations have been contaminated with agricultural sprays, car fumes, and roadside impurities. They are pretty to pick for table displays, but never eat them. When using edible flowers, make sure that you strip the petals off the stamen and pistils. Only cook with and eat the petals of a flower.

Wild Edibles Available from the Seashore

Like other plants, seaweeds are subject to seasonal growth changes. They produce shoots in the spring, grow quickly in the summer months, and wither in the winter. Late April, May, and June are the best months to gather fresh, edible seaweeds.

Most edible seaweeds can be eaten raw in salads or cooked and added to stews or soups to thicken them. Seaweeds obtain their nourishment from the surrounding seawater and thus do not have roots like other plants. They attach themselves to rocks and shells by holdfasts, from which a stripe grows. You can gather seaweeds that have broken free from their "home," or you can cut part of the plant. If you choose to do the latter, make sure that you do not cut too close to the holdfast so that the sea vegetable can regenerate itself and does not perish.

Before cooking or preparing a sea vegetable for eating, wash it thoroughly in fresh water to remove any sand or small shells that may have adhered to it during the tidal changes. Most seaweeds contain alginates, a kind of vegetable gelatin that is released during long periods of cooking.

Seaweeds are low in calories but rich in minerals, particularly the iodides. Include them in salads, stir-fries, and soups. I have eaten seaweeds all my life and found them especially important to my pregnancy diet because of their valuable ocean-rich mineral content of silicons, iodine, bromine, and carotene. Sea lettuce, kelp, carragheen, dulse, and wakame are common seaweed varieties, which can be purchased dried at most health foods stores. I eat seaweed as a condiment and as an ingredient staple in many recipes.

MY SPROUTING KITCHEN 🌾

I've been a vegetarian for about nineteen years: during that time, I've researched and tested many different kinds of food for their nutritional, medicinal, and cosmetic benefits. During one of my pregnancies, I began experimenting with sprouted and fermented foods, which, I quickly discovered, provided many of the benefits I was looking for. And not only that, they were cheap. How cheap? Imagine being able to eat a nutritious, appetizing, health-promoting, inner-healing, and energy-boosting menu for a whole week for less than twenty-five dollars.

Sprouted and fermented foods provide a pleasant, light alternative to dairy products, meats, fast food, and microwaved meals. For the pregnant woman, these high-energy foods offer nutritious, light eating that is filling, easily digestible, and varied enough to tempt even the most fanatic junk food addict. I still continue to make and drink these delicious sprouted beverages three years after my last pregnancy, and weaned my children off animal milks completely by the time they were two years old. I made tasty, nutritious, child-friendly beverages with sprouted seeds and nuts.

Making Sprouted Beverages

Sprouted beverages can be added to fresh fruit juice, muesli, and vegetable broth, or drunk alone as a refreshing midmorning drink (they do not, however, complement coffee, tea, or other hot commercial beverages). Take a few minutes to think about how much you will spend making your "milk" for the day (probably fifty cents). And you will have enough seeds, nuts, or grains to make a whole week's worth of milk. You will have wasted nothing, because the sprouted water can feed your houseplants, and the pulp of these grains, seeds, and nuts can be used to make savory cheeses and sweet spreads.

Basic Recipe for Sprouted Beverages

A delicious, light alternative to dairy for drinks, cereals, and shakes.

> *2 cups nuts, grains, or seeds*
> *8 cups mineral water*

> Put the nuts, grains, or seeds of your choice (wheat berries, pine nuts, and almonds are the most versatile and nutritious) in a glass jar, and cover with 3 cups of the mineral water. Let soak for 6 to 12 hours, or overnight. Wheat berries, barley, and rice need 2 soaks, while most other seeds need only 1. The nuts will sprout, swelling until approximately double in size, in about 8 hours. Once they have sprouted, strain them through a fine-mesh sieve (save the water to nourish your house plants).

Place the sprouts in a blender and add the remaining 5 cups of mineral water. Blend for I minute on a high speed. Strain this mixture through a sieve again.

Making Sprouted Cheeses and Spreads

Sprouted cheeses and spreads make a delicious low-fat, high-energy alternative to dairy or other commercial products. If you're looking for pure living nutrition for you and your baby, look no further than these simple and nutritious foods.

Savory Sprouted Cheese

Ideal for a midmorning break, this snack can be garnished with fresh basil and vegetable sticks.

> *1 cup day-old wheat sprout water*
> *1½ cups day-old sprouted seeds or nuts (pinenuts, sunflower seeds, or cashews)*
> *½ cup chopped mixed vegetables of your choice*
> *½ cup fresh herbs of your choice*
> *Cheese Base (recipe follows)*

In a medium bowl, mix the water, seeds or nuts, and fruit. Season with the spices. Add the cheese base, place in a sealed container, and refrigerate. Serve chilled.

Makes enough for I meal

Making the Cheese Base

> *1 cup wheat berries*
> *4 cups mineral water*

In a small bowl, soak the wheat berries in 3 cups of the water for 12 hours. (Doing this overnight is a good idea, so that you are able to make up the cheeses and spread the following morning.) Strain the sprouted wheat berries through a fine-mesh sieve, and set aside the soak water in a glass-lidded bottle or jar. (Refrigerated, it will keep for up to 4 days.) Wash the sprouted berries with cold running water; then return to the jar, covered, with the remaining 1 cup of mineral water. Soak for another 12 hours.

Once the wheat berries have soaked for the first 12-hour period, the soak water will turn a translucent tan color (like cold tea) and will have a sweet aroma. This makes a refreshing drink in itself, sweetened with a little honey or molasses to taste. (Personally, I like it raw, unsweetened.) This grain soak water is so nutritious; it contains all the B vitamins and purifies the digestive flora in your intestines, which often become malnourished with poor eating habits. Wheat fermentation water contains most of the minerals the skin requires on a daily basis to regenerate and rejuvenate cells.

Take the sprouted nuts or seeds and place them in the blender with 2 to 3 tablespoons of the wheat-berry soak water and blend slowly for 30 seconds. This is your cheese base.

MAKES ENOUGH FOR 1 MEAL

Sweet Sprouted-Cheese Spread

A delicate sweet spread ideal for crackers, fruit, dips, and salad toppings.

> 1 cup day-old wheat sprout water
> 1½ cups day-old sprouted seeds or nuts (pinenuts, sunflower seeds, or cashews)
> ½ cup dried fruit of your choice, diced
> ¼ teaspoon spices of your choice
> Cheese Base (pages 96–97)

Chop the dried fruits finely and put in a medium bowl. Season with the ¼ teaspoon spices. Add the cheese base and mix thoroughly. Place in a sealed container and refrigerate. Serve chilled.

MAKES ENOUGH FOR 3 SNACK MEALS
(APPROXIMATELY 1 CUP)

The above recipes are just starting points: other great combinations included almond and sesame, and pine nut and sunflower (which makes a good sweet, fruity spread). Experiment and discover which combinations please your taste buds!

Making Sun-Dried Breads

Here's another product you can make from your leftover sprouted seeds, nuts, and grains.

Giving Texture, Taste, Aroma and Color to Cheeses

So you're having bread and cheese for your garden picnic. That's okay! But how about adding further nutrition and texture with edible flowers and decorating your feast quite spectacularly at the same time?

If you have a soft cheese, the flowers can be pressed in, then refrigerated before serving. Or you can make an aspic layer to go over the cheese, and then place the flowers on top. This second method takes a little more preparation time, but the results are well worth it. Adding an aspic layer also lets you use just about any edible flower or herb with any variety of cheese.

Cheese in Aspic

2 cups dry white wine
1 ounce agar
A cheese to be decorated
Edible flowers for garnish

Combine the wine with the agar in a small saucepan. Heat the mixture over low heat until the gelatin powder has completely melted and the mixture is clear, about 5 minutes.

Place the saucepan inside another saucepan filled with ice. As the mixture cools, stir it carefully, making sure no bubbles form. Remove from the ice-filled saucepan when it has thickened, about 5 minutes.

Place the cheese in a shallow dish. Spoon the aspic over the cheese, covering all surfaces. Let stand for about 5 minutes, until the jelly is tacky to the touch.

Now you can place and arrange your flowers. Once your decorating is complete, place the newly adorned cheese in the refrigerator for 10 minutes. Then remove and reglaze with a layer of the gelatin mixture over the decoration.

Experiment with the different colors and textures of flowers or gelatin. Use herbs as well: select tastes that you like to eat, and colors that appeal to your moods and appetite.

MAKES ENOUGH TO DECORATE 1-POUND BLOCK OF CHEESE

Basic Recipe for Sun-Dried Bread

A light, crunchy (and filling) bread, which is ideal for either the sweet or savory sprouted spreads.

> *1 cup day-old sprouted wheat berries, plus ¼ cup soak water*
> *1 teaspoon chopped fruits/spices (dates, raisins, banana chips, or coconut for sweet breads) or vegetables/herbs (onions, grated carrots, celery, basil, sundried tomato, or garlic for savory breads)*
> *½ teaspoon seaweed/spices*
> *¼ cup fresh raw wheat-germ flakes*
> *Seeds (sunflower, pumpkin, sesame, or poppy)*

Wash the wheat berries in cold water. Place them in a blender with the fruits/spices or the vegetables/herbs. Add the wheat-germ flakes. Blend on low for 30 seconds.

Dust a work surface with more wheat-germ flakes, and scoop the mixture out of the blender.

Knead the mixture with your hands: if it is too wet, add more wheat-germ flakes. If too dry, add a little wheat-berry soak water.

Dust a rolling pin with some ground mixed spices (for the fruit bread) or ground herbs (for the savory bread) and the seaweed. Roll the dough to a thickness of about ¼ inch.

Cut into 4-inch squares. Press in some raw sunflower, pumpkin, sesame, or poppy seeds for extra nutrition and texture. Do this on both sides of the dough.

Place all the cut bread on a drying mesh and dry in the sunshine on a dry day, or in a warm, dry, well-ventilated room where it won't be disturbed (a ventilated sunroom works well). You can even place the bread in an oven with just the pilot light left on for heat and light.

Let bake for 8 to 12 hours, turning frequently so that both sides dry completely.

Pack each bread square in greaseproof paper, such as confectionary bags or sheets, then place in a covered plastic container in the refrigerator until ready to use. These breads taste much better if they are removed from the refrigerator 1 hour before eating and sit in the warm sunshine or in a warm oven for 5 to 10 minutes.

MAKES APPROXIMATELY 12 SQUARES

As soon as you become accustomed to the taste of these fermented and sprouted foods, you can begin experimenting with a variety of garnishes. I like eating the breads with a sea-vegetable broth, or steamed vegetables seasoned with vinegar and garden herbs. These foods are a wonderful addition to your pregnancy diet because they are light yet filling, low in calories but high in essential nutrients, and they taste as good as grandma's homemade pasties and pastries.

Making Your Own Live Yogurt

Yogurt is another nutritious fermented food that is simple to make at home and a valuable supplement to your wholesome pregnancy diet. Your own yogurt, made fresh daily, will taste much sweeter than the commercial, supermarket varieties. It will have the added bonus of ample supplies of "friendly," health-giving bacteria, and no added preservatives. (It won't actually last long enough to spoil, since being as versatile as it is it will be gobbled up before the end of one day!) All you need is an oven with a pilot light or a high shelf that is exposed to warm sunlight for about 8 hours a day.

Basic Recipe for Yogurt

A delicious condiment and a base for my baby formulas.

> *1 pint fresh goat's milk, or 1 cup dried milk to 1 pint water (for best results, begin making the mix with 1 tablespoon of hot water, then add the remaining cold water)*
>
> *2 teaspoons Yogourmet (See Note), or 1 tablespoon plain active goat's yogurt*

Pour the goat's milk into a pitcher and add the Yogourmet. Whisk gently.

Pour the mixture into a sterilized glass jar. Cover with a piece of cotton cloth or paper toweling and fasten it to the rim with a rubber band or string.

Leave the fermenting yogurt in a warm place for about 8 to 10 hours, or overnight. Strain through a fine-mesh sieve, and gently whisk again.

Spoon the yogurt into a ceramic pot with a lid and store in the refrigerator until ready to use. Wash to sterilize the glass jar.

Set aside 3 tablespoons of your fresh yogurt as a starter for your next batch. If yogurt is going to be a staple food throughout your pregnancy (it won't take you long to discover its versatility), you will need to make a new batch every day. Letting it ferment during the night—while you sleep—means you can strain, rebottle, and use it the following day, continually using one batch as a starter for the next.

MAKES I PINT

NOTE: YOGOURMET IS A FREEZE-DRIED YOGURT STARTER AVAILABLE FROM HEALTH-FOOD STORES.

Make Your Own Baby Formula

After feeding my children a pure, natural diet while they were inside my womb, I wouldn't entertain the idea of introducing them to chemically altered food substances like commercial formulas. So after breast-feeding, I placed them on a homemade formula.

I made this formula every day from fresh yogurt, spirulina, goat's milk, and freshly extracted pear or apple juice. It must have tasted better than it looked! My babies enjoyed their formula so much that they were often sucking only air at the end of each bottle. I also made toasted-rice milk and mixed that with spirulina and pear juice. The following recipe is named for my third child.

Tamara's Formula

I made enough fresh yogurt and milk before refrigerating to last through a whole day. I added the spirulina and mixed in the pear juice just before each of her feeds. Although breast-feeding was more convenient and pleasurable for me, I found that she was very satisfied with this substitute.

> *2½ cups fresh yogurt*
> *2½ cups goat's milk*
> *¼ teaspoon spirulina*
> *½ cup pear juice or purée*

Make the yogurt (see basic recipe, page 102). Place the yogurt, goat's milk, spirulina, and pear juice in a blender. Blend for 30 seconds on low. Strain twice. Pour mixture in a bottle.

MAKES ENOUGH FOR 1 FEEDING

This formula works. While I was pregnant and nursing, I daily drank a combination of wheat-grass and barley-grass juice (I sprouted and grew the grasses in my bathroom) and spirulina for 6 months. This protected my children from ear infections. Then I introduced whole-grain and cereal-milk formulas.

I have discovered that natural grains and other whole natural foods are used to imitate the natural production of a mother's milk, which is made from the cereal grains and other natural foods that we eat. In terms of the micronutrients, brown rice and wheat grains come very close to natural breast milk. Pure coconut milk is the same consistency and contains the same vital nutrients a newborn infant requires (but imagine just how many coconut trees you would have to climb to get enough milk for 8 to 10 feeds a day!).

EATING FOODS TO HARMONIZE WITH YOUR MOODS

During pregnancy, the daily insanity can be overwhelming, to say the least. You may wonder if your brain circuitry has blown a fuse as you fumble through your day, tripping over your own feet, thinking and worrying about everything and nothing all at the same time. Don't add to the stress your changing body is going through: feed your moods and emotions the nutrients they need. Don't light that short fuse you're on with hot spicy chili for lunch, washed down with icy cold soda and followed by two or three sticky donuts. You need to be fully in control of your emotions, especially when everything else in your life seems to be out of balance. Eat healthily for yourself and your growing baby. After all, your responses to the foods you eat are shared with your baby, too.

Sit down for a few moments and think about your daily moods. What types of reactions are triggered by various foods? How do you feel upon awakening each morning—are you joyous, decisive, passionate, relaxed or assertive; or are you shy, timid, irritable, worried, confused, tired, or compulsive?

For a week, keep a record of your feelings upon awakening, after breakfast, midmorning, lunchtime, midafternoon, and dinnertime. Beside each heading, describe the snacks and meals you consumed. Be specific: read all the labels on purchased items, and look for the additives, coloring, and preservatives. Are you eating too many processed or prepared foods? Are you eating in pleasant surroundings? How do you feel twenty minutes to an hour after eating? Which foods make you feel bloated and uncomfortable? Which ones make you feel light and energized?

Ask yourself these 5 questions:

1. How do the foods I eat affect the way I behave every day?
2. Who am I when I eat junk foods?
3. Who am I when I eat whole grains, seaweeds, vegetables, wild edibles, and herbs?
4. Who am I when I eat processed, chemically manipulated foods and meat?
5. How am I willing to change the way I eat and the way I feel?

When you find the foods that change your moods in a negative way, slowly eliminate them from your diet.

Choosing a Basic Mood Meal Plan

How you are feeling and what you are eating greatly affect your reactions to situations and circumstances. Harsh foods, such as meats, contain the fear of the killed animal, which can lead to violent outbursts and frustration. Gentle foods, such as fruits and vegetables, come from Mother Earth and lead to inner balance and humility. You need to be in complete control of your emotions so that you can respond to situations that need your full attention—driving, cooking, and playing with children, for example. During every minute of the day, your body is under the influence of the foods you ate at your last meal. So treat it with respect. Give your growing body foods that harmonize, heal, and promote growth.

The foods you eat on a daily basis can reduce sweet cravings, regulate blood-sugar levels, settle indigestion, tone the lungs, cleanse the blood, increase stamina, restore energy, rejuvenate sexual vitality, reduce cholesterol, dissolve accumulated fats and mucus, relieve hay fever and sinus trouble, relieve stress, loosen tension in muscles and tendons, and bring a sense of wellness to your whole body. The most energizing and beneficial diet is one that brings you closer to Mother Earth and all her natural resources.

When thinking about your meal plan, ask yourself how you want to feel an hour after eating. In fact, how do you want to feel each day throughout your pregnancy? Have faith in your intuition when making decisions, and remember to keep meals simple and natural.

A pure, natural, mood-enhancing diet is based on seasonal vegetables and cooked whole grains, sprouted foods and beverages, herbs, wild greens, edible flowers, sea vegetation, and pure well or mineral water. Nothing added, nothing taken away—just as nature intended human beings to eat. Following is an appetizing spread of recipes and meals built around the positive, mood-enhancing benefits of natural foods.

You will see from the ingredients included that these recipes pack a powerful nutritional punch, in addition to helping you deal with the many moods of pregnancy, from exhilaration to feelings of overwhelming sadness. You'll suffer minor symptoms of bodily imbalances, but these foods will start you off to a self-healing lifestyle, helping to bring your body into a renewed state of balance. Mood foods teach you three principles:

1. Eat in harmony with nature.
2. Use foods to create desired effects.
3. Balance natural forces in cooking.

Keep your meals simple. Your body and lifestyle during pregnancy are unique. There is no other woman quite like you. No other woman will experience her pregnancy the way you will. So make it an adventure of tastes, aromas, and textures, and begin a fresh approach to diet and emotional healing.

The following wonderful recipes take full advantage of the herbal pantry and the principles discussed thus far in the book. I've included a sample menu at the end of this section, which I urge you to try. You will be amazed at the results, and the energy you will have.

RECIPES ~

Chickweed and Wakame Curry

A light Asian dish enhanced with succulent, crisp garden vegetables and meadow greens.

> *2 strips wakame*
> *3 tablespoons extra-virgin olive oil*
> *1 teaspoon cumin seeds, cracked*
> *1 teaspoon ground turmeric*
> *4 wild mushrooms, such as parasol, caesar's, chanterelles, giant puffballs, saffron milk or caps, chopped*
> *1 small fennel bulb, diced*
> *2 broccoli florets*
> *1 tablespoon tamari*
> *1 tablespoon cider vinegar*
> *3 cups fresh chickweed, chopped*
> *4 cherry tomatoes, halved*
> *20 fresh dandelion leaves*

In a small saucepan, boil the wakame in a little spring water; then simmer for 15 minutes.

Heat the oil in a large saucepan over medium heat. Add the cumin, turmeric, mushrooms, fennel, broccoli, tamari, and vinegar. Add the wakame and cook the mixture for 10 minutes on low heat. Add the chopped chickweed, stir well, cover, and remove from the heat. Let sit for 5 minutes. Serve with tomatoes on a bed of dandelion leaves.

MAKES 4 SERVINGS

Wild Rice and Burdock

A hearty herb dish that's filling and cleansing.

1 burdock root
4¼ cups pure mineral or filtered tap water
1 cup wild rice
1 cup brown rice
¼ teaspoon dried dulse
¼ teaspoon dried nori
½ sweet onion
15 dandelion leaves, rinsed and drained
6 fennel stalks with feathered fronds

Wash the burdock root gently; then chop into 10 small pieces. In a small bowl, soak the burdock in 2 cups of the water for 5 to 10 minutes. Transfer to a medium nonreactive saucepan with a secure lid and bring to a boil. Add the remaining 2½ cups of water, wild and brown rice, and the dulse and nori. Return to a boil, then reduce to a simmer and cook for 35 to 45 minutes. Dice the onion.

Decorate a serving dish with the dandelion and fennel. When the rice and burdock are cooked, spoon them into the dish and sprinkle with the diced onion. Serve hot.

MAKES 2 SERVINGS

Dandelion Cheese Bake

A great-tasting bake for the whole family.

6 small new potatoes
4 to 6 cups fresh dandelion leaves, rinsed

2 tablespoons extra-virgin olive oil
2 small sweet white onions, diced
10 small tomatoes, quartered
thyme, basil, fennel, peppercorns, and garlic, ground, to taste
kelp, powdered, to taste
½ cup ricotta cheese
½ cup sharp Cheddar cheese
4 fresh dill flower heads

Wash the potatoes, leaving on the skins. Chop into small chunks. Place in a large saucepan with enough water to cover; then place the dandelion leaves on top of the potatoes. Cover the saucepan, bring to a boil over high heat, lower the heat, and simmer for 10 minutes.

In a wok, heat the oil and sauté the onions and tomatoes until soft and transparent. Drain the potatoes and dandelion leaves (save the water for a refreshing evening facial wash), and add the sautéed onions and tomatoes. Add the ground thyme, basil, fennel, peppercorns, garlic, and powdered kelp.

Transfer to an ovenproof dish and crumble the ricotta and Cheddar cheeses on top. Decorate with the dill flower heads and bake at 350°F until the cheese melts. Eat with savory sprouted-seed sun breads and a cold-pressed peanut or almond butter.

MAKES 4 SERVINGS

Leek and Violet Leaf Soup

An exquisitely creamy and satisfying soup to eat on a cool, moon-lit night under the stars.

½ cup wild mushrooms

1 cup wild leeks

1 small sweet onion, diced

1 pinch powdered kelp

1 pinch powdered dulse

3 tablespoons extra-virgin olive oil

4 cups fresh violet leaves

4 cups mineral water

5 cups fresh goat's milk

Pinch of ground nutmeg

In a skillet or wok, sauté the mushrooms, leeks, onion, and powdered kelp and dulse in the olive oil over medium heat for about 4 minutes. Chop the violet leaves and add to the pan. Stir well, then add the water. Lower the heat and simmer for 15 minutes; then put into a blender for 30 seconds at high speed.

Return the mixture to the saucepan, add the goat's milk, and reheat. Sprinkle with a few violet flowers and a pinch of ground nutmeg. Serve hot, with sprouted-grain bread, and seed butter.

MAKES 4 SERVINGS

Arame Oriental

Rich in calcium and iron, this dish is filling and warming.

1 cup fresh arame seaweed, or dried

1 small sweet onion, diced

¼ cup diced red bell pepper

1 celery rib, diced

10 baby carrots, diced

2 teaspoons sesame seed oil (cold pressed)

1 teaspoon cider vinegar

1 teaspoon tamari

Wash the seaweed if fresh; if dried, soak in a little water before cooking. Place in a small saucepan, cover with cold water, and bring to a boil over medium heat. Lower the heat and simmer for 3 to 5 minutes; then add the onion and pepper. Cover and simmer for 15 minutes. Add the celery and carrots with a little more water, if needed, to keep the seaweed moist, but not saturated. (When you're done cooking, most of the water should have evaporated.) Simmer for another 5 minutes. Add the oil, vinegar, and tamari. Stir again; then serve hot.

MAKES 4 SERVINGS

Root Vegetable Stew with Wakame

1 4-inch strip wakame

1 small onion, diced

1 small burdock root, sliced

1 parsnip, cubed

3 baby courgettes

1 cup cooked green lentils

1 pinch herbal seasoning, such as garlic or fennel

1 tablespoon tamari

8 whole outer spinach leaves

½ cup diced celery

1 teaspoon mirin

Soak the wakame seaweed in mineral water for 5 minutes.
Cut into ½-inch pieces and place in a medium saucepan
with the soak water. Bring to a boil over medium heat. Add
the onion, burdock root, parsnip, courgettes, and lentils.
Lower the heat, cover, and simmer for 10 minutes. Sprinkle
with the seasoning, add the tamari, and cover with the
spinach leaves and celery. Cover with a lid and simmer for
another 10 minutes. Add the mirin, stir, and serve.

MAKES 2 SERVINGS

Pansy and Chicory Garden-Patch Salad

A delicate and colorful spring salad dish.

2 small fennel bulbs, chopped
20 fresh young dandelion leaves
6 beet greens
15 sprouted buckwheat greens (6 days' growth)
¼ cup wheat-grass sprouts (5 days' growth)
3 tablespoons extra-virgin olive oil
1 teaspoon balsamic vinegar
1 tablespoon pineapple juice
1 pinch celery salt
1 pinch powdered kelp
15 pansy flowers
7 chicory flowers
20 broccoli flowers

Gently wash the fennel, dandelion leaves, beet greens,
buckwheat greens, and wheat-grass sprouts. Spin the larger
leaves; then place all of them in a large salad bowl. Toss
gently; then add the oil, vinegar, juice, salt, and kelp. Toss

with a fork; then add the pansy, chicory, and broccoli flowers. Chill. Serve with sprouted sun breads and nut cheese.

MAKES 4 SERVINGS

Herbed Potato and Sprouted-Seed Salad

A light but satisfying seasonal salad dish, ideal with freshly steamed corn or nut bread.

8 new potatoes
1 pinch of dulse granules
1 pinch of powdered kelp
1 pinch of coarse sea salt
¼ cup diced green bell pepper
¼ cup diced red bell pepper
5 sprigs fresh parsley, chopped
4 chives, chopped
1 tablespoon extra-virgin olive oil
1 teaspoon balsamic vinegar
Juice of 1 small lime
½ cup sprouted sesame seeds (1 day's growth)
½ cup sprouted sunflower seeds (1 day's growth)
10 Johnny-jump-up flowers (assorted colors)
5 nasturtium flowers
Freshly ground black pepper

Steam the potatoes in a little mineral water. Strain; then cool. Chop into small chunks. Dust with the dulse, kelp, and salt; then place in a wooden salad bowl. Decoratively layer the green pepper, red pepper, parsley, and chives. Add the oil, vinegar, and lime juice. Toss with a fork, sprinkle with the sprouted sesame and sunflower seeds, and toss again. Chill before adding the Johnny-jump-up and nasturtium flower petals. Sprinkle with freshly ground black pepper and serve with steamed corn on the cob.

MAKES I SERVING

Nasturtium and Carrot Slaw

A colorful, mood-enhancing salad that's low fat, low guilt, and utterly delicious.

½ cup grated pumpkin
¼ cup grated rutabaga
8 baby carrots, thinly sliced
1 tablespoon fennel herbed vinegar
¼ cup raisins, soaked overnight in water
½ cup homemade yogurt
¼ cup homemade mayonnaise
1 cup alfalfa sprouts (5 days' growth)
10 fennel fronds
10 nasturtium flower heads (assorted colors)

Place the pumpkin, rutabaga, and carrots into a small bowl and toss with the vinegar. Add the raisins, yogurt, and mayonnaise. Refrigerate for 10 to 15 minutes until cold.

Meanwhile, mix the alfalfa sprouts and fennel fronds in the bottom of a salad bowl. Decorate with the nasturtium flower heads.

When when ready to serve, remove the slaw from the refrigerator and place I teaspoon into each flower head. On each serving plate, lay a bed of alfalfa and fennel leaves, then 2 nasturtium flower heads packed with the slaw. Dust with poppy seeds and dulse granules.

MAKES 5 SERVINGS

Dandelion and Chickweed Fritters

A light and crunchy deep-fried snack in a tasty corn batter.

1 cup corn flour (organic)
1 pinch sea salt
1 pinch powdered kelp
1 free-range egg, lightly beaten
1 cup fresh goat's milk or dried goat's milk and pure mineral water
12 whole large dandelion flower heads, plus the petals from 5 heads
12 chickweed flowers
10 large dandelion leaves
10 large basil leaves
10 beet greens
½ cup buckwheat sprouts (5 days' growth)
½ cup sunflower-seed sprouts (7 days' growth)
5 fresh parsley sprigs
1 teaspoon extra-virgin olive oil
1 teaspoon lime juice
Vegetable oil for deep-frying

Start by making the corn batter: Sift the flour with the salt and kelp. Make a well in the middle of the mixture. Add the egg and ½ cup of the milk. Beat well, then add enough of the remaining milk to make a loose, yet not too runny, batter. Let stand 20 to 30 minutes.

Meanwhile, carefully wash the dandelion and chickweed flower heads. Remove the leaves near the flower heads, but leave a little of the stalk. Make a decorative salad using the dandelion leaves, basil, beet greens, buckwheat and sunflower sprouts, and parsley. Lightly toss with olive oil and lime juice.

Add enough oil to a deep saucepan to reach a depth of 3 inches. Heat until it reaches a temperature of 365°F. Dip the dandelion and chickweed flower heads in the batter. Deep-fry the flower fritters until golden brown on all sides. Drain on paper toweling. Sprinkle with the dandelion petals and serve hot.

MAKES 6 SERVINGS

Ginger and Dill Flower Broth

An Asian aromatic broth that's warming and filling.

2 tablespoons extra-virgin olive oil
1 small onion, diced
¼ cup diced bell pepper
1 teaspoon finely grated gingerroot
1 teaspoon ground turmeric
2 teaspoons vegetable stock
1 teaspoon cumin seeds, cracked
½ cup diced celery
2 sprigs fresh parsley
2 baby spring carrots, thinly sliced
5 dill flower heads, plus extra for garnish
1 cup homemade yogurt
¼ cup raw sweet corn kernels
Dill leaves for garnish

Place the olive oil in a medium saucepan over medium heat and add the diced onion, pepper, ginger, turmeric,

vegetable stock, and cumin. Cook, stirring occasionally,
until the onions are soft and transparent. Lower the heat
and add the celery, parsley, carrots, and dill flowers. Cook
for 15 minutes. Allow to cool for 10 minutes; then place
in a blender. Blend the mixture for 30 seconds on a low
speed; then return to the saucepan. Add the yogurt and
sweet corn and cook over low heat for another 10 minutes.
Garnish with whole dill flowers and leaves, and serve hot
with sprouted savory sun breads or a toasted pita bread.

Makes 2 servings

Red Clover and Wild Rice Salad

A light, tangy-flavored salad ideal with grain bread or stuffed
field mushrooms.

> 1 cup wild rice
> ¼ cup brown rice
> 2 cups mineral water
> 1 teaspoon dulse granules
> 1 pinch powdered kelp
> 1 tablespoon extra-virgin olive oil
> 1 tablespoon freshly squeezed orange juice
> 1 cup red-clover leaves
> 5 fresh spearmint leaves, minced
> 2 cups red-clover blossoms

Place the wild rice and brown rice in a medium saucepan
or rice cooker. Add the water, dulse, and kelp. Bring to a
boil over medium heat. Lower the heat and simmer until
tender. Drain while still hot and transfer to a medium
bowl. Add the olive oil and fresh orange juice.

Place the clover leaves and mint in a salad bowl; then add the rice and combine well. Toss in a few of the clover blossoms. Chill before serving and garnish with the remaining clover blossoms.

Eat as a refreshing snack with lightly steamed root vegetables, seasoned with fresh dill and fennel herb vinegar and sprouted sunflower seeds. Great for a summer picnic!

MAKES 2 SERVINGS

Tansy Pancakes and Cherry Tomato Salad

A zesty, sweet snack with a plentiful blend of color and taste.

12 cherry tomatoes, quartered
1 cup sprouted sunflower seeds (1 day's growth)
1 cup sprouted pine nuts (1 day's growth)
1 teaspoon molasses
2 cups unbleached all-purpose organic flour
2 free-range eggs
1 cup half-and-half
1 teaspoon blossom honey, plus extra for drizzling
1 teaspoon grated orange zest
1 teaspoon grated lemon zest
2 teaspoons balsamic vinegar
½ cup chopped fresh tansy flower heads
6 graham crackers, crumbled
1 tablespoon unsalted butter, melted
1 tablespoon salted butter
lemon slices for garnish

Sprinkle the tomatoes with the sprouted sunflower seeds and pine nuts, and glaze with the molasses. Set aside.

Sift the flour into a medium bowl, and beat in the eggs and half-and-half to form a smooth batter. Add the honey, orange and lemon zests, vinegar, tansy flowers, graham crackers, and melted butter and mix thoroughly. Set aside for 15 minutes.

Heat the salted butter in a skillet. Drop several tablespoons of the batter into the hot butter and cook for 2 to 3 minutes, turning the pancakes over to cook on both sides. Serve each pancake hot with a slice of lemon, a drizzle of honey, and 1 tablespoon of the cherry tomato salad.

MAKES 4 SERVINGS

Spring Flower and Fruit Salad

A refreshing celebration dish dancing with summertime flavor and colors.

12 chamomile flowers
6 bee balm flowers
12 violets
2 honeysuckle flowers
1 ripe peach, pitted and sliced
1 ripe pear, cored and sliced
6 ripe strawberries, hulled and halved
1 sweet, juicy orange, sliced
2 small apples, cored and diced
1 cup fresh pineapple juice

Remove the petals from the chamomile, bee balm, violets, and honeysuckle and lightly mist with cold water. Put on a plate and refrigerate for 5 minutes. Place the peach, pear, strawberries, orange, and apples in a salad bowl and pour in the pineapple juice. Sprinkle with the flower petals, and serve with sweet or savory sprouted sun-dried breads, drizzled with blossom honey.

MAKES 2 SERVINGS

Lavender and Lime Zest Cookies

One of my favorite childhood memories is sitting on my grandmother's lawn eating these zesty cookies.

½ cup brown sugar
1 cup unbleached all-purpose flour
4 free-range egg whites
½ cup melted unsalted butter
¼ cup sprouted sesame seeds (1 day's growth)
Grated zest of 1 lime
¼ cup finely chopped fresh lavender blossoms

Preheat the oven to 450°F.

Blend the brown sugar with the flour in a medium bowl and beat in the egg whites. Stir the butter into the mixture and refrigerate for 10 minutes. In the meantime, lightly oil a cookie sheet.

Sprinkle the chilled dough with sprouted sesame seeds. Spoon onto the cookie sheet by the tablespoon, leaving about 1 inch of space between each dollop.

Bake for 1 to 2 minutes. Remove and sprinkle with the lime zest and lavender flowers and return to the oven for 3 minutes, or until lightly browned. Transfer cookies to a rack to cool. Enjoy with a refreshing cup of Earl Grey tea.

MAKES 8 TO 10 COOKIES

Tomato and Nasturtium Fritters

A great-tasting, crunchy midafternoon snack.

> 2 tablespoons plain flour
> 1 pinch sea salt
> 1 free-range egg, beaten
> 1 cup fresh goat's milk
> 12 nasturtium flowers (assorted colors)
> 6 fennel flower heads, chopped
> 2 large tomatoes, each cut into 6 slices
> 3 tablespoons baked pine nuts (see Note)
> Vegetable oil for deep-frying

Make the batter: Sift the flour and salt into a bowl and make a well in the middle. Add the beaten egg and a little of the milk. Mix to form a stiff paste, then add more milk, a little at a time, until a batter consistency has been reached. Cover and let stand for 20 minutes.

Mist the nasturtium flowers; then allow to air-dry on paper toweling. Dip each one in the batter and deep-fry 350°F. until golden brown. Sprinkle the fennel flowers over the tomato rounds on a bed of baked pine nuts. Serve the fritters hot, garnished with fennel flowers.

MAKES 6 SERVINGS

NOTE: TO BAKE PINE NUTS: PLACE THE PINE NUTS ON A BAKING SHEET. BAKE IN A 400°F. OVEN FOR 5 MINUTES, OR UNTIL GOLDEN BROWN.

Carrot and Calendula Spring Broth

A dazzling, crunchy and cheerful carrot soup.

4 tablespoons unsalted butter

1 small sweet onion, chopped

2 cloves garlic, crushed

1 tart apple, such as Granny Smith, cored and chopped

5 cumin seeds, cracked

½ teaspoon freshly ground nutmeg

2 cups vegetable stock

¼ cup sprouted sunflower seeds (1 day's growth)

8 baby carrots, chopped

1 teaspoon baked pine nuts (see Note, page 122)

½ cup goat's milk

1 cup fresh calendula petals

Melt the butter in a saucepan over low heat. Add the onion, garlic, apple, and cumin seeds and sauté for 5 minutes, or until the onions are tender and translucent. Add the nutmeg, stock, sprouted sunflower seeds, and carrots. Lower the heat to medium and cook for 25 minutes, stirring the mixture frequently.

Remove from the heat and carefully pour into a blender. Add the baked nuts and blend for 30 seconds on high, then 10 seconds on low, or until you have a smooth purée.

Return the purée to the saucepan and add the milk. Heat the broth on low heat for 5 to 10 minutes (do not allow to boil). Just before serving, sprinkle with the calendula petals. Enjoy with sprouted grain sun-dried breads or pita halves with sprouted-nut cheese.

MAKES 4 SERVINGS

Herbal Tea Combinations

Serve morning and evening teas warm, and midday teas cool with ice and edible flowers.

MAKING A GREAT CUP OF HERBAL ICED TEA

Even the smallest details can make the difference between a mediocre iced tea and a sublime one.

+ Always use fresh herbs or flowers.
+ Use a small cotton bag to tie the herbs.
+ Brew the tea in a glass or ceramic teapot.
+ Never, ever boil an herbal tea.
+ Use spring water instead of filtered tap water.
+ Make your herbal tea double strength to allow for dilution caused by the melting ice.
+ Use 2 generous tablespoons of fresh, crushed herb leaves or flowers for each glass of iced tea.

MORNING TEAS

Comfrey leaf and peppermint leaf
Comfrey leaf, ginseng root, and spearmint leaf
Comfrey leaf, red-raspberry leaf, and rosehip
Dandelion flower and spearmint leaf
Peppermint and red-raspberry leaf
Red-raspberry leaf and spearmint leaf

LUNCHTIME TEAS

Basil leaf, gingerroot, and ginseng root (after four months of pregnancy)
Catnip leaf and chamomile flower (before nap or meditation)
Chamomile flower and ginseng root

   Ginseng root and red-raspberry leaf
   Lemon balm and red-raspberry leaf

DINNER AND EVENING TEAS
   Anise seed and comfrey leaf
   Basil flower, comfrey leaf, and dill leaf and flower
   Chamomile flower and fenugreek seed
   Chamomile and lavender flower
   Comfrey leaf and red-raspberry leaf
   Dill leaf and red-raspberry leaf
   Dill leaf, fennel seed, and rosehip
   Fennel seed and red-clover flower
   Fennel seed and red-raspberry leaf

Some herbs seem to have been created especially to make hot summer days more tolerable. Try making a refreshing herbal iced tea from the mint family. It not only enlightens the spirit but also encourages intellectual thinking. One of my favorite mint teas is spearmint and lemon balm. Chamomile has a sweet taste of apples and is refreshing for headaches, but if you have a pollen allergy, beware: it will turn your slightly annoying headache into a pounding migraine. For a beautiful complexion, try calendula tea. For those days when you can't seem to get organized, sip a cup of warm rosemary tea; it will stimulate your memory.

   Caffeine is not recommended in any stage of a woman's life, especially during pregnancy and menopause. But please do not assume that drinking herbal teas is safe in unlimited quantities. Herbs may be natural, but they do contain tannins and other extracts that have soporific or stimulating properties.

   Enjoy your herbal tea times wisely.

SAMPLE MENU: A High-Energy, Body-Cleansing, Skin-Regenerating Day of Herbal Meals, Juice Combinations, Shakes, and Teas

Upon Awakening

2 cups fresh apple and papaya juice
30 minutes before breakfast, 3 cups pure water

If morning sickness is a problem, drink I cup of warm red-raspberry-leaf tea or hot water with the juice of I lemon. Take small sips, and swish each one around your mouth thoroughly before swallowing (do this for all juice, shake, and herbal tea recipes) to predigest before it enters the stomach.

Breakfast

Fresh pear, berry, and orange fruit salad sprinkled with
    2 spoonfuls of sprouted sunflower seeds (12 hours'
    growth) and sprouted wheat berries (2 days' growth)
I cup sprouted-almond milk, pine-nut milk, or pineapple juice
2 to 3 sliced ripe strawberries

Do not substitute cow's or goat's milk for the nut milk. If you are unable to sprout the nuts or are allergic to nuts, drink pineapple, mango, papaya, or orange juice.

Midmorning

Freshly Made Fruit Yogurt Shake

1 cup of fresh yogurt
6 fresh berries (of your choice)
¼ cup fresh juice (of berry used)

Prepare the fruit, and make the juice. Blend mixture for 15 seconds on a high speed. Pour the yogurt shake into a cooled glass. Sip small mouthfuls, thoroughly chewing 20 to 30 times before swallowing.

MAKES 3½ CUPS

OR

Protein Green Shake

1 teaspoon wheat grass juice
2 tablespoons fresh dandelion juice
2 tablespoons fresh alfalfa sprout juice (from 6 days' growth)
1 teaspoon parsley juice
½ cup apple juice
½ teaspoon spirulina powder
¼ cup soy sprout juice
2 cups green grape juice

Process all the ingredients in a blender for 1 minute 30 seconds on high, and 30 seconds on low. Pour into a cooled glass, and drink slowly. Remember to take small sips, and swish them around your mouth 10 times before swallowing.

MAKES 4 CUPS

30 minutes before lunch, 6 to 9 ounces pure water

Lunch

A large green salad with herbs and wild edibles

4 sprouted grain and seed sun-dried breads with goat cheese
or sprouted-nut spread

Small bowl of steamed vegetables seasoned with thyme, dill,
marjoram, and cider vinegar

4 to 5 ounces chamomile, comfrey, dandelion, and red-
raspberry-leaf herbal tea

I hour after lunch, 3 to 5 ounces pure water

Take an early-afternoon nap in the warm sunshine or in a warm,
well-ventilated room.

Midafternoon

Fruit yogurt shake or fruit juice combination

Carrot and celery sticks

I cup of rich sea vegetables and noodle broth

I hour before dinner, 3 to 5 ounces of pure water

Dinner

Eat this meal before 6:30 P.M. so that you can digest your food
before bedtime.

Spinach pasta with steamed broccoli and garlic-marinated
mushrooms

Fresh green salad with sprouted alfalfa and radish seeds
(6 days' growth), dressed with freshly squeezed lemon

juice and olive oil, and seasoned with marjoram, fennel,
and other fresh herbs

2 sprouted savory sun-dried breads spread with almond
or peanut butter

Fresh mango and apricot slices with chopped dates
and/or fresh figs

Chamomile flower, catnip, and lemon-balm-leaf herbal tea

1 hour after meal, 3 to 5 ounces pure water

Bedtime

Chamomile and red-raspberry-leaf herbal tea

MAINTAINING SEXUAL HEALTH

A woman's sexual happiness and fulfillment is heavily influenced by
her diet. Good physical health is a primary condition for the maintenance of your reproduction ability. When your body is balanced,
the electromagnetic current charges trillions of cells throughout
your body, igniting them with a living, electric energy that animates
your entire life. Your health is a reflection of your inner vitality.

To maintain sexual health, energy blockages and toxic-waste accumulations, caused by digestive stagnation, need to be eliminated.
Your diet influences the production of excess mucus and unwanted
fat deposits, which diminish the intensity of your life and the quality of your sexuality. The single most important factor influencing
sexual health is your diet. A naturally balanced diet of simply prepared foods will contribute to a sound physical and mental plateau
that promote a happy sex life. On the other hand, a chaotic, unbalanced diet of refined, processed, and overcooked foods con-
tributes to a variety of sexual problems, as well as ill health.

Problems of sexual weakness and desire can usually be solved simply with a natural diet, adjusted to fit individual needs. It may take a few months, maybe even a year, but sexual vitality and full enjoyment can be restored by changing your eating habits.

A WONDERFUL (NATURAL) PREGNANCY DIET 🖎

So far you have created menus out of garden herbs, edible flowers, seaweeds, fungi, fresh seasonal fruits and vegetables, sprouted beverages, yogurt, sun-dried breads, herbal teas, sprouted savory cheeses, protein shakes, and many more fruit, flower, and herb combination drinks.

What else could you possibly want? A few candies? A glazed donut? A tub of ice cream or a spicy chili? Those are your hormones talking. Remember the promise you made to your unborn child? Satisfy your cravings for junk food after your baby is weaned. Now is the time to make sure your growing, changing body receives the nutrition it needs in the most healthful, natural way possible.

The Influence of Diet on Newborn Appearance

There are many aspects of newborn features that are directly linked to the foods and liquids consumed during pregnancy. Genetics has an influence, but a baby's physical features have a stronger relationship to what the mother ate when each part of the body was developing. If angled ears, thick dark hair, a pixie nose, or bridged eyebrows do not run in your family, read on.

HAIR COLOR

Hair color and length give surprisingly accurate clues to maternal nutrition. A lot of long hairs on the baby's head indicates a good diet of vegetables, fruits, and their raw juices. Dark hair color points to the consumption of vegetable-derived foods, while blond and lighter colored hair results from a greater consumption of animal-derived foods, including dairy products and eggs.

EYEBROWS

Eyebrows with a downward slant indicate that the mother ate a predominantly vegetable diet. Those with an upward slant indicate that the mother ate a predominantly animal-derived food diet, with refined and/or overly sweetened foods. Brows that peak in the middle indicate that during the first few months of gestation, the mother's diet was predominantly meat derived, and that during the latter stages of pregnancy, she changed to a more vegetable-derived diet. Smoothly curved eyebrows with a balanced angle indicate a maternally balanced diet throughout pregnancy.

NOSE

A nose that points upward at the tip shows a diet that consisted of a great proportion of animal derived foods, especially fish. Look at Eskimo babies! This type of nose reflects a baby's potential for clarity of thought in later life.

Large nostrils displays a masculine character. Small nostrils indicate a feminine character. Boys with small nostrils may develop a feminine character, while girls with larger nostrils may develop a masculine one.

EARS

Ears that begin at eye level, with lobes that end on a level with the mouth (the middle part of the ear is at the level of the nose) indicate that the maternal diet was well balanced with living micronutrients.

Small, pointed ears positioned higher than the nose indicate a predominantly meat and processed-food maternal diet. Ears with tiny lobes reflect a maternal diet lacking in essential minerals.

SKIN

Healthy caucasian newborns have skin of a deep red color, clear and free from marks. The appearance of small yellow or white dots over the nose, cheeks, or chin indicates a maternal diet consisting of too many fatty, greasy foods, especially during the last few months of pregnancy.

Small red blotches on the upper eyelids, bridge of the nose, or back of the neck reflect the consumption of too many sugared foods, coffee, medications, or drugs. Babies born with a strawberry mark (strawberry nervus) on the face or neck are usually small at birth and the mark can indicate that the mother used a medication.

Another form of discoloration is a red diamond that begins on the forehead and extends downward over the nose. This is caused by the consumption of medications and drugs, and the use of chemicals such as food preservatives or dyes during the fourth month of pregnancy. The same is true of any purple birthmark.

HANDS AND FINGERS

The strength of a baby's grasp corresponds to the contracting power of the heart. A weak grasp indicates a weaker heart.

Long fingers indicate the potential for artistic or intellectual excellence. Shorter ones indicate the potential for social and physical grace.

The lines on the palms correspond to the major systems of the body. If the lines are deep and clear, the baby has a sound constitution. Right palm lines are influenced by the mother's heredity, while the left palm lines are influenced by the father's.

3

Thyme
for Healthy
Herbal Living

THE MEDICINAL USES OF HERBS

As you have read, most aromatic herbs also have medicinal properties, making them valuable natural healers. They can be used in teas, poultices, compresses, tinctures, decoctions, infusions, and gruels. There are herbs to soothe a fretting mind, induce a restful sleep, calm heartburn and indigestion, curtail morning sickness, increase energy levels, encourage skin tone and elasticity, and promote relaxation—even when everything else in your life seems to be in a state of organized chaos. All of these herbs can be grown in your garden, planter, or window box, to be picked fresh whenever you develop a condition that calls for their healing powers.

Once a plant is established, the leaves and flowers can be picked anytime, although peak flavor and aroma is reached just before flowering. Each time you pick and use a leaf or flower from an herb, it stimulates further growth of the plant. Once the leaves, flowers, and seeds are harvested from the plant, they can be used fresh or else dried for future use.

Herbs practically take care of themselves from season to season. Their requirements are small in comparison with their benefits. Having a planter in a protected environment, such as a sunny windowsill, porch, or greenhouse will guard them against winter frosts. Left outside, however, herbs tend to hibernate during the cold winter months. When spring arrives, the dormant herbs send up shoots to the surface of the soil. Maintenance is limited to snipping off the leaves and flowers, and digging a few roots whenever a remedy calls for that herb part. Again, the more you cut, the more you'll stimulate growth.

I began my medicinal garden with the happy chamomile (the children's healer), dainty feverfew (the women's healer), graceful lavender (the "all" healer), and many varieties of pungent mint. I started out making delicious teas, floral waters, and simple compresses, with live plants obtained from mail-order and organic nurseries (see Resources at the back of this book). I bought plants that had been established for two years or more, and would easily take to being transplanted either in an inside or outside environment. Outside, I planted many cultivated "wild" species of herbs, which I'd become familiar with while living in

England, such as nasturtiums and chickweed. Inside, I planted a window box, which took up the whole length and half the height of the glass. I also had three terra-cotta planters on my back deck for herbs that needed extra growing space. I have managed to keep all three healing gardens for over three years, and still (even though I am not pregnant) use the herbs for myself and my family.

Making a Pregnancy First-Aid Garden

You will need:

A small plot of land about 4 feet square
2 pounds small stones
10 to 12 pine cones
Organic and garden waste
5 earthworms
11 medicinal and nutritional herb plants (see page 136)
2 × 16-foot fencing to go around garden edge
Fine mesh or netting to cover the garden area,
    protecting it from pets and children

Dig a 2-foot trench the dimensions of your garden, piling the soil at the side. Place the stones on the bottom; then cover with the pine cones, and organic and garden waste, and add the worms. Break up and sift the garden soil through your fingers, removing any roots and debris. Fill the hole with the soil and pat it down. Remove the plants from their pots, and make some small holes with a stick or a spade, and you are ready to plant the herbs. Make sure that the plants are pressed securely into the holes; then water. Place the smaller herbs around the edges, and the plants of medium height around the middle. The tallest plants go in the center, so that each plant receives adequate light, warmth, nutrition, and shade. Once all the plants are in place and have been sufficiently watered, push in the fencing and attach the mesh or netting.

HERBS FOR YOUR GARDEN PATCH

Borage	Rich in minerals; stimulates milk production in nursing mothers.
Burdock	Promotes the appetite through the stimulation of digestive juices.
Chickweed	Helps nutrients to be absorbed in the body. As a poultice, it reduces hemorrhoids.
Cucumber	A fast-acting diuretic; soothes sunburn.
Dandelion	Reduces exhaustion in the first few months of pregnancy.
Marsh mallow	Relieves diarrhea and rebuilds vitality.
Rosemary	Brings good luck; antiseptic.
Scented geraniums	Relieves stress and emotional anxiety.
Skullcap	Relaxes nervous tension; sleep inducer.
Strawberries	Teeth whitener; soothes sunburn.
Violets	Best source of vitamin A; makes great eye washes.

Growing your herbs inside does add a few complications to the gardening process. For one thing, herbs fare better in garden soil than potting soil. To make my first window box, I filled a lined wooden box (with cracks for drainage) with small gravel stones, pine cones, and a layer of organic waste. Then I added a few worms and some finely sifted garden soil, filling the box three-quarters full. The box was about I × 4 feet with a 2-foot depth. Even though it took up half my window, its green hues looked brilliant and its scents filled my whole house, especially on warm evenings.

Another complication I had to deal with and one which you may face too: pets. I had to distract my cats from chewing on my plants, so while the herbs were becoming established, I used 2-foot bean poles around the edges of the box; then hung some light netting over the top. The plants still got warmth and light from the sun, but they were shielded from curious paws and whiskers. To further distract the cats, I started growing small pots of wheat and barley grass for nutrition and amusement in the hope that they would lose interest in the window garden. All went as I had planned, until I realized that they were using the wheat and grass pots for a litter box! So I had to construct a cover that would let in the light and warmth, but shield the plants from those other curiosities.

As my children grew, I transplanted most of the window box into the outside plot, and replanted my indoor boxes with a few smaller, more floral herbs like valarian, aloe, bergamot, thyme, and marjoram, which are fragrant and have relaxing, soothing qualities. We all use them for bathing infusions, teas, and "booboo" poultices.

Making a Pregnancy First-Aid Window Box

Make a wooden or plastic windowbox lined with cloth, with drainage holes punctured through the bottom. You can design one that is I × 4 × 2 feet, or make it to fit your window. Personalize it with folk art pictures and plant names (optional).

You will need:

5 pounds of common garden soil

1 pound organic and garden waste, broken up or finely
   mulched.

2 pounds small drainage stones

10 small pine cones

9 medicinal and nutritional herbal plants

9 ice-cream sticks

8 to 10 thin sticks and nylon or mesh netting

3 to 5 earthworms

See page 136 for putting together your Pregnancy First-Aid
Window Box.

HERBS FOR YOUR PREGNANCY FIRST-AID WINDOW BOX

Aloe vera	Good for burns, cuts, insect bites, skin blemishes.
Dwarf chamomile	Relieves headaches, promotes gum health, induces relaxation.
Fennel bulb	Relieves flatulence, stimulates the appetite.
Lavender flowers	Relieves stress headaches, promotes natural sleep, heals bites.
Melissa	Relieves tension and stress, reduces fever.
Sage	Good for tooth powders; stops bleeding gums, reduces the production of breast milk.
St. John's wort	Relieves anxiety, reduces inflammation.
Skullcap	Relieves anxiety.
Stinging nettle	Strengthens and supports the whole body.

Making a Pregnancy First-Aid Deck Planter

Construct using the same soil layers as in your window box—stones, organic waste, worms, soil, then plants. Make sure you have adequate drainage holes in the bottom of the planter so that excess rainfall does not become trapped. Anchor the netting to sticks to protect the plants from pets, wild critters, and children. (See the instructions on pages 135–36.) Try not to cram too many plants into a small space: if you have a small planter or limited space, try 2 pots with 5 to 6 plants in each.

HERBS FOR POTS OR DECK PLANTERS

Alfalfa	Contains all the known vitamins and minerals for life.
Chamomile	Promotes a good night's sleep, aids digestion and oral health.
Comfrey	Repairs body tissues, strengthens bones, and promotes healthy skin.
Dandelion	Good source of calcium and potassium.
Lavender	All around healer: relieves stress and headaches, soothes insect bites, prevents infections.
Marjoram	Spreads happiness, reduces stress, clears clogged sinuses.
Rosemary	Relieves headaches, aids poor circulation and digestion.

HERBS FOR YOUR PHARMACY

With the herbs listed above, you will have a wonderful herbal pharmacy. The following herbs are categorized by medicinal effects on the body. Review them and decide which ones would benefit your family the most; then add them to your garden.

Diuretics

Diuretics increase the output of urine and detoxify toxic substances from the system. Diuretic hebs include: asparagus, borage, burdock, chamomile, corn silk, dandelion, mugwort, nasturtium, nettle, parsley, plantain, sweet basil, sage, strawberry, thyme.

Expectorants

Expectorants cause expulsion of the mucus and break up congestion. Herbs with this property include: anise, bee balm, boneset, borage, chervil, costmary, garlic, horseradish, hyssop, Irish moss, lemon balm, lobelia, mullein, nettle, prickly lettuce, sassafras, sweet cicily, St. John's wort.

Astringents

Astringents are antibiotic in nature and natural cleansers. Astringent herbs include: bee balm, borage, calendula, chervil, cinnamon, comfrey, eyebright, garlic, hyssop, lemon balm, mullein, nettle, plantain, rosemary, sage, shepherd's purse, sweet basil, thyme, witch hazel.

Nervines

Nervines relieve nervousness caused by strain and tension. They include: basil, blue cohosh, borage, catnip, cayenne, chamomile, chicory, comfrey, cornflower, lavender, lobelia, motherwort, passion flower, pennyroyal, rosemary, sage, skullcap, valerian, willow, yarrow.

RECIPES FOR YOUR HERBAL PHARMACY 🐾

Tonics

There is nothing more natural than adding herbal tonics to your daily life, as they are good to take all year round. They can become part of your health-protecting pregnancy diet, and they'll really pick you up anytime you're feeling sluggish. Tonics are herbs that strengthen and enliven a specific organ, a system, or even the whole body (see basic recipe, page 27). For each system of the body, there are plants that are particularly beneficial.

Here are a few of my favorite pregnancy tonics. I used to make them daily in the springtime, when flowers and herbs carpeted our front lawn. Spring tonics were an annual event in our family because they act like a system spring cleaning. They didn't always taste good, but with a little honey, molasses, or lemon juice they were palatable. Generally, tonics increase the appetite and make you feel healthy and robust—ready to take on another year.

Pregnancy Tonic

Red raspberry is the best-known and most widely used uterine and pregnancy tonic herb. Before and during pregnancy, this herb has outstanding health-promoting properties that deserve serious consideration.

Among its merits: it prevents miscarriage, eases morning sickness, and reduces pain during labor. Red raspberry also allows the contracting uterus to work more efficiently, making for an easier and faster birth; and it helps to bring down an undelivered placenta.

1 cup freshly picked young red-raspberry leaves
2 cups freshly boiled distilled water

Bruise the raspberry leaves with the back of a spoon. Place them in a medium bowl and cover with the hot water. Cover the bowl and allow to steep for 1 hour. Strain through a cheesecloth-lined strainer, funnel into a glass bottle, cover, and refrigerate. Drink as often as required.

Dandelion and Violet Tonic

Whenever your body feels in need of an internal cleansing, try this blood-purifying tonic.

10 to 15 dandelion flower heads
1 cup violets
2 cups freshly boiled distilled water

Place the dandelion heads and violets into a medium bowl and cover with the hot water. Steep for 10 minutes, covered. Strain through a cheesecloth-lined strainer and sweeten to taste.

Drink 2 to 3 glasses a day. Dandelions are a great whole-system cleanser.

MAKES 2 TO 3 CUPS

Citrus Tonic

Here is a tasty, light tonic full of vitamins that your body needs throughout pregnancy, so drink it as often as you like.

Zest of 3 lemons
Zest of 2 oranges
8 cups distilled water
4 tablespoons hops

1 whole clove
½ cup violet flower heads
¼ cup violet leaves
Lemon juice (optional)
Honey (optional)

Place the lemon and orange zests into a saucepan. Cover with the water. Bring to a boil over medium heat, lower the heat, and simmer for 20 minutes. Remove from the heat and add the hops, clove, violet flowers, and leaves. Cover and steep for another 15 minutes. Strain through a fine-mesh sieve.

Pour the liquid into a glass bottle, adding either lemon juice or honey. Drink cool cupfuls throughout the day.

MAKES 4 SERVINGS

Bowel Tonic

This great tonic acts as a bowel regulator, efficiently clears up any bladder infections, cleanses the blood, and rids the body of toxic waste.

2 cups fresh cranberry juice
1 cup fresh aloe juice
½ cup sheep sorrel—leaf infusion, cooled (see basic recipe, page 27)
½ cup strawberry-leaf infusion, cooled (see basic recipe)

Mix the juices and infusions together and pour into a glass bottle. Cover and store in the refrigerator.

Pour 2 tablespoons of the tonic in 1 cup of spring water. Drink throughout the day.

MAKES 8 CUPS

Herbal tonics are all gentle remedies that have mild, yet profound effects on the body. You will find that as your family grows, your medicinal needs change. The plants you had for pregnancy, although still beneficial for minor home remedies, will be replaced with others that meet the needs of your children. My outside pharmacy garden has become so varied in color, texture, and fragrance that I have come to view it as a sense-stimulation and butterfly garden. It gives pleasure to everyone and anyone. Even visiting cats just love to brush up against the catnip—it makes them wild!

TYPES OF HERBAL PREPARATIONS USED ROUTINELY DURING PREGNANCY

In addition to the specific applications mentioned in chapter I, you can use your medicinal garden to make the following types of preparations:

Uterine Tonics

Tonics with these herbs tone and strengthen the uterus. They're often used when there is no obvious disease but rather an overall weakness in the sexual organs, which has a degenerative effect on the rest of the body as a whole. All of these herbs, used alone or in combination, make excellent uterine tonics: motherwort, red-raspberry leaf, life root, and blue cohosh.

Astringents

These help normalize hormonal activity, specifically, estrogen and progesterone activity. All of these herbs make excellent astringents: periwinkle, lady's mantle, and shepherd's purse.

Demulcents

These heal and soothe the mucous membranes, especially those inside the vagina and urinary tract. They can be used to treat cases of cystitis and urethritis. All of these herbs make excellent demulcents: couch grass, Irish moss, bearberry, and corn silk.

Herbal Teas

Herbal teas (iced or warm) make an invigorating beverage with many associated health benefits, including some specific to pregnancy. Many varieties are commercially available, but you can grow your own quite easily. Your herbal tea planter will become (much like your first-aid garden) an at-home "living" drugstore. No more pills, capsules, powders, or syrups, and no more potentially harmful side effects for either you or your baby. Herbs are naturally free of toxins. They contain living, active, and easily absorbed ingredients that nourish and heal you from the inside out.

After reaping the medicinal benefits from my first-aid gardens, I made myself a delightful little planter full of herbs for tea. It gave me great pleasure to go outside in the morning sunshine to see, smell, and pinch off a few leaves or flowers for a first-thing, pick-me-up brew. There was no tea bag or wrapper to dispose of, and I was able to recycle the infused herbal pulp for composting. Nothing went to waste.

Making Your Kitchen Herbal Tea Garden

You will need:

I half-size wooden barrel (available at nurseries, garden centers, and lumberyards)

3 to 5 pounds small stones
I pound organic and garden waste
3 to 5 earthworms
3 to 4 pinecones
I pound sand
I0 to I5 pounds garden soil
I pound sphagnum peat
7 two-year-old, well-established herb plants, such as lavender,
    sweet woodruff, chamomile, calendula, bee balm, catnip,
    and rose geranium

Drill a few holes in the bottom of your barrel for drainage.
Layer the garden soil with the same materials you used in
your window box and deck planter (small stones, organic and
garden waste, a few worms, and some pinecones). Add the
sand and soil.

On top of those layers, spread some sphagnum peat (it's a
little more expensive than compost peat, but well worth it).

For my kitchen herbal tea garden I chose chamomile, raspberry
leaf, clover, dill, parsley, basil, alfalfa, and comfrey. I decided to
place the chamomile, clover, parsley, and alfalfa in the front so
that they would trail over the sides. I placed the basil, raspberry,
comfrey, and dill in the center, so they would have the height and
width they required to spread out their shoots and stems. As the
plants began to grow thicker and taller, I snipped the tops to
contain them below 2 feet.

After two years, the comfrey, alfalfa and raspberry leaf can
be replanted in single planters or in the garden, so their long-
reaching roots can forage for nutrients in the soil.

MAKING A FRESH CUP OF HERBAL TEA

Take time to brew a fresh cup of cold, clear, and refreshing herbal tea; you may never go back to drinking those heavily sugared tanned ice teas again. Herbal teas are a beautiful, crystal-clear, green or golden liquid with a subtle taste and the aroma of an English country garden.

There is a right and a wrong way to make an iced herbal tea, so see page 124 to refresh your memory and make a wonderful cup of tea.

HERBAL TEAS FROM YOUR GARDEN

Alfalfa leaves and chamomile flowers	Calms nerves, induces sleep.
Chamomile flowers and dill leaves	Soothes digestion, induces sleep.
Chamomile flowers and parsley sprigs	Induces sleep, produces milk.
Chamomile flowers and red-raspberry leaves	Induces sleep, promotes womb health.
Comfrey leaves and red-raspberry leaves	Tones the uterus, heals wounds.
Raspberry leaf and red-clover flowers	Promotes womb health, brings labor relief.

Following are three health-promoting teas. Use the basic recipe on page 27 for guidance.

Relaxation Combination

A delicate tea that soothes your emotions.

> *2 sprigs rosemary*
> *3 peppermint leaves*
> *2 catnip leaves*
> *6 chamomile flower heads*
> *3 cups freshly boiled distilled water*

See the basic recipe for herbal infusion or tea tonic on page 27. Allow the infusion to steep for 1 hour and drink warm or cold.

MAKES 2 TO 3 CUPS

Diuretic Combination

A sweet-tasting tea to regulate and tone the kidneys.

> *1 teaspoon dried uva ursi*
> *4 red-raspberry leaves*
> *1-inch piece gingerroot, diced*
> *2 parsley sprigs*
> *3 cups freshly boiled distilled water*

See the basic recipe for herbal infusion or tea tonic on page 27. Allow the infusion to steep for 1½ hours and drink cold.

MAKES 2 TO 3 CUPS

Decongestant Combination

A soothing, lightly spiced tea that eases chest congestion.

1 teaspoon dried marsh-mallow root
1 teaspoon fenugreek seeds
3 rose hips
4 mullein leaves
3 cups freshly boiled distilled water

See the basic recipe for herbal infusion or tea tonic on page 27. Allow the infusion to steep for 30 minutes and drink warm or cold.

MAKES 2 TO 3 CUPS

Making Herbal Skin Mists

Cosmetic herbal mists are skin nourishing and body refreshing. They can be made from a cooled herbal infusion, fizzed floral waters, or essential oils diluted in distilled water. During pregnancy, I was living in a hot and humid climate. I made fresh skin mists daily, and took them with me whenever I was away from home, whether out walking, gardening, or driving. They made me feel feminine, clean, and refreshed, anytime and anywhere. There are many more recipes in Chapter 4, but here are a few of my favorite combinations to try.

Chamomile and Comfrey Skin Mist

Chamomile renews cells, while comfrey repairs tissues. This is an ideal mister for facial blemishes, acne, and sallow skin.

5 young comfrey leaves
½ cup fresh chamomile flowers
2 cups freshly boiled distilled water

Bruise the young comfrey leaves with the back of a spoon. Put in a medium bowl and add the chamomile. Cover with the hot water, and allow to steep for 1 hour. Strain through a cheesecloth-lined sieve. Funnel the herbal infusion into a spray bottle.

Refrigerate the herbal mist for 10 minutes. Mist yourself generously and air-dry your skin for 20 minutes. Rinse off with warm water and pat dry. Repeat as often as required.

MAKES 2 CUPS

Fennel and Rose Hip Body Mist

Fennel is cell restorative and toning, while rose hips promote healthy collagen (a protein in the skin that makes up the fibrous support system from which the skin is made) production.

½ cup finely chopped and crushed fennel
5 crushed rose hips
2 cups freshly boiled distilled water

Place the fennel and rose hips in a medium saucepan and cover with the hot water. Simmer the mixture on low heat for 10 minutes. Remove from the heat and set aside to cool, covered.

Strain through a cheesecloth-lined sieve. Funnel the herbal infusion into a spray bottle and refrigerate for 10 minutes. Use as required.

MAKES 2 CUPS

Elder Flower and Marigold Antiseptic Mister

Elder flowers are cleansing and emollient, while the marigold is astringent and antiseptic. This is a good wound-healing mister.

2 elder flower heads
½ cup fresh calendula petals
2 cups freshly boiled distilled water

In a medium bowl, mix the elder and calendula flowers. Pour the hot water over them and cover. Steep for 2 hours.

Strain through a cheesecloth-lined sieve and funnel into a spray bottle. Refrigerate for 10 minutes before use.

MAKES 2 CUPS

TERATOGENS

Teratogens are either naturally occurring or synthesized substances, compounds, or energies that can cause physical and/or mental defects in unborn babies through electromagnetic transmission, absorption, contact, or inhalation.

A mother is especially susceptible to their influence during the first three months of pregnancy. Exposure to these sometimes invisible dangers can cause a wide range of mental and physical deformities in your baby, such as blindness, deafness, loss of limbs, and harelip, to name but a few.

Herbs

The following herbs should be used sparingly, especially during the first three months of pregnancy, when a miscarriage can be induced: basil, caraway, celery seed, gingerroot, fresh horseradish, marjoram, nutmeg, parsley, rosemary, saffron, sage, tarragon, thyme, and watercress.

Avoid goldenseal root throughout your pregnancy. It raises the white-blood-cell count, places stress on the kidneys and liver, and can cause uterine contractions.

High Temperatures

Avoid prolonged exposure to high temperatures, especially hot tubs over 104°F, because they will increase your body temperature, too.

Dangers of Prepregnancy Birth Control Methods

The birth-control pill has a history of causing birth defects. Use of the pill should be discontinued for three months, or at least two menstrual cycles, prior to a planned pregnancy.

The use of an IUD (intrauterine device) may cause a miscarriage or premature birth, especially if left in place after conception.

Diaphragms, used with spermicides, have been linked to miscarriages and birth defects.

Alcohol

There is no minimum amount of alcoholic beverages that is considered safe to drink during pregnancy and nursing. Alcohol causes not only physical defects but also learning difficulties, emotional trauma, and in some cases, blindness. It takes only two fluid ounces a day to cause a permanent fetal defect: a single, one-night binge can cause fetal alcohol syndrome, resulting in permanent behavioral and/or physical abnormalities. For both of your well-beings, avoid the consumption of alcohol altogether.

Caffeine

Recent scientific research has indicated that the consumption of caffeine, whether in liquid or solid form, may contribute to infertility, miscarriage, stillbirth, and fetal death. Three cups of coffee a day (or the equivalent) is considered a high level of caffeine intake. Caffeine and xanthine alkaloid—coffee's principal active ingredients—stimulate the nervous system and can cause nervousness, irritability, anxiety, insomnia, and heart-rhythm disturbances. It also influences blood pressure and the secretions of gastric acids. Reduce your intake (if elimination is just too much) during prepregnancy and understand that there is no safe level of caffeine consumption during pregnancy. By becoming an observant label reader, you can switch to a decaffeinated brand of tea or coffee or drink caffeine-free soda and cocoa.

As an alternative, try a warm, herbal beverage made from chicory, artichoke, beet, carrot, parsnip, burdock, or dandelion root. Roasted barley was a very common coffee substitute during World War II. Coffee substitutes do not taste exactly like your favorite coffee, but they can be mixed with a variety of spices, such as cinnamon, caraway, cloves, and nutmeg, to wean you from your caffeinated brew.

Drugs

Speed and uppers (amphetamines) are stimulants that are very dangerous to the unborn baby's nervous system.

Using cocaine and crack can produce an addicted baby, who will experience very painful withdrawal at birth. A mother's long-term cocaine usage is known to cause behavioral, developmental, and neurological dysfunction.

Heroin-addicted mothers will give birth to heroin-addicted babies, who will have to suffer extremely painful and traumatizing withdrawals, with probable blood transfusions at birth.

LSD and other psychedelics increase the risk of late-pregnancy miscarriage with the further possibility of genetic abnormalities.

Quaaludes have been known to cause physical deformities if taken during the first three months of pregnancy.

Marijuana smoked in even the smallest quantities can cause severe complications during pregnancy and increase the possibility of a stillbirth or infant death.

Obviously, drug use of any kind should not occur during pregnancy.

Smoking

If you were a smoker before your pregnancy, giving up cigarettes now is one of the best gifts you can give yourself and your unborn baby. A woman who smokes during pregnancy reduces the amount of oxygen her baby receives. Smoking can also contribute to low birth weights.

Sipping a strong herbal infusion of fresh gingerroot and licorice sticks each time you feel the urge to smoke will quickly (in about 7 to 9 days) and naturally break your nicotine habit.

If you just can't break the habit (not even for the sake of your unborn child), there are ways to cut down on consumption. If you smoke for oral gratification, suck a lollipop or chew some nuts and dried fruit instead. If you have been smoking more than ten cigarettes a day, make a conscious effort to reduce the number by half, and then further still, until you smoke only two or three a day. Once this feels good, reducing the number even further will be easier and less likely to cause withdrawal.

Since smoking is a contagious habit, stay away from friends and colleagues who smoke, and if you must continue, buy yourself one of the brands that is lowest in tar and nicotine. If you buy one pack at a time and keep them out of easy reach, you will have to make more of an effort to smoke, and hopefully, you won't bother. Last, when you do puff away, smoke your cigarette only halfway down, as the tar and nicotine concentrations tend to be in the end of the cigarette, near the filter. Just remember that the gradual method for quitting still allows nicotine to get into your bloodstream—and your baby's, too.

If you really want to stop smoking, but do not feel you can do it alone, there are many programs available. Talk with your doctor.

USING HERBAL PREPARATIONS AROUND THE HOUSE 🍃

Modern household cleansers include a variety of ozone-debilitating aerosols that smell bad and are harmful to the environment, to you, and to your baby. But there are alternatives: the cleansers, polishes, and detergents you use in your home have many age-old, effective herbal counterparts—for instance, you can use yucca root to wash linens. Use your herbal pregnancy as an opportunity to rediscover these natural cleansers.

There is a popular, spiky cactus known to absorb electromagnetic radiation if placed near televisions or computers. Spider plants cleanse the air of formaldehyde, a common agent in fiberboard, plywood, resins, and wall coverings. Formaldehyde irritates the mucous membranes in the throat, eyes and mouth, making life intolerable for asthma sufferers (this pollutant can even cause throat cancer). Hanging spider plants throughout your home can lessen the effects of the formaldehyde.

Do take caution though: some familiar houseplants are irritating to the skin and are fatal if eaten. Hyacinth, chrysanthemum, ivy, and poinsettia, to name a few, all contain deadly toxins. Again, use your botanical dictionary to make certain of your identification.

Insect Repellents

There are many herbal alternatives to the commercial bug repellents sold in every grocery store and farmer's market. On those occasions when you want to be outside in keeping with your healthy, herbal pregnancy, but fear the ever-present swarms of biting insects, nibbling moths in your clothes, whispering weevils in your food containers, scampering ants under your windows, and mosquitoes tangled in your hair, here are some herbal protectors and preventions. Talk with your grandmother, she'd know that hanging bunches of fresh tansy by windows and doors discourages flies, and that dusting an ant trail with dried tansy leaves drives them out of their home.

The tiny, bushy herb called "rue" is a powerful protectant against fleas, bed bugs, and flies. Common mint is another repellent for flies. Ants can be deterred by sprinkling cayenne pepper near the entrance of their home, and weevils are controlled by placing a dry bay leaf into each storage container of rice and flour. Placing pots of live herbs in your kitchen or bathroom window will keep the rooms sweet smelling (most green plants recycle pollutants) and repel pesky insects. Another herbal repellent for fleas and moths is southernwood.

There are many such repellents, all of which can be used dried, as essential oils, or even picked fresh and left sprinkled in your carpets, animal beds, and other areas in your home. Catmint, tansy, lavender, rosemary, wormwood, and sage can be used summer or winter with great results in fighting off pests.

If you are a frequent "feast" for mosquitoes, like myself, you can become quite ill, due to the accumulating poison in your system. Not a summer has gone by since I came to America when I haven't been maddeningly attacked by swarms of these biting pests.

Most commercial mosquito deterrents contain a very powerful chemical called DEET (diethyltoluamide), which should be avoided during pregnancy. My grandmother used to make a smelly infusion of feverfew, lemon balm (the main ingredient of oil of citronella, an effective mosquito repellent) and tansy flowers. From the infusion, she made a lotion, which she washed over her exposed skin before gardening. She swore by its effectiveness in repelling biting insects, and I have used it on my children with great effect. Onion is another powerful mosquito repellent, if you don't mind smelling like a garden salad. Just massage a small amount of almond oil over your exposed skin; then slice a fresh onion and rub its pungent oils into your skin. You can also place a few slices near your open window at night; it's an ideal remedy for your baby's nursery on those hot summer evenings.

Thankfully, there are many aromatic (aromatherapy) insect-repelling recipes that you can easily and safely make at home. Those that I use most include oils of the faithful lavender, rosemary, eucalyptus, patchouli, and citronella. These potent oils can by diluted in a light cold-pressed oil, and sprayed either directly on your skin or on your clothing for protection when you're outside. These oils can also be diluted in spring water or dabbed on a ball of cotton and placed inside your pocket or hair band.

Here are a few safe and effective herbal remedies for controlling seasonal pests in your home.

Flea and Tick Carpet Repellent

An aromatic dusting powder ideal for your pet's bed, blankets, and favorite spot.

> *1 cup borax powder*
> *5 drops sweet orange essential oil*
> *5 drops lavender pure essential oil*
> *5 drops pennyroyal pure essential oil*
> *Finely ground zest of 1 lime*

Place the borax in a small bowl and add the orange, lavender, and pennyroyal essential oils. Gently mix. Add the lime zest, then place into a shaker container.

   Dust your carpets, especially areas where your pets sleep and lounge. Let set for 1 hour; then vacuum.

MAKES ENOUGH FOR 1 TREATMENT FOR AN
AVERAGE SIZE HOME

Clothing Insect Repellent Spray

A pleasing, aromatic combination of natural repelling oils.

> *3 drops peppermint essential oil*
> *3 drops patchouli essential oil*
> *3 drops citronella essential oil*
> *3 drops rose geranium essential oil*
> *½ cup spring water*
> *1 teaspoon vegetable glycerin (optional)*

Place all the ingredients in a small spray bottle and shake well. If you are using this recipe on your skin, add the glycerin to your blend and be careful not to spray your face. One spray to your clothing or skin is enough to keep you bug free for many hours of leisurely, outdoor activity.

MAKES 2 TO 3 OUNCES

Insect-Repelling Hat Pin

This novel idea could catch on! If your skin is sensitive to oils or sprays, you can still repel biting bugs by tying a small bunch of thyme, basil, and mint leaves and a few blossoms of lavender to your hat, scarf, or sweater.

MAKES 1 PIN

Vanilla-Scented Moth Repellent

Moths are another household pest that can cause mayhem in your kitchen and closet. Fill self-sealing tea bags with dried cloves, lemon peel, sweet woodruff, or rosemary; then add a few drops of lavender essential oil, and store them in food cupboards or clothing drawers. They will offer you some degree of protection and give a wonderful, spicy vanilla scent to your rooms. Or use the following repellent in place of commercial mothballs, which contain polydichlerobenzene and may be carcinogenic.

Herbal Moth Repellent

This mixture can be placed in paper or fabric pockets and tucked into drawers, chair creases, and other places where wool is found. The pouches (self-sealing tea bags or muslin bags) should be renewed twice a year.

   1 tablespoon dried camphor-basil
   1 tablespoon dried pennyroyal

1 tablespoon eucalyptus leaves
1 tablespoon southernwood
1 tablespoon rosemary leaves

Mix the ingredients in a bowl. Divide among small fabric or paper pouches and bind them with ribbons or rubber bands.

MAKES 5 SMALL BAGS

Insect Bite Reliever

For all those times when you need to cool and anesthetize picnic bug bites.

5 tablespoons ground oats
1 tablespoon dried cleavers herb
1 tablespoon dried peppermint leaves

Put the oats in pantyhose, securely knotted to seal, and set aside.

Place the cleavers herb and peppermint and 8 cups of water in a large saucepan over high heat. Bring to a boil, lower the heat, and simmer for 5 minutes. Remove from the heat, cover, and steep for 15 minutes.

Strain the infusion and discard the herbs. Drop the oatbag ball into the warm infusion and allow to steep for another 5 minutes.

With a hand whisk or fork, whip the infusion gently; then pour into a warm bath. Soak for 15 to 20 minutes twice a day.

MAKES ENOUGH FOR 1 BATH

Bee and Wasp Sting Soother

Bee and wasp stings are painful, and if you are allergic to their venom, you might require hospitalization. For an emergency herbal remedy, try the following recipe.

1 unrolled (nonmenthol) cigarette or 1 large pinch of pouch tobacco

You'll need to bruise the tobacco for this remedy to work. Chewing is the easiest way to do this, but beware, tobacco has a bitter, horrible taste. If you're at home in your garden, the tobacco can be moistened with water and bruised by chopping.

Remove the insect stinger from the wound; then place the moistened wad of tobacco over the sting and hold in place with slight pressure for 5 minutes. Remove. You should see a noticeable reduction in swelling and redness. Replace for another 5 minutes; then allow the sting to heal in the open air. This remedy works for children as well.

MAKES 1 TREATMENT

Quick Kitchen Tips

Just as herb preparations can benefit your health and emotional stability, they can benefit your home environment, too. You can make herbs an active part of your pregnancy lifestyle by bringing them into your home and enjoying their aromas and appearance, which will bring you closer to your natural world. On the following pages you will find a variety of my own household recipes.

Try a few of these tips:

- Put a small bouquet of fresh basil, red clover, and sweet bay on your food-preparation area to keep flies away and make the room smell fresh and clean.

- Crush cinnamon sticks and put them in small muslin sachets. Place the sachets in containers of dried beans and peas to deter the fungus that infects them in storage.

- If stray dogs or cats constantly rummage through your garbage during nightly excursions, deter their antics by lining a few empty cans with a dusting of cayenne pepper.

- Scrub damp copper pots with a handful of fresh sorrel leaves to restore their shine.

Laundry Detergent

Do your laundry with herbs that cleanse and soften without harsh chemicals. Yucca and soapwort root, when chopped and crushed, produce cleansing suds that make the best herbal alternative detergent for delicate fabrics. The best time to harvest soapwort roots is when the plant is in bloom.

> *1 cup soapwort root and leaves*
> *2 quarts warm water*

Chop the roots and add some fresh leaves; then mix with warm water to make soft suds. This simple formula cleans silk and other delicate fabrics and restores their natural sheen.

MAKES ENOUGH FOR 2 WASHES

NOTE: STALE DAMP CLOTHING CAN BE RESTORED TO AN AROMATIC FRESHNESS BY PLACING IN A DRYER WITH A SELF-SEALING TEA BAG OR

MUSLIN BAG FILLED WITH FRESH SPEARMINT AND LEMON VERBENA LEAVES.

Furniture Polish

This recipe makes an ideal natural polish, which can be whipped up in minutes and used again and again, giving a lustrous, polished shine to all your wooden shelves, cupboards, and furniture.

> *½ cup linseed oil*
> *½ cup malt vinegar*
> *1 teaspoon lime oil*
> *4 drops peppermint oil*

Pour the linseed oil and malt vinegar into a glass bottle, seal tightly, and shake. Add the lime oil and peppermint oil and shake again. Pour some of the fragrant oil onto a clean cotton cloth and rub the mixture into the wood. This remedy polishes and dusts at the same time, and there is no need to buff the surface after polishing.

MAKES I CUP

Another way to polish your wooden furniture: rub liberally with fresh lemon balm leaves. This naturally scents the wood and provides an excellent polished shine.

Disinfectants

Herbal disinfectants protect against infectious microorganisms in your bathroom, kitchen, and children's rooms, especially during periods of sickness.

Wash your refrigerator with a solution of freshly squeezed lemon juice and water to protect it from domestic infestations.

Infusions of thyme and rosemary make excellent disinfectants for counters and cupboards, while ten drops of lavender and tea tree essential oil diluted in 2 cups warm water will disinfect bathroom and kitchen floors.

A child's sick room can be misted with a few drops of geranium and lavender essential oils mixed with water in the morning and evening to keep infectious bugs at bay. By using these healthful and safe herbal preparations in your home, you can create an inviting atmosphere to welcome your new baby.

PHYSICAL ACTIVITY DURING PREGNANCY

Exercise

Along with your herbal lifestyle, exercise increases the benefit of healthy living. It goes without saying that staying physically fit during your pregnancy is essential to both your health and the health of your growing baby.

But what if you didn't exercise before? Should you start now, seven months into pregnancy, feeling as if any moment you might topple over from your unbalanced shape? The answer is yes: any form of exercise during pregnancy can do you a lot of good, but do talk with your doctor first.

Exercise can relieve many of the moans and groans associated with your changing shape, such as backache, constipation, and varicosis. Getting back into shape after giving birth is easier if you exercise during pregnancy. Exercise will make you feel good about yourself: I found that walking 30 minutes to 1 hour daily (especially prior to a meal) was exhilarating: it made me feel as if I'd earned the right to be hungry. I walked the day before my first son was born. During my second pregnancy, I walked with a

baby jogger; in my third, I walked wearing a baby sling and push-
ing a stroller.

It was during my third pregnancy, however, that I also started
driving, which led me to search for an alternative form of exercise
to make up for the energy I was no longer expending walking.

Yoga

The alternative type of movement and agility training I found
was yoga, and its associated color meditations. In fact it was during this period of my pregnancy that I starting using color to
express my feelings through art. A friend who was an adept yogi
guided me through a program that I could practice at home. The
exercises and postures he showed me took into consideration the
physical limitations of my pregnancy: I began a short, daily routine of postures, stretches, and color-energy meditations, which
I continue to use to this day.

Now, instead of screaming at my children, I think a color and
pose a position I know will calm and reenergize me. I have put
my children into a sound sleep by creating for them calming
color meditations, such as resting in a field of yellow (happiness)
buttercups, or bathing in the blue (tranquillity) waters of the
ocean. We all (even my three-year-old daughter) practice simpli-
fied yoga poses first thing in the morning and before bedtime.

Learning yoga increases your body awareness, strength, and
suppleness and boosts your sense of well-being (make sure that
you find a professional instructor before attempting difficult
contortions). Both forms of yoga (*Hatha yoga*, which develops the
physical body, and *Karma* or *Bhaki*, which focus on meditation
and breathing) fill your whole being with positive energy forces.
Yoga teaches you to listen to your body and focus your energy.
There are eight basic postures (which will need to be modified

throughout your pregnancy). There is nothing complicated about practicing yoga. Begin by learning how to breathe.

BREATHING TECHNIQUES

Human beings can live without food for over a month. We can live without water for over a week. But deprived of oxygen, we die in minutes.

Many cultures believe healthy breathing techniques play an important role in preventing illness. The correct way to breathe is to take air in and breathe it out through the nose. The mouth is not for breathing, it is for eating and talking.

In India, the Hindu word *prana* means "breath of life" and refers to an energy source that energizes all life. *Pranayama* is the ancient art of breath control and regulation. It consists of three separate phases: *pukaka*, to inhale; *kumbhake*, to retain or hold; and *recake*, to exhale. Breathe this way while doing yoga, and, in fact, become conscious of it at all times.

Meditation

Meditation is an ancient Eastern technique, similar to self-hypnosis in that it induces a trancelike state, relaxing both mind and body at the same time. Sleep allows your body to rest and recharge, but your mind remains active, dreaming and fretting to such an extent that you often wake feeling less rested than before you fell asleep. Meditation allows your mind to rest, allowing you to let go of the worries associated with our competitive, fast-paced, material world. You can achieve this state of relaxation through the repetition of words (chanting) or thoughts.

Meditating throughout the physical and emotional transitions of pregnancy lessens your tensions and anxieties. It allows you to go beyond your normal daily imagery and create visions that instill tranquillity and comfort. Meditation is a recognized way of combating stress and stress-related physical conditions. It has become a way of life for thousands of people.

Follow the guidelines below to achieve a successful meditation.

1. Find a quiet place to retreat and shut off your senses.
2. Find a comfortable posture, either standing, sitting, or lying down.
3. Make sure your back is erect, controlled, yet relaxed.
4. Mentally command your muscles to relax, releasing all tension.
5. Practice breathing deep, steady inhalations and exhalations.
6. Meditate on your breathing, following its journey in and out of your body.
7. When you feel refreshed, open your eyes.

Make a concerted effort to steal away from the demands of your life at least once a day to meditate.

Color Meditation

Try color meditations once you're comfortable with the practice of meditation. Choose a relaxation position, close your eyes, and concentrate on your breathing. Once it is deep and even, blank out thoughts of anything but the sound of breathing. Now using your imagination, create an environment of serenity:

You are sitting on a white marble platform. There is no color around you; everything is white. In the distance you see a brilliant shining ball of light. You watch as it moves closer to you. You feel the light dance upon your skin; it feels warm and energizing. It rests above your head, and as you look up, you see it burst into a shower of rainbow colors. One at a time, each color showers over your skin.

The light energy of red stimulates vitality.

The light energy of orange fills you with a sense of
   well-being.

The light energy of yellow sparks happiness within you.

The light energy of green nurtures a sense of body balance.

The light energy of blue relaxes and inspires love.

The light energy of indigo stimulates your intuition.

The light energy of violet calms you and inspires creativity.

Take a few seconds to absorb all the positive charges of these colors. Then slowly straighten your arms over your head. As you do so, you will see a ray of colored light from each energy beam from within you and gather together within the ball of light. Watch as it ascends once again to a brightly colored ball in the sky.

Take a few deep breaths. Open your eyes, and blink a few times. Stretch completely, before returning to your normal activities.

Usually after an energizing meditation like this, I like to lie down in dappled sunlight and nap in the fresh open air, enjoying the smells of my nearby herb garden and reveling in my blissful pregnancy.

4

Thyme
for Pregnancy
Pampering

To neglect your skin during pregnancy is to neglect an integral part of your being. Taking care of your body suit every day is no less important than eating right for you and your baby. The best way to achieve your "body beautiful" is not by purchasing pretty bottles of hormonal and vitamin time-release creams—which were probably manufactured over a year ago, shipped halfway around the country, and all too often have a repelling chemical or artificial aroma. Instead, do as I did during my pregnancies: make your own facial and whole-body treatments.

This chapter is offered in the hope of provoking change, by proposing that you reevaluate the hazardous ingredients in commercial skin-care products. The most prudent and healthful approach is to choose body-care treatments as carefully as you choose the foods you eat.

TREATMENTS FOR A BEAUTIFUL PREGNANT BODY

If you've been buying the nutritious food sources outlined earlier in the book, you already have many of the ingredients you will need for these skin treatments: most of the natural foods you love to eat are as healthy for the outside of your body as they are for the inside.

Grain, seed, and rice flours make excellent body powders and deodorants. Nuts, seeds, and berries make deliciously aromatic facial scrubs, steams, and packs. And while you wouldn't eat the pit from a tropical fruit, it does make for a wonderful exfoliating tool.

Below are some recipes I used during pregnancy to keep my skin well cleansed, soft, and supple. Remember, preserving your skin's moisture balance of secretions is a matter of following two basic skin care principles:

1. Keep your skin hydrated from the inside by drinking enough water.
2. Seal in that moisture with external skin protectors and barriers.

There's an added bonus that comes with taking care of yourself in this way: at a time when the physical changes to your body and the emotional upheavals associated with pregnancy can make you feel increasingly lonely, unloved, and sad, pampering yourself is a fun and rewarding way to feel special.

Allergy Testing

Even natural ingredients can cause a problem for some people, especially those with sensitive skin types. If you have a known food allergy, take it as a hint that you will have a reaction to the same ingredients when applied externally. Even if you are normally without allergies, your skin is much more sensitive during pregnancy than at any other time in your life. Always, always test a new ingredient on your skin before including it in a recipe that will cover a large portion of your body. (Better to have a reaction on a small patch of skin than an entire body that's itching, irritated, and swollen.) Highly concentrated ingredients, such as pure essential oils, mined clays, herbal powders or barks, animal fleece oils, and bee and dairy by-products, are most likely to cause problems.

To test, apply a small amount of the preparation or new ingredient to be tested on a soft area of skin (upper arm, breast tissue, inner arm, elbow, or behind the knee). Then cover it with a Band-Aid or patch of cotton gauze. Leave the test ingredient or recipe in place overnight. Any reaction, such as a constant itch, rash, or irritation indicates an allergy to the substance or combination of ingredients. Bathe the affected area in a very weak solution of bicarbonate of soda, then apply aloe gel or a healing skin salve of comfrey or calendula.

Skin-Cleansing Recipes for Your Pregnant Body

Berry and Oats Breast Scrub

This slightly gritty pack sloughs off dead cells on the skin's surface. It's a wonderfully refreshing and invigorating way to improve your skin's texture and tone, especially at this time, when your breasts are expanding and are often sore.

> *½ cup finely ground oatmeal*
> *1 tablespoon slippery-elm-bark powder*
> *6 ripe strawberries, hulled*
> *10 ripe blackberries, stemmed*
> *¼ cup ginseng-root infusion (see the basic recipe, page 27), chilled*
> *¼ cup rose-hip-seed infusion (see the basic recipe), chilled*

Put the oatmeal, slippery-elm powder, and strawberries in a small bowl and combine well with a fork. Place the blackberries in another bowl.

Cleanse your breasts with warm water. Pat dry. Mist your upper neck, breasts, and shoulders with the ginseng and rose-hip infusions, then air-dry.

Crush the blackberries slightly; then rub them against your skin. Allow the juice to dry.

Apply the strawberry and oat paste. Use your hands to spread the paste over your breasts and upper neck. Cover a comfortable chair with an old towel and lie back and relax for 10 minutes. Rinse off in a warm shower.

Apply more of the herbal-infusion mists; then air-dry again. Repeat twice weekly.

MAKES ENOUGH FOR 1 APPLICATION

Fruity Belly Mask

This multifunction pack brings nourishing blood to the skin's surface, exfoliates and eats away dead skin cells without harming the new cell growth underneath, and helps prevent stretch marks. Performing this treatment outside, in the fresh air, is ideal if weather and privacy conditions permit.

1 mango
1 avocado
1 cup seeded chopped watermelon

Chop enough of the mango to get ¼ cup. Set aside all of the skin.

Chop enough of the avocado to get ¼ cup. Reserve the pit.

Put the melon and mango flesh into a small bowl and mash well. Put the avocado flesh into another bowl and mash with a fork to form a smooth paste.

Place a large top sheet or old towel on a lounge chair or deck chair. Undress so that your belly is exposed. Using a natural-bristle skin brush or hemp mitt, lightly brush your abdomen until it turns a warm pink and feels silky soft.

Spread the avocado paste over your belly gently, using sweeping massaging movements in an upward direction. Allow to air-dry.

Pile the mango and watermelon mixture on top, especially around your protruding belly button. Allow to set for 15 minutes.

Using the avocado pit, massage the mask with small, circular, upward movements, covering your whole belly. Leave for another 5 minutes.

Rinse off with warm water, leaving your skin moist. Massage the mango skin over your belly and leave to air-dry for 5 to 10 minutes. Rinse thoroughly with warm water, mist with cold water, and pat dry.

MAKES ENOUGH FOR 1 TREATMENT

Yogurt and Honey Breast and Nipple Cleanser

This recipe exfoliates, cleanses, and moisturizes your nipples and breasts. Performing this treatment outside, in the fresh warm sunshine, is ideal if weather and privacy conditions permit. If not, use a well-ventilated, warm room.

¼ cup honey
1 cup homemade yogurt or commercially prepared plain yogurt
2 teaspoons fresh aloe gel or juice (see Note, page 175)
½ cup dandelion-leaf infusion, chilled (see basic recipe, page 27)
½ cup ginseng root infusion, chilled (see basic recipe)

Pour the honey and yogurt into a small bowl. Add the aloe and whisk together. Set aside.

Cleanse your breasts with warm water and pat dry. Mist them with the dandelion and ginseng infusions. Allow to air-dry.

Using your hands, apply the honey-yogurt cleanser in small, circular massaging movements in an upward direction, completely covering the nipples.

Leave the cleanser on your breasts for 10 minutes. Rinse off with warm running water, and pat dry.

MAKES ENOUGH FOR 1 APPLICATION

NOTE: FRESH ALOE GEL MAY BE EXTRACTED FROM THE ALOE PLANT BY BREAKING OFF A LARGE LEAF NEAR THE ROOT, SPLITTING IT OPEN, AND SCRAPING OUT THE CLEAR GEL.

Egg and Aloe Firming Belly Mask

Speeds up skin cell renewal for your expanding belly and breasts, thus reducing stretching.

½ cup goat's milk, warmed
3 egg whites
¼ cup fresh aloe gel (see Note, page 176)
½ cup calendula infusion, chilled (see basic recipe, page 27)
½ cup dandelion infusion, chilled (see basic recipe)
½ cup gingerroot infusion, chilled (see basic recipe)

Cleanse your belly with the warmed goat's milk, and allow to air-dry. Rinse with tepid water, and pat dry.

Beat the egg whites gently and mix with the freshly extracted aloe gel in a small bowl.

Mix the infusions together in a pitcher and pour the mixture into a spray bottle.

Cover a chair or bed with a top sheet or large towel; then seat yourself comfortably. Massage the egg-aloe mask over your belly, using sweeping, upward strokes with your hands. Leave on for 10 minutes.

Spray the infusion mist over the mask and stand near an open window or outside in the fresh air for 5 minutes more. Rinse off in a warm shower; pat dry with a soft, warmed towel. Repeat as often as desired.

MAKES ENOUGH FOR 1 APPLICATION

NOTE: FRESH ALOE GEL MAY BE EXTRACTED FROM THE ALOE PLANT
BY BREAKING OFF A LARGE LEAF NEAR THE ROOT, SPLITTING IT OPEN,
AND SCRAPING OUT THE CLEAR GEL.

Chamomile-and-Dandelion-Infusion Belly Mist

A pore deep-cleansing mist that improves skin texture and nourishes your growing skin.

> *1 egg white*
> *1 tablespoon vegetable glycerin*
> *3 teaspoons dandelion stalk juice, chilled (see Note, page 177)*
> *1 cup chamomile flowers*
> *1 cup fresh dandelion flowers*
> *2 cups freshly boiled distilled water*

In a small bowl, lightly beat the egg white and mix with
the glycerin. Add the dandelion juice and set aside.

Place the chamomile and dandelion flowers into a heat-
resistant pitcher or bowl and add the distilled water. Allow
to steep for 10 minutes. Strain the infusion through a
cheesecloth-lined sieve and pour it into a long-neck bottle.

Seat yourself or lie in a comfortable position. Place a
sterilized cotton cloth over your belly; then pour the warm
infusion onto the cloth, completely saturating it. Leave the
herbal-infused cloth on your skin for 5 minutes; remove
and set aside.

Apply the dandelion juice and egg white paste to your
moistened skin, using your fingertips. Cover your belly
with the paste, using small, circular massaging movements
in an upward direction.

Use up the remaining infusion by soaking the cloth again and placing it over your pasted belly. Leave for 10 minutes more.

Remove the cloth, rinse your skin with warm water, and pat dry.

MAKES ENOUGH FOR 1 APPLICATION

NOTE: DANDELION STALK JUICE MAY BE EXTRACTED BY REMOVING THE DANDELION HEAD FROM THE STALK AND SPLITTING THE STALK WITH YOUR NAIL. SCRAPE THE STICKY WHITE FLUID OUT WITH THE BLUNT EDGE OF A KNIFE AND PLACE IT IN A SMALL DARK GLASS BOTTLE. IT WILL TAKE APPROXIMATELY 25 TO 30 PLANTS TO PRODUCE 3 TEASPOONS OF JUICE. TRY NOT TO TOUCH IT, AS IT OXIDIZES QUICKLY AND LEAVES DARK BROWN STAINS ON YOUR SKIN. REFRIGERATE UNTIL READY TO USE.

Acid-Enzyme Breast Peel

Rich in alpha-hydroxy acids, this peel loosens the skin surface glue that binds the outer skin layers together. It also increases the shedding of skin cells and encourages the formation of new cells underneath. Ideal for upper-body skin, breasts, and thighs, where cellulite can form.

½ cup homemade or commercially prepared plain yogurt
3 tablespoons fresh aloe gel (see Note, page 178)
1 fresh fig skin
1 fresh plum skin
1 papaya skin
1 mango skin

Wash your breasts in warm water. Dry in the sunshine or air-dry in a warm, well-ventilated room. Using your hands or a clean make-up brush, apply the yogurt to your breasts in sweeping, circular strokes. Let it set for a few minutes; then wash off and pat dry.

In a small dish, mash the extracted aloe gel with a plastic fork. Spread over your nipples and breasts.

Massage the fig skin over your breasts and air-dry for 1 minute. Do the same with the plum, papaya, and mango skins, one at a time. Mist cold water over the fruit residue. Let dry for 5 minutes, and rinse off with a warm shower. Pat dry with a soft, warmed bath towel.

MAKES ENOUGH FOR 1 APPLICATION

NOTE: FRESH ALOE GEL MAY BE EXTRACTED FROM THE ALOE PLANT BY BREAKING OFF A LARGE LEAF NEAR THE ROOT, SPLITTING IT OPEN, AND SCRAPING OUT THE CLEAR GEL.

Avocado-Pit Scrub

This is a grainy exfoliation for hard skin areas of tired feet that lifts dead skin cells and encourages new cell growth. You can also use it to exfoliate the upper back, knees, elbows, and hands.

4 clean whole avocado pits
3 tablespoons honey or molasses

Place the avocado pits in a plastic zip-top bag. Put the plastic bag inside a cloth bag.

On a hard, outdoor surface (concrete, stone, brick, etc.), bash the pits with a wooden mallet into small pieces the size of dried lentils. Wash them and air-dry on a drying rack in a warm, dark, well-ventilated room for 2 days. Grind the dried pit pieces, a few at a time, in a coffee or mechanical grinder until they are tiny granules.

Use immediately, or place the granules into a sterilized, wide-mouth glass jar. Seal and label the contents.

Massage the honey or molasses into your skin. Apply a handful of the avocado granules over your pasted skin and rub gently. Leave on for 1 to 2 minutes. Wash off with warm running water.

MAKES ENOUGH FOR 1 APPLICATION

Violet Upper-Body Milk

Here is a sensually refreshing and feminine cleanser that lifts your spirits while moisturizing and toning your skin; it soothes skin blemishes and dry patches, which often occur on hands and arms during pregnancy.

4 tablespoons violet floral water (see basic recipe, page 24)

2 tablespoons orange-flower water (see basic recipe)

3 teaspoons freshly squeezed lemon juice

½ cup whole unhomogenized milk

2 teaspoons fresh aloe gel (see Note, page 180)

2 tablespoons chamomile infusion (see basic recipe, page 27)

20 freshly picked spring violets

Place all the ingredients into a large china bowl or wash basin. Beat gently with a plastic whisk or fork.

Put the bowl on a small, low table or a chair outside. Place a few towels or a small quilt on the ground (if the weather is too cold or you lack privacy, perform this exercise inside, in a warm, well-ventilated room near an

open window). Secure your hair so that it is off your face.
Undress to the waist.

Kneel facing the table (or chair) and begin splashing the
violet wash on your skin, using your hands. Smooth it over
your neck, shoulders, breasts, and arms. Then let your
lower arms and hands soak in the wash for a few minutes.

Air-dry for 5 to 10 minutes; then wash your face, and
pat dry with a warm facial towel. Relax for a few moments:
breathe in the nourishing fresh air. Dress lightly.

MAKES ENOUGH FOR 1 APPLICATION

NOTE: FRESH ALOE GEL MAY BE EXTRACTED FROM THE ALOE PLANT
BY BREAKING OFF A LARGE LEAF NEAR THE ROOT, SPLITTING IT OPEN,
AND SCRAPING OUT THE CLEAR GEL.

Floral Waters That Cleanse, Refresh, and Heal Different Skin Types

Choose from the following floral waters when making your natural skin-care packs, scrubs, and splashes, to adapt the formulas
to your individual needs.

For dry skin: rose and lavender
For normal skin: peppermint, spearmint, lemon balm,
      and thyme
For oily skin: rosemary, sage, orange, and linden

"Scenteous"-Touch Body-Massage Oils

While pregnant, I drew a great deal of pleasure from creating
sensuous, infused massage oils, which made the whole experience

Skin Care from the Refrigerator

Most of the natural foods you love to eat are as good for the outside of your body (in the form of facials, cleansers, and scrubs) as they are for the inside. To preserve your skin's natural moisture balance through sebum-secretion regularity, observe the following two rules:

1. Keep your skin hydrated from the inside by drinking enough natural water, which refreshes the inner skin layers. On a cellular level, pregnancy can either make you look your best, or your worst. If you have never suffered with dry skin or acne throughout your teenager years, you just might find facial clusters appear throughout the whole nine months, and disappear again as quickly as they appeared, after the birth of your baby.

2. Seal your skin's moisture in with external skin protectors and barriers. Use the ingredients you already have in your refrigerator. For example, fresh apricots are delicious to eat, and skin nutritious, too. Full of active vitamins and minerals, apricots can be applied as a gentle facial scrub. Or they can be juiced and mixed with an eyebright, violet, and chamomile infusion for a refreshing eye wash. The often-discarded pit contains tiny seeds, which can be macerated with oil or glycerin (see pages 21–22) for bathing recipes. The pit can be ground into tiny granules and mixed with yogurt or oatmeal and honey for a light exfoliating scrub for your breasts.

   Avocado pits can be crushed and ground, then mixed with a little molasses to make an excellent foot and hand scrub. Orange and lemon peel can be finely grated, mixed with rice or corn flour, and brushed through your hair as a dry shampoo. There are many more suggestions throughout this chapter.

Pregnancy can be a very needy time; it's easy to overlook your need to feel and look feminine. Pregnancy isn't just about the birth of your baby; it is about living through trimesters of physical, hormonal, and emotional changes that affect you, the woman behind the mom-to-be. You want to be nurtured, too. It is vital that you take time out for pleasures and beauty rituals that reinforce your sense of self.

Skin health is essential during pregnancy, as it is during any transitional stage of growth. Dry-skin brushing, moisturizing after showering, fruit or natural cleansing products, scrubs, peels, and baths all help to aid skin renewal through the process of detoxification and tissue hydration. They promote elasticity and tone as you grow and stretch to accommodate the two bodies growing in one suit.

of receiving a massage more special and beneficial. You, too, can make these oils at home, saving yourself quite a bit of money, especially if you can harvest the basic ingredients from your own garden.

Most of these recipes are designed to yield enough oil for one treatment: you won't need to worry about storing these valuable botanical oils.

Vitamin E and Rosemary-Leaf Belly Oil

Rosemary leaf is a skin-oxygenating botanical that increases energy levels and tones the three layers of the skin. Comfrey is a skin-healing, tissue-binding herb that leaves the skin soothed and soft. Chamomile has a sweet apple scent that is relaxing to the body and mind and has cell-renewing properties. This is an ideal combination for a healing massage oil. This oil will help keep those stretch marks at bay, and nourish and tone your stretching skin.

3½ tablespoons wheat-germ oil
1 sprig fresh rosemary
1 sprig chamomile flowers and leaves
5 small young comfrey leaves

Pour 1 tablespoon of the wheat-germ oil into a small jar with a close-fitting lid.

Break up the rosemary leaves, chamomile leaves and flowers, and comfrey leaves, and crush them, if necessary, with the back of a plastic spoon. Add them to the oil, shake vigorously, and place in a sunny, warm spot for 3 days.

Strain the infused oil through a fine-mesh sieve; then line it with cheesecloth and strain again.

Pour the oil into a ceramic bowl, and add the remaining 2½ tablespoons of wheat-germ oil.

Warm your hands by washing them in hot water, or clapping them together 5 times. On your cleansed belly, use your warmed hands to massage the oil into the taut skin, using small circular movements in an upward direction for 3 to 5 minutes. Make sure that the whole belly has been massaged; then cover with light cotton clothing.

MAKES ENOUGH FOR 1 TREATMENT

Rose and Orange Flower After-Shower Oil

This is one of my favorite feminine scented oils: it acts to free the body and spirit. I recommend making your own herbal flower waters—their sweet aromas will fill your house before, during, and after the massage. If you don't have the time, you can purchase them from herbal suppliers.

2 teaspoons rose-flower water (see basic recipe, page 24)

1 tablespoon plus 1 teaspoon orange-flower water (see basic recipe)

2 teaspoons evening-primrose oil

1 tablespoon vegetable glycerin

Pour all the measured ingredients in a small bowl and gently blend with a whisk or plastic fork. Pour into a long-neck bottle, and leave at room temperature until ready to use. (If tightly sealed, it will keep for 3 to 4 days at room temperature.)

Take a hot shower. Remain standing in the warm steam after the water has been turned off. Splash your moistened body with the after-shower oil; then hug, caress, and massage yourself from your neck to your feet (if you can reach). Or you could ask your partner to help. Massage all your oily wet skin and feel utterly indulged by this luxuriating body treat (you won't want to stop). Carefully step out of the shower, air-dry, wrap yourself in a soft, warm bath sheet, and curl up for a 15-minute nap.

MAKES ENOUGH FOR 1 TREATMENT

Hand and Foot Reflex-Workout Oil

A delightful feet treat. It not only exercises those tired, pregnancy-burdened "tootsies" but also balances and charges all the reflex points, which, in turn, stimulate the associated organs, nerves, and glands.

If you don't have time to make the infused oils, you can buy them from mail-order herbal suppliers (see Resources at the back of this book).

2 teaspoons wheat-germ oil

2 teaspoons comfrey leaf—infused oil (see basic recipe, page 21)

2 teaspoons lavender flower—infused oil (see basic recipe)

1 teaspoon St. John's wort—infused oil (see basic recipe)

4 teaspoons sweet almond oil

Pour the ingredients into a small bowl. Mix together with your fingertips.

Warm the oils by placing the bowl inside a larger one half-filled with hot water for 5 minutes. Test the temperature of the oil before applying.

If you can reach your feet comfortably without placing undue pressure on your expanding belly, you can do this massage yourself. Otherwise, have a friend or partner pressure-point massage your feet and hands for you (lie down comfortably or sit, reclined). Wash your hands thoroughly with warm water, dry them, and then oil your hands with a little of the recipe. Spend about 5 minutes on each hand and each foot, using your thumbs and forefingers to lightly massage. Press and hold for 5 seconds, then release. Massage both the palms, wrists, balls, heels, all ten toes, and all ten fingers in this way.

MAKES ENOUGH FOR 1 TREATMENT

Aromatic Temple Massage Oil

This oil is especially soothing for thumping headaches or migraines.

2 teaspoons sweet almond oil

5 drops lavender pure essential oil

5 drops cajeput pure essential oil

Measure the oils into a small bowl. Place a compress pad or piece of pure cotton linen into a bowl of cold water.

Pull your hair back from your face with a hair band, barrettes, or a towel turban (whatever you use, make sure it doesn't constrict the scalp). Remove any restrictive clothing.

Wash your hands in hot water, then thoroughly dry. Using your fingers, begin massaging the oil over the temples and forehead with small, circular movements, for about 5 minutes. Rest, then repeat for another 5 minutes. Gently squeeze the excess water from the compress; then place it over your eyes, temples, and forehead. Close your eyes and relax for 15 minutes.

MAKES ENOUGH FOR 1 TREATMENT

Shea Butter and Pure Olive Breast Oil

A luxuriating oil treatment that nourishes and soothes enlarged breasts.

> 3 tablespoons sweet almond oil
> 2 teaspoons shea butter
> 1 teaspoon royal jelly granules
> 2 teaspoons finely ground comfrey root
> 2 cups distilled water
> 1 tablespoon plus 1 teaspoon olive oil
> 2 teaspoons fresh aloe gel (see Note, page 187) or preservative-free
>   bottled aloe juice

Add enough water to a small, stainless-steel saucepan to come a quarter of the way up the sides of the pan.

Place the almond oil and shea butter in a small ceramic bowl; then place the bowl inside the pan. Place the saucepan over low heat until the oil is warm and the shea butter has melted. Add the royal jelly, and stir until it melts. Remove from the heat, keep stirring, and allow to cool.

Make a comfrey root decoction: Put the root in a small saucepan and add the distilled water. Bring it to a boil; then adjust the heat and allow it to simmer for 20 minutes (or until a third of the water has evaporated). Allow to cool.

Add 2 teaspoons of the comfrey-root decoction to the shea butter and royal jelly mixture (reserve the rest for another use). Add the olive oil and aloe. Beat gently; then transfer to a small bowl.

Undress to the waist. Cleanse your breasts with a warm soaked and rinsed towel, rubbing them vigorously; then allow to air-dry before applying the treatment.

Using both hands, gently massage the oil into your skin, using small circular movements in an upward direction, toward the heart. Spend about 5 minutes on each breast, including the nipples, as well as the underarms and shoulders.

Leave the oil on your skin and dress lightly.

MAKES ENOUGH FOR 1 TREATMENT

NOTE: FRESH ALOE GEL MAY BE EXTRACTED FROM THE ALOE PLANT BY BREAKING OFF A LARGE LEAF NEAR THE ROOT, SPLITTING IT OPEN, AND SCRAPING OUT THE CLEAR GEL.

A Relaxing, Herbal-Infused, Meditative Massage

THE MASSAGE

Dim the lights. Put on some soothing music (perhaps Tibetan chants with bells and chimes). Make sure the room is warm and well ventilated—not too hot, not too cold. Place four folded blankets on the floor on top of each other, making a support mat. Place some cushions nearby, one for under your knees and another for your neck. The objective of the exercise is to completely relax your whole body (and your baby, too!). For this massage to be most beneficial, you will need a willing assistant (a close friend or partner). Otherwise, in a sitting position, you can massage your legs, arms, abdomen, lower back, and breasts. I prefer to receive a massage so that I can fully benefit from the lovely mood, good company, and conversation.

Select your massage oil. Vitamin E and Rosemary-Leaf Belly Oil (page 182) or Shea Butter and Pure Olive Breast Oil (page 186) is a good choice. Heat the oil, so that it is warm when applied.

Lie on your back with your neck and head elevated on a cushion and your knees slightly propped up on another one, releasing any tension placed on your abdomen. Take a few deep breaths and begin clearing your mind of any nagging thoughts. Repeat the words "relax" and "let go."

Your assistant or partner may now begin. The massage strokes should be flowing and smooth, beginning with the feet and moving up to the ankles, calves, knees, thighs, nether regions, and abdomen. While you feel the massage around your belly, use your mind's eye and roam inside to where your baby is cozy and snug. Talk to her or him, sing a lullaby, smile—then release the vision.

Become mindful of the massage. Feel without thinking; become part of each touch, each stroke, from the inside of your body. Even though they are not your hands, become the hands stroking your body. Be the movements. Say to yourself, "I am falling into a state of deep relaxation, all tension is leaving my body. I am each stroke. I am completely relaxed."

Continue feeling and being the massage as it moves up toward your breasts, shoulders, down your arms, hands, gently around your neck, then your face and forehead. Now begin to feel total relaxation, a sense of full-body well-being. You feel weightless and fully harmonized with your body, mind, and spirit, all functioning on the same level to bring about total relaxation. (What pregnant woman wouldn't want to feel light and weightless every day?)

As the massage comes to a conclusion, spend a few minutes running your fingers through your hair and over your scalp. Pretend to crack a raw egg over the crown, and let the yolk roll down over the hair.

Exit assistant!

Place a light blanket or sheet over your oiled body, and begin the following color-energizing visualization.

THE VISUALIZATION
You are resting in a field of buttercups. You look around and you notice the brilliant yellow surrounding you—at your left, right, in front, and behind. The air is sweet; the sky is blue; the sun is warm on your skin. Reaching down, you pick a single buttercup and bring it up to your face. Notice the simplicity and beauty of its structure, so delicate.

Your eyes catch a red butterfly swooping and fluttering toward you, and you get to your feet and begin walking toward it. In the distance there are three large bubbles moving toward you; they are so big that a house could fit in each.

As they get closer, they merge into one bubble, which stops just in front of you. Inside the bubble you see all the colors of the spectrum dancing and glistening in the brilliance of the light within. It looks so inviting, you decide to step inside. Once you do, you begin to feel a floating sensation, and as you look down at your feet, you see that you are floating high above the treetops. There is no fear, you are safe. Inside the bubble, you are showered by each color. From the tip of your head, you feel each color go inside and travel throughout your functioning, breathing, regenerating body, leaving all their vibrational strengths within you.

The red color energy makes you feel courageous and strong.

The orange color energy leaves you feeling free spirited and independent.

The yellow makes you feel confident and happy.

The green color energy leaves you feeling full of compassion with a strong love of and connection with nature.

The blue color leaves you feeling inspired: the darkest blue, indigo, makes you feel a heightened intuition.

The final color energy, deep purple, surrounds your head and makes you feel at one with the universe.

As the bubble descends to the ground, you step out, leaving all your negative thoughts behind, all your negative attitudes and feelings within the bubble. You walk away, confident, refreshed, energized, and in harmony, emotionally, physically, and spiritually.

After this visualization, you can nap in the room or go for a short walk in the fresh air.

This was one of my favorite self-nurturing rituals during the latter stages of pregnancy. Sometimes, I chose not to have my husband massage me. I took time, caressing and hugging my pregnant form. These stolen moments of pleasure were sacred to my spiritual well-being, and gave me a special maternal-bonding experience.

AROMATHERAPY

Aromatherapy, using the scents of essential oils to promote well-being, is an exciting, growing field of study. The best way to bring aromatherapy into your pregnancy is to make a choice of fragrances that appeal to your nature, please you, and have a beneficial effect on a condition that may be bothering you. If you are having problems sleeping peacefully at night, using the essential oils of lavender and chamomile will help immensely. All you need do is place a cotton ball soaked in a few drops of each oil under your pillow, in a small flower arrangement near your bed, or even in your bathwater in the evening. You will be pleasantly surprised at just how refreshed and energized you feel in the morning.

Here are ten other ways to incorporate aromatherapy into your pregnancy lifestyle.

1. Take a small ball of cotton, saturated with a few drops of an appealing pure essential oil fragrance, like neroli or anise, and place it inside your vacuum cleaner bag. This will scent your whole house while cleaning.

2. Deodorize your carpets by mixing a few drops of a pure essential oil of your choice with 1 pound of baking soda. Stay away from an overly pungent fragrance, such as ylang-ylang, which could bring on a headache. Try clove, fennel or bergamot. Mix well; then sprinkle over your carpets (don't

forget your car rugs). Leave on for about 1 hour then vacuum it up.

3. To dispel pesky mosquitoes, place a few drops of concentrated citronella pure essential oil on melting candle wax. Works wonders for picnics, barbecues, and garden parties.

4. To deodorize shoes, sneakers, and boots dip a ball of cotton in your favorite pure essential oil, and leave it tucked inside the offending footwear overnight.

5. To ease a pounding headache, add a few drops of cateput pure essential oil into 2 teaspoons cold-pressed wheat-germ or extra-virgin olive oil, and massage into your temples.

6. Place a few drops of lavender and Mandarin pure essential oils on a warmed radiator or switched-on lightbulb and fill your home with memories of summer picnics and walks in the open countryside.

7. Revive the fragrances of potpourri by adding a few drops of pure essential oil and placing the dried herbs and oil in an airtight jar for 3 days; then place in small ceramic bowls around your home. Repeat once a month for best results.

8. To scent your towels, sheets, and clothing, place a few drops of either lemon, tangerine, pine, or jasmine pure essential oil on an old flannel shirt, and throw it into the dryer with your damp laundry.

9. Scent your bathroom by soaking a cotton ball in a pure essential oil of your choice and tucking it inside a small silk flower arrangement or bowl of glass marbles.

10. While bathing, enjoy the relaxing qualities of pure essential oils by placing a few drops of your favorite fragrance in the melting wax of a candle.

Making an Herbal Sock Face

During the latter months of pregnancy, when your abdomen is growing bigger and you find it increasingly difficult to get comfortable, whatever position you try, make yourself a sleep buddy in the form of an herbal sock face, which you put under your pillow. (You'll be using it long after the baby is born: I made myself these little sleep-aid gems for all my pregnancies, and now my children have them, too.)

THE HERBS

3 scented geranium leaves

6 catnip leaves and a few flowers

10 lavender flower heads and a few leaves

12 chamomile flowers

12 sweetly perfumed rose petals

5 drops lavender essential oil

5 drops jasmine essential oil

Grated zest of 1 orange, plus a few seeds

Grated zest of 1 lemon, plus a few seeds

3 whole cloves, crushed

OTHER SUPPLIES

An old, clean cotton sock (any color will do, but check for holes!)

Styrofoam chips

1 rubber band

Colored wool for hair

Paint or thread for eyes, nose, mouth, and cheeks

Colored ribbon

Bruise the geranium, catnip, lavender, chamomile, and rose (leaves and flowers) to increase their aromatic potencies. Place in a glass jar with a tightly fitting lid. Add 2 drops each of the lavender and jasmine oils, and the orange zest and seeds, lemon zest and seeds, and cloves to the fresh herbs.

Leave for 5 days.

In the meantime, fill the sock with a handful of tiny foam chips to shape the face. Secure the leg of the sock with a rubber band, and sew on some colored wool for hair. Paint or sew on eyes, a nose, a smile, and rosy cheeks.

After 5 days, add the remaining 3 drops of each oil to the herbs. Transfer the mixture from the jar to the sock, combining it with the Styrofoam chips. Reseal the sock face, and bind some colored ribbon around the rubber band, tying it with a loose bow.

Your herbal sock face is ready for use!

Each month, empty the contents of the sock and replace with fresh herbs, new foam chips, and pure essential oils. You can vary the materials and herbs that you use to fill your sleep sock face, according to your own preferences. You don't even need to use a sock: I did, because for one thing, I was recycling something old into something new. And for another, using a sock didn't require any sewing skills.

NOTE: IF YOU ARE UNABLE TO HARVEST FRESH HERBS, YOU CAN PURCHASE THEM IN DRIED FORM FROM MAIL-ORDER SUPPLIERS (SEE RESOURCES AT THE BACK OF THIS BOOK). THE PROCEDURE IS THE SAME, EXCEPT YOU DO NOT NEED TO BRUISE THE LEAVES OR FLOWERS. JUST CRUSH THEM IN YOUR HANDS AND PLACE IN THE JAR WITH THE PURE ESSENTIAL OILS. LEAVE FOR 5 DAYS, THEN ADD MORE OIL AND COMBINE WITH THE FOAM CHIPS BEFORE SEALING THE SOCK FACE.

Essential Oils

Essential oils have many, many remarkable healing and relaxing powers. Nonetheless, it's important to remember that all pure essential oils are for external use only, *and must be kept out of the reach of pets and children.* All of these oils are highly concentrated: you need only a few drops for a recipe or remedy. It will be well worth your time to read through an introductory book on aromatherapy (*Complete Book of Essential Oils and Aromatherapy,* by Valarie Ann Worwood, and *Aromatherapy: A Complete Guide to the Healing Art,* by Kathi Keville and Mindy Green, are two good references), before experimenting at home. It is vital that you understand each oil and its origin before using its beneficial active properties.

The use of certain essential oils should be avoided during pregnancy, as they can affect your hormonal balance and possibly stimulate early uterine contractions. My advice to you is to refrain from using any pure essential oils on your skin until after your fourth month of pregnancy, and even then, use sparingly. The following varieties are too overpowering for use during pregnancy:

ESSENTIAL OILS TO AVOID USING ON YOUR SKIN
DURING PREGNANCY

> Aniseed
> Basil
> Cedarwood
> Cinnamon
> Coriander
> Cypress
> Hyssop
> Juniper berry
> Lemongrass

Marjoram
Myrrh
Nutmeg
Pennyroyal
Peppermint
Sage
Tansy
Wintergreen

Aromatherapy in the Bath

Bathing is always a wonderful, whole-body, relaxing treat, but during pregnancy, it is probably the only time you can completely relax and take the weight off your tired, swollen feet. Aromatherapy can be used in bathing by adding a few drops of essential oil to the running water, or by splashing aromatic moisturizers on moistened skin. I liked to add chamomile, neoril, and lavender to my pregnancy baths. If you do not wish to use the concentrated, pure essential oils, you can make small fresh herb wash balls by dropping in running bathwater one tablespoon combined herbs in a tied muslin bag or teabag (you then wash your skin with the bag as you bathe). Add some loose rolled oats to the water to moisturize and relieve itchy skin conditions.

A bath is one of the simplest and best ways to promote a restful sleep. I went through two pregnancies in a very hot, humid climate and found that I needed to bathe in the early mornings and evenings, and sometimes take a refreshing herbal sitz bath or shower in the afternoon.

AN HERBAL PREGNANCY JOURNAL 🖎

Throughout each trimester of your pregnancy, you'll experience many dreams, fantasies, anxieties, joys, and fears. One of your most pressing concerns will undoubtedly be your need to know if your baby is okay, what she or he looks like, and whether all the limbs and digits are accounted for and are in the right place. By the eighth month of my first pregnancy, all I could think of was hugging and nurturing my newborn: the more I agonized about whether he was fully formed and safe, and who he was going to take after, the more vivid my dreams became.

When I became pregnant for the second time, I decided to keep a record of these dreams. I mapped my pregnancy journey from the day I found out to the day my son was born. It was a journey that involved a great deal of self-discovery. I grew from the mother of one infant into the mother of a growing toddler with another life developing inside of me. I was no longer in my own world. I was becoming the head of a family. My whole existence had turned around. Who was I, who was I becoming? These questions needed answers. Beyond that, I wanted to map the journey so that when my children were grown, I would be able to share this very exciting time with them.

You can do this, too. Your pregnancy journal will give you the opportunity to understand the changes you are going through and to celebrate your personal, individual pregnancy experience. You don't have to write in it every day, like a diary. Ask yourself what you want to say to your newborn. If you are not comfortable talking aloud to your expanding belly, then you can write or draw messages in a journal.

For my journal, I chose to take advantage of a wonderful holistic therapy used in psychiatry called "psycho-aromatherapy," which stimulates patients to get in touch with their deepest feelings using their scent memory. This therapy is based on the fact that each person has a scent memory in the brain, and the olfactory nerve is linked directly to the part of the brain where memories and emotions are stored. You can use this information as you journey through your pregnancy, using scents and fragrances as future reminders of how you experienced situations and circumstances. You will discover how simple it is to respond to a smell memory. I chose to use seasonal herbs throughout each month of my pregnancy as reminders.

Since I learned of my pregnancy in early spring, I collected 10 different varieties of herbs, all pungent, all brightly colored. For each herb, I made a self-sealing tea bag, and placed the herb inside whole. I placed each bag in an airtight, dark-colored glass jar and left it for 2 to 4 days. All together, I had 10 jars, with 10 different herbs, for ten months of pregnancy.

I began compiling a record of this transitional stage of my life with the aid of color and the aroma of freshly collected herbs and their seasonal flowers. I formed associations in my mind between important events and a particular aroma. Important dates, anniversaries, happy and sad times, joyous and rewarding times, challenging and demanding times, lonely times, divinely indulgent times—they all went into my journal. As one month passed into another, and as I journeyed from trimester to trimester, my journal grew with me. Everything I wanted to say to my unborn child, I wrote or painted.

My pregnancy journal was packed with drawings and flower presses from each "monthly-reminder herb." Now, as I look back on those months of pregnancy, I need only smell a fennel bulb to be reminded of buying my son's first baby clothes, or smell basil and remember repainting the nursery.

For the journal pages, I used 20 brown paper bags, 2 for each month, stapled together. Then I stapled 5 sheets of onion paper between each bag. I chose the paper bags so that I could store collected memorabilia inside for each month. I wrote or drew on the onion paper. Inside the top of each paper bag, I stapled the herb collection for that month. I made a small pressed flower print for each herb on the front of the bag.

It sounds like it is time-consuming, but once all the materials are ready, it takes only about an hour to put the journal together. As each month unfolded, I took another dried herb bag from the cupboard and stapled it into the journal.

Of course, your materials can vary: you can paint a front cover for your journal, and you can make some home-recycled paper covers, bound with pastel-colored ribbon, or brightly colored craft paper of different shapes, stapled together or strung on string. Be creative about personalizing your journal.

As you keep your journal, month by month, begin connecting with your inner self. Start looking at life from a child's point of view. I found this a wonderful way to reclaim innocence. Open your eyes. Speak freely and openly, and enter the realms of true knowledge. Being pregnant will offer you a great opening for personal growth and full transformation.

Enjoy every insane and rewarding aspect of this transitional journey. Jot down everything and anything. Collect, stick, paint, and write. Use all your senses, and make a family heirloom you can share with your children, your children's children, and many generations to follow.

How to Make a Pregnancy Journal

Use fresh herbs or whole dried leaves and flowers. You may be pregnant throughout a different sequence of seasons, so make your own choice of the herbs you want to fill your journal. Make it individual and special; after all, it's your journey.

THE HERBS

    Basil leaves

    Catnip leaves

    Chamomile flowers, stems, and leaves

    Diced gingerroot

    Fennel leaves

    Jasmine flowers

    Lavender flower heads and a few leaves

    Rosemary leaves

    Scented geranium leaves

    Sweet thyme leaves

THE SUPPLIES

    50 sheets (6 by 10 inches) onion paper, colored craft paper, or tissue paper

    10 self-sealing (paper, hemp, or linen) herbal tea bags

    Stapler

    Scissors

    20 small, recycled brown-paper bags

    Colored string, ribbon, or cord

    Paper puncher

    10 small 4-by-5-inch zipper-top bags

Measure and cut the onion, tissue, or craft paper, and set aside. You should have 5 sheets for each month.

Put the herbs into 10 small piles on paper towels. Take the self-sealing tea bags and fill each one with a different herb. Place the filled bags in a small, tightly covered, colored glass jar, and place in a cupboard until ready to use.

Staple 2 paper bags together at the top and bottom corners for each month. Staple 5 sheets of paper to the front bag. Do this for all ten months. Once you have a small book for each month, staple all the books together.

Make a floral design using the herbs you have collected (1 piece per herb) for your front cover. Cover it with clear tape to protect and preserve the herbs.

Each month, take an herbal bag from your cupboard, hold it in your hands, and breathe in its pungent aromas. Each time you write something that month, the thoughts, quotes, pictures, and collectibles become associated with this scent. After writing, place the herbal bag into a small zipper-top bag, and seal the aromas for another trip down memory lane. Or, just leave it clipped on the paper bag, so that each time you open the journal, you smell the aromas.

NURTURING YOUR MIND, TOO

Obviously, it's not just your outer self that needs to get revitalized during pregnancy. As I have said throughout this book, keeping a healthy mind and healthy attitude is just as important, if not more so. The following techniques are designed to keep you feeling good about yourself and your baby.

Daily Affirmation

Repeat the following affirmation in front of a mirror: the idea is to be positive, complimentary, and nurturing toward yourself and your baby.

I am a very special woman, doing a very important job.

I love and cherish my changing body.

I recognize the miraculous duty my evolving being is creating inside my womb.

I welcome this, our baby *(you and your partner's names, or just your name)*, as part of our world.

With all my heart, with all my love, I am at peace.

I am happy.

I am joyful.

I am healthy.

I am beautiful.

Visualization

The idea of the next exercise is to use both your imagination and your memory (remembered smells, sights, tastes, etc.) to get in touch with your sense of self.

Using your mind's eye, "see" a reflection of yourself, as in a mirror. Visualize your changing form, from the front and the back, below and above, inside and out.

Feel the texture of your skin and hair. Touch your expanding belly and breasts. Kiss your belly.

Look inside yourself to see your baby, all cozy and snug, looking back at you. Speak to your baby, see him or her acknowledge you by blinking and smiling. Hold this bond for a few seconds, then let go.

Open your eyes. Wiggle your toes, stretch your arms above your head, and flex your fingers. Take a few deep breaths, breathe out slowly, then wash your face in cold water. Pat dry.

Color Meditation

Here's another powerful color meditation, like the one I included in the section on massage. This is a longer meditation than the two outlined above, so take some time to find a comfortable setting in which to perform it. Dress in loose and comfortable clothing, making sure that you are warm and that your movements are not constricted.

To ensure you stay both relaxed and alert for this meditation, assume a lotus position, with your feet crossed and tucked beneath your thighs (if you are supple enough, rest your feet on top of your thighs). Keep your back straight and head up. Flex your neck from side to side, and up and down. Once the meditation begins, keep it steady, however.

Close your eyes. Take a few deep breaths to relax your body, and clear your mind.

Think about silence, tranquillity, and solace.

Think of water.

Put yourself at peace with your soul, your deepest feelings, instincts, and intuitions.

In your mind's eye, begin viewing your "surroundings."

You are sitting in a castle ruin. The walls and floor are covered with light golden yellow satin drapes. You are seated between two green marble pillars.

In front of you is a blue-green clear ocean; to your left, acres of orange-yellow flowers; to your right, rambling hilltops, covered in red and purple blossoms. The sky above you is dark blue.

All of these colors have their own individual energy, their own individual meaning. You have the power of each of them inside your changing being.

Feel the power of red, orange, yellow, green, blue, violet, and dark blue (indigo), and be courageous, energetic, independent, creative, free spirited, generous and loving, faithful, intuitive, and instinctive. Allow your body to be showered in these powerful color energies: feel them touch your skin and go inside your body, dancing and resonating, uplifting you to a state of true energized alertness.

Now see the energies come out of you, dull in color, bringing with them all your negative thoughts and feelings, and leaving all their positive powers inside.

Take another look at your surroundings; then look down at your pregnant form and see a ribbon of these brilliant colors tie a bow around you and your baby.

Lose the vision: close your mind's eye, and let your thoughts go blank.

Place your arms around your belly and hug your baby within. In a soft tone, say a short prayer or affirmation, one that you create, or that speaks to you directly, confirming the love you have for your baby and your changing form. Acknowledge the evolution you are both experiencing.

Open your eyes. Take a few deep breaths, twitch your nose, wiggle your toes, stretch your arms above your head, and blink your eyes.

Stand up. Wash your face in cold water. Pat dry.

AN HERBAL SPA DAY 🍃

Being pregnant gives you the perfect opportunity to pamper your changing form with a home-herbal spa treatment experience. Make a weekly appointment with yourself to enjoy a luxurious day of beauty enchantment for the body, mind, and spirit. Yes, you can do this within your own home at a fraction of the cost of commercial salons and European spas.

I indulged in a full spa day once a week during my first pregnancy, when I had only myself to look out for. During my second pregnancy it was one whole day, once a month. During my third, when I had two small children, I was able to steal only a few hours two nights a week, but even this brief period of time allowed me to preserve my sanity and recharge my psychic batteries.

To create the proper mood for your spa time and make it as relaxing (and refreshing) as possible, stick closely to the following rules.

PREPARE THE DAY BEFORE

Make up your spa treatments and snacks (sandwiches and salads, herbal teas, juices) the day before, so your self-pampering can proceed uninterrupted. Get assistance with this if you can.

BE UNAVAILABLE

If you have small children at home, lend them out to relatives, friends, or neighbors for a full or half day. Let other household members know that you are off-limits for everything (except an absolute emergency). You do not want to be disturbed. Take the phone off the hook, or switch on the answering machine (mute the volume, or turn it down low). This is your special time.

CREATE PLEASANT SURROUNDINGS

This is going to be a special day for you: create a special space in
which to experience it. Start by filling your house with fragrances
that appeal to your inner self, instinct, creativity, and femininity.
Use pure essential oils dropped in the melting wax of a candle,
or place small bunches of fresh herbal bouquets on small tables
or night tables. Make up some floral waters (see page 24), and let
the aromas flow through your house. Or leave small bowls filled
with various herbal infusions in those rooms where you are either
relaxing or applying a treatment.

Sound is important, as well. If you live in the country, let the
morning songbirds be your sound track. If you live in a city or
on a busy street, shut out the hustle and bustle by putting on a
tape of whale songs, or a trickling creek with birdsongs. Classical
instrumentals, bells, chimes, and Tibetan chants are also soothing and mind calming.

If you are not alone in the house, shut yourself in your bathroom or bedroom and use headphones. If you are completely
alone, and it feels a wee bit strange and uncomfortable, put all
the lights on, lock the doors, and have music resonating throughout the house.

Use color to enhance your spa day: Decorate with soft pastel
shades (pinks, whites, lilac, lime, turquoise, primrose) in the
areas where you want to relax, and brighter, more passionate colors (red, orange, violet, cobalt blue, emerald green, golden yellow) in the areas of activity and application. You don't need to
go out and buy new furnishings—use pillows, scarves, towels,
sheets, and your own clothing. Bed quilts tend to be white on the
underside: turn yours over and put it on the sofa or the floor;
then place colored pillows on or near it. Use towels in a variety of

colors on work surfaces and application areas. Experiment. Be imaginative.

Use your space creatively: I was fortunate enough to have a large bathroom, where I could shut myself in for a whole morning of pampering, and a sun-drenched living room, where I could spend the afternoon relaxing. If your house is small and compact, use all the rooms—bathroom and kitchen for application, living room and bedroom for relaxation, the garden or ventilated rooms for air baths.

If you do not have a bathtub in your bathroom, perform the bathing and washing treatments outside in the open fresh air, using a bowl and pitcher, or inside in a warm, well-ventilated room, near an open window. If your bathroom doesn't have a window, hang wind chimes around the room, with a small fan on low speed, creating sound. Use scented candles for light. If you have windows, open them out and let in the fresh morning air, hang some quartz crystals in the natural light, and catch the hundreds of rainbows dancing through the energy of daylight.

At the end of your special day of pampering, you'll look like you've gone to an expensive European health spa—and who's to know you didn't?

Below is a menu of treatments and exercises for your personalized spa day:

Full-Body Dry Skin Brush

For this you will need:

> 1 natural-bristle body brush with handle, or a dry luffah or hemp mitt

Start by drinking 8 ounces of water and then undress completely. Take the brush in your hand, sit down on the ground or floor, and begin brushing the balls of your feet, first the right, then the left; move up your body to your ankles, calves, knees, and thighs, first doing the right side, then the left.

Stand up, and brush your buttocks, lower back, and lower abdomen (be careful on your expanding belly; use only soft, circular brush strokes), breasts, shoulders, lower and upper neck, arms, and finally, your hands. The whole exercise should take no more than 10 minutes. Your skin will have a pinkish glow and will feel warm and soft.

Dry skin brushing activates the removal of waste product accumulations from the cells and tissues, unclogging the pores and removing dead skin cells on the skin's surface. Internally, it increases the metabolism and stimulates lymphatic drainage. To nourish the skin after brushing, mist with an herbal infusion of comfrey and ginseng (see basic recipe, page 27); then let air-dry. Next, do a Seashore Body Wrap.

Seashore Body Wrap

This is one of my favorite whole-body wraps: it is so deep cleansing that you feel refreshed and energized within minutes. I first heard about these types of body wraps from a friend visiting from Israel, where the recipe includes saltwater from the Dead Sea, to increase body buoyancy. I decided to use the sweet-smelling botanical aromas of chamomile and the skin-oxygenating qualities of rosemary to enhance the benefits to be gained from this delightful treatment.

THE HERBS

> 1 cup fresh or dried kelp
> 1 cup fresh or dried wakame
> ½ cup fresh or dried arame
> 2 cups fresh seawater, or Celtic sea salt dissolved
>   in 2 cups distilled water
> 4 teaspoons chamomile infusion
>   (see basic recipe, page 27)
> ¼ cup rosemary infusion (see basic recipe)
> 2 cups Rhassoul powdered mud
> 3 teaspoons fresh lemon juice
> ½ cup each comfrey and dandelion-leaf infusion
>   (see basic recipe), chilled

SPECIAL EQUIPMENT

> 1 queen size cotton sheet
> 1 warm wool blanket

If you're using fresh seaweeds, thoroughly wash the kelp, wakame, and arame in cold running water. If using dried, hydrate the seaweed with enough water to cover for 10 minutes. Finely chop the fresh or dried seaweed. Put it in a large bowl along with the seawater, chamomile and rosemary infusions, mud, and lemon juice.

Run a piping hot bath. Close the bathroom door, and let the heat and steam warm the room for at least 15 minutes. In the meantime, whip the ingredients in the bowl; then set aside for the application.

Dampen your hair with cold water, and brush it back, off your face.

Exfoliate your body completely by dry brushing; then mist

your skin with a spray bottle filled with the infusion of comfrey and dandelion leaf.

Begin applying the paste with your hands. Start with your hair, then work down over your face and neck, being very careful not to cover the skin surrounding your eyes or lips. Cover your breasts, shoulders, arms, abdomen, and swollen belly, and continue down to your legs and feet. Keep your skin moistened by spraying more infusion over the paste.

Once you are completely pasted (be careful not to slip!), wrap yourself in the cotton sheet, leaving your head uncovered.

Place a towel turban over your hair, and cotton gauze patches on your facial skin. Try and cover all areas of pasted skin with the sheet or gauze, but do not wrap your belly, breasts, or any area with swollen veins too tightly.

Test the bathwater; it should be warm.

Immerse your wrapped body. Lie back, dipping the towel turban in the water, and relax for 10 minutes. If you don't have a bathtub, stand, covered in the wrap, under a warm shower for 5 minutes.

Remove the sheet, gauze patches, and towel turban; then shower in warm water, rinsing off all of the paste, and finish with a few seconds of cold water.

Step out of the bath and air-dry, either in the warm sunshine or a well-ventilated, warm room near an open window. Wrap yourself in the warm wool blanket, and put your feet up. Or snuggle into bed for a 15- to 20-minute nap.

Next is the scalp and hair massage, but first, try this herb-flower refreshing splash:

Herb-Flower After-Shower Splash

Morning or night, this after-shower splash will leave you feeling refreshed, cleansed, moisturized, and very feminine. If you use it on your moistened skin in the morning, you will be accompanied by its sweet, delicate aroma throughout the day. If you use it at night, it will induce a relaxed, restful, and sound sleep.

THE HERBS
> ¼ cup glycerin
> ¼ cup rose-flower water (see basic recipe, page 24)
> 3 teaspoons lavender-flower water (see basic recipe)
> 3 teaspoons violet-flower water (see basic recipe)
> 3 teaspoons orange-flower water (see basic recipe)
> ¼ cup sweet almond oil

Pour the rose-, lavender-, violet-, and orange-flower waters into a sterilized, long-neck bottle. Mix the glycerin and sweet almond oil in a small bowl, using a plastic hand whisk or fork; then transfer to the bottle.

Take a hot shower. Stay in the warm steam and splash the moisturizer on your skin. Begin massaging it in with sweeping movements, always directed toward the heart. Once completely covered from neck to feet (spend a little time massaging around and over your pregnant belly), air-dry in a warm room or outside, if the sun is not too hot.

Scalp and Hair Massage

This exercise is ideally performed by a willing assistant, so that you can enjoy the full benefits of mind/body relaxation. Dress lightly, in loose, comfortable clothing.

Sit on the floor in a lotus position, feet tucked under your thighs, arms resting at your side, hands placed over your expanding womb. Close your eyes.

Run your fingers through your hair, from the roots to the

ends, and begin softly weaving. Do this all around your hair for about 10 minutes.

Using your fingertips, gently knead the scalp, starting at the nape of the neck and making your way up to the crown (don't forget the backs of the ears!). Once you have finished, crack an imaginary egg over the top of your head and let the yolk fall over and down the hair.

Perform this exercise at least twice a week, but always as part of your herbal spa day, especially during the later months of pregnancy, when some of the other treatments may be uncomfortable.

You may want to use a basic herbal shampoo to wash your hair.

All-Purpose Herbal Shampoo

An excellent herb-infused mild baby shampoo, it will leave any kind of hair soft, shiny, and tangle-free.

> *2 cups of freshly boiled distilled water*
> *1 tablespoon fresh young nettle leaves, or 2 teaspoons dried*
> *1 tablespoon chopped rosemary*
> *1 tablespoon chopped comfrey leaves*
> *5 fresh calendula flowers*
> *Grated zest of 1 orange*
> *Grated zest of 1 lime*
> *20 drops lavender pure essential oil*
> *½ cup unscented mild baby shampoo*

Pour the distilled water into a heat-resistant pitcher. Add the nettle, rosemary, comfrey, calendula, and orange and lime zests. Let steep for 2 hours, covered. Strain the mixture through cheesecloth or a fine-mesh sieve. Return the liquid to the pitcher (save the herbal pulp for compost). Add the lavender oil and stir well. Let cool. Add the unscented baby shampoo and stir again. Pour into a recycled plastic container with a pop-up top. To preserve freshness, store in the refrigerator (keep it away from fresh produce).

Apply 1 to 2 tablespoons on wet hair once a day, or however frequently you wash your hair. Condition the hair after thoroughly rinsing with warm water.

MAKES ENOUGH SHAMPOO FOR ABOUT 3 WEEKS

Warm/Cold Showers and Air-Drying "Baths"

Perform these skin-rejuvenating techniques each time the skin has been exfoliated, deeply cleansed, or dry brushed. If doing my recommended day spa, try these between the dry brushing and seaweed wrap.

These simple, self-explanatory techniques not only feel refreshing but actually increase circulation in the skin layers and promote detoxification and rejuvenation.

The first exercise is quite simple: after finishing your normal warm or hot shower, simply stand for a few seconds in cold water to invigorate your skin.

If you don't have a shower, it makes life a little more complicated, but you can still partake by washing in warm water at a basin, then splashing your skin with icy cold water.

The second technique is even more basic: don't towel dry, let the air do the job for you. After using this method a few times (whether you stand outside, or near an open window), you won't want to towel dry again.

Even when the weather is cold, if you stand in a warm room near an open window, you can reap the benefits of this utterly indulgent, yet extremely simple and effective treatment.

Herb-Infused Hair Steam

This treatment allows you to resuscitate damaged hair and combat scalp irritations/scaling. Use it twice a month to give your hair a silky shine and lustrous texture. It also encourages circulation and promotes hair growth. Use fresh or dried herbs. For this you will need:

> 1 gallon pure mineral or distilled water
> Grated zest of 2 lemons
> 1 tablespoon lavender
> 1 tablespoon comfrey
> 1 tablespoon ginseng root
> 1 tablespoon rose hips
> 1 tablespoon basil
> 1 tablespoon fennel seeds
> 1 tablespoon lemon balm
> 1 large stainless-steel saucepan

Bring the water to boil in a large stainless-steel saucepan. Remove from the heat, and let cool for 10 minutes. Immerse the remaining ingredients. Let steep for 5 minutes, then stir.

Place a folded towel on a small table near your sofa or bed; then put the saucepan with the hot infusion on the towel.

Pin your hair back with bobby pins or clips (you do not want it to fall into the infusion). Get into a comfortable, relaxed position, so that you can lie or sit up with your head 10 inches above the steaming pot.

Place a large towel over your head and around the saucepan (to catch the steam and aromatic vapors). Keeping your head a comfortable distance from the saucepan, let the herbal steam circulate through your hair and scalp. Stay covered for 10 minutes.

NOTE: YOU MAY FIND THAT THIS TREATMENT MAKES YOUR SCALP ITCH. THIS IS A NORMAL REACTION, AND SHOULD NOT CAUSE YOU ALARM (YOU ARE NOT ALLERGIC TO THE STEAM).

Refreshing Foot-Workout Bath

If possible, perform the whole exercise outside in the warm sunshine for an extra-refreshing treat for your often-swollen, tired, "pregnancy-burdened" feet.

> 5 cups fresh, clean seawater, or 2 teaspoons of sea salt
>   dissolved in 5 cups of distilled water
> 3 tablespoons hot, freshly made lavender-flower infusion
>   (see basic recipe, page 27)
> 3 tablespoons hot, freshly made rosemary-leaf infusion
>   (see basic recipe)
> I teaspoon fresh lime juice
>
> I foot bath or rectangular "washing-up" bowl
> I seeded luffa (see page 25)
> 100 small rounded black pebbles or glass marbles

Pour the seawater in the footbath. Add enough small pebbles or marbles to cover the bottom of the bath (make sure the stones are thoroughly washed before immersing them in the bath, and remove any sharp stones that could cut the skin).

In a small bowl, mix the lavender and rosemary infusions with the fresh lime juice. Gently stir this mixture into the seawater.

Place a large, folded bath towel under the bath and a few small towels within reach.

Immerse both feet in the water, and begin rolling the balls of your feet and your heels over the stones or marbles. Stretch and wiggle your toes and try picking up a few pebbles with them. This will stretch, exercise, and manipulate all ten toes, while the herbal infusions will relax and rejuvenate the skin.

Continue the workout for 15 minutes.

Immerse the luffa and rub your soles and ankles before stepping out and air-drying.

MAKES I FOOT BATH

Between-Treatments Shakes and Juices

Choose your shakes and juices according to your body's needs on your herbal spa day. All of these recipes are healthful and rejuvenating. Just be sure, after consuming a juice or shake, to wait 30 minutes before drinking pure water and at least 1 hour before eating any food.

Protein Shake 1

This is a high-energy, whole food drink that allows you to accomplish those extra hours of activity during the day when sleeping through the night is uncomfortable.

½ apple
5 large dandelion leaves

10 feathery dill leaves

2 teaspoons molasses

3 tablespoons plain yogurt

½ cup buttermilk or sprouted-almond beverage

½ banana

½ teaspoon brewer's yeast

5 ripe strawberries

1 teaspoon powdered spirulina

Prepare the apple, dandelion, and dill with a pulp-extractor juicer, or macerate the herbs with water in a blender. Bruise the leaves before placing them in the water, then blend on a high speed for 30 seconds. Add molasses, yogurt, buttermilk, banana, brewer's yeast, and strawberries, and blend for another 30 seconds.

Pour the shake into a tall glass. Add the spirulina, and mix with a spoon. Take small sips. Chew thoroughly before swallowing.

Drink this shake on an empty stomach (2 hours after eating a solid meal). Within 1 hour drink 1 cup of pure mineral water so that digestion is complete.

MAKES 1 SHAKE

Protein Shake 2

Another full meal in a shake.

Barley Tea

½ cup barley grains

3 cups distilled water

1 teaspoon honey
½ teaspoon powdered spirulina
½ teaspoon fresh aloe gel (see Note)
½ teaspoon powdered propolis
½ teaspoon powdered royal jelly
1 cup chopped watermelon with seeds
2 cups seedless red grapes
10 ripe strawberries

Make the barley tea. Place the barley grains in a medium saucepan with the distilled water. Bring to a boil, then simmer on low heat for 20 minutes, stirring occasionally so that the grains do not stick to the bottom of the pan. Remove from the heat; then strain through a fine-mesh sieve. Save the grains to eat later with a little oil and fresh basil, and pour the barley tea into a blender.

Add the remaining ingredients to the blender. Blend for 30 seconds on low speed. Add four ice cubes; then blend for another 15 seconds on high.

Pour into a glass. Take small sips. Chew thoroughly before swallowing.

Drink this shake on an empty stomach (2 hours after eating a solid meal). Within 1 hour drink 1 cup of pure mineral water so that digestion is complete.

MAKES 1 SHAKE

NOTE: FRESH ALOE GEL MAY BE EXTRACTED FROM THE ALOE PLANT BY BREAKING OFF A LARGE LEAF NEAR THE ROOT, SPLITTING IT OPEN, AND SCRAPING OUT THE CLEAR GEL.

Ageless-Skin Juices

Youthful-Likeness Juice

This juice gives your skin an inside-out cleansing and boost as your hormones weaken collagen production. All the fruits in this juice are beneficial for cell and tissue renewal and give your complexion a vibrant, healthy glow.

>   1 tablespoon mango purée
>   1 tablespoon passion-fruit purée
>   3 tablespoons pink apricot purée
>   3 tablespoons red grape juice

Mix the ingredients together in a glass. Drink 1 recipe (½ cup) daily. Then follow with 9 ounces of water 30 minutes later.

MAKES ½ CUP

Laughter-Line Smoother Juice

All the fresh produce in this juice combination works at flushing out and hydrating the skin tissues. The produce is high in the essential A, C, and E skin vitamins and rich in silicon, iron, and potassium. This juice is excellent for bags under your eyes and dry, flaking skin on your hands, feet, and scalp.

>   2 tablespoons carrot juice
>   2 tablespoons lettuce-leaf juice made from outer leaves
>   4 teaspoons pear juice
>   2 teaspoons parsley juice
>   2 teaspoons apple juice

Mix the ingredients together in a glass. Drink 1 cup in the morning. Then follow with 9 ounces of water 30 minutes later. Remember to chew each small mouthful thoroughly before swallowing.

MAKES ½ CUP

Spots, Pits, and Pimple-Eraser Juice

This is a spicy combination that warms and soothes. Full of active vitamins and enzymes it detoxifies the deeper skin layers so that the accumulated wastes that contribute to spots and pimples, which are common in pregnant women, is eliminated from the skin through sweating.

2 tablespoons carrot juice
2 teaspoons gingerroot juice
4 teaspoons green-bell-pepper juice
1 teaspoon fresh aloe gel (see Note)
1 teaspoon parsley juice
4 teaspoons pear juice

Mix the ingredients together in a glass. Drink 1 cup in the afternoon. Then follow with 9 ounces water 30 minutes later.

MAKES ½ CUP

NOTE: FRESH ALOE GEL MAY BE EXTRACTED FROM THE ALOE PLANT BY BREAKING OFF A LARGE LEAF NEAR THE ROOT, SPLITTING IT OPEN, AND SCRAPING OUT THE CLEAR GEL.

Complexion Clear Juice

Kiwi, cantaloupe, and peach are considered excellent skin fruits because they are rich in vitamin A and beta-carotene. The vegetable juices are packed with skin-essential iron, potassium, and sodium—all important pregnancy foods for your growing and stretching skin.

> *2 tablespoons carrot juice*
> *2 tablespoons kale juice*
> *2 teaspoons spinach juice*
> *4 teaspoons peach juice*
> *2 teaspoons kiwi juice*
> *2 tablespoons cantaloupe purée*
> *4 teaspoons celery-stalk juice*

Mix the ingredients together in a glass. Drink 1 cup in the afternoon or early evening. Then follow with 8 ounces of water 30 minutes later.

MAKES APPROXIMATELY 2 CUPS

A Sample Herbal Spa Schedule

8 A.M. or upon awakening:
> 10-minute sunbath (be as lightly dressed as possible)
> Herbal infusion (peppermint, spearmint,
>   or red raspberry—6 ounces)
> Light breakfast of fresh seasonal berries with
>   sprouted seeds
> Tall glass (6 to 8 ounces) water, drunk in sips
> Daily Affirmation (page 202)

10 A.M.

> Full-Body Dry Skin Brush (pages 207–8) and herbal infusion mist
>
> 15-minute air-dry (either outside or in a warm, well-ventilated room)
>
> Belly and breast massage (take time to communicate with baby, too) with rosemary and chamomile massage oil
>
> Tall glass (8 ounces) water (drink in sips)
>
> Protein Shake (pages 216–17) or light yogurt and sprouted seed snack
>
> Daily Affirmation

Noon

> Warm shower, followed by a 5-second cold shower
>
> Herb-Flower After-Shower Splash (pages 210–11)
>
> Herb-Infused Hair Steam (page 214) and Refreshing Foot-Workout Bath (page 215)
>
> Lunch and herbal tea: mixed green salad with grain or seed sprouts (six days' growth), sun-dried bread, and spearmint tea
>
> 30- to 60-minute color meditation and breathing exercise

2 P.M.

> Dandelion and rose-hip herbal facial mist
>
> Violet Upper-Body Milk (page 179)
>
> Juice and raw vegetable snack
>
> 6 ounces water
>
> Fruity Belly Mask (page 173)
>
> Daily Affirmation

4 P.M.

> Scalp and Hair Massage (page 211)
> Protein Shake
> Seashore Body Wrap (page 208)

5 P.M.

> Light early dinner with 2 to 3 cups of warm herbal tea
> Herb-Flower After-Shower Splash (page 210–11)
> Daily Affirmation

6 P.M.

> Color Meditation (page 203–4)

8 P.M.

> Full-Body Skin Brush
> Warm/Cold Showers and Air-Drying "Baths" (page 213)
> Lavender and chamomile herbal infusion mist
> Daily Affirmation and Visualization (page 202)

9 P.M.

> Bedtime (if possible, leave a small window open while
>   sleeping)
> Shakes, juices, and herbal tea snacks throughout day,
>   as needed

What to Do When You're Pressed for Time

As my third pregnancy progressed into its seventh month, I could snatch only a few hours a week to pamper myself. An aromatic foot-workout bath was always first on my list (my toes felt as though they were about to pop and throbbed at the prospect of walking the floors for yet another restless night with a teething infant). I couldn't do without open-air skin brushing and herbal infusion mists; and I just had to squeeze in an herbal bath (to energize my little gray cells) followed by a moistened skin massage. Having rose floral water around, so that the aroma dispersed throughout my house and gave every room I went into a light, feminine fragrance, was also important to me.

My spa time consumed less than two hours. I had a raw veggie snack before starting, herbal teas during, and a protein shake as I concluded.

I gave the start of my day definition and its end a conclusion: I began every morning with an early sunbath, meditation, and affirmation. Each night before sleeping, I performed a short color meditation and affirmation. On the mornings when it was cloudy or raining, I stood by an open window and breathed deeply in and out 20 times to start my day refreshed and alert (even if the rest of the day degenerated into chaos).

5

Thyme After Your Baby Is Born

POSTPARTUM CARE

Congratulations! You are now a new parent (whether this is your first, second, or fifth baby). Never again will you be that carefree, career-oriented, self-centered person you were ten months ago. You have a new role in life: the next few weeks may be the most physically and emotionally draining experience of all.

How you cope with these trying weeks depends heavily on you, your partner, your support system, your birth experience, and not least of all, your darling baby. It is all too easy for you (and others) to get caught up in your newfound role, and suddenly find yourself tangled in a screaming mass of self-neglect and physical exhaustion.

My advice: Take it slow. Pace yourself. Focus on your needs and the needs of your new baby (let the laundry and dishes pile up). Continue to pamper yourself. Share some of your luxurious escapes with your infant. Anything that isn't vital to you or your baby's health and happiness can wait. This special time right after the birth of your child deserves to be fully enjoyed.

Learn to make the most of doing nothing for short (or long) intervals throughout each day. Nap between feeds. Meditate to relax and center yourself, and restore your energies.

You will have physical changes to deal with. Your breasts may feel congested, full, and heavy. Your abdomen (uterus) will shrink rapidly. By the end of the first week, especially after a vaginal birth, you may not be able to feel your uterus while pressing your abdomen (five to six weeks after birth, it will shrink back to its normal size). Your vagina will need to heal from the stretching and possible tearing it went through, while your liver and kidneys must cope with an increase of "buzzing" hormones as you adjust to the sleep-deprived rhythm of being a new mom.

If you had a cesarean birth, it will take a few more weeks, perhaps even months, to regain your prepregnancy shape. Remember, recovering from a cesarean birth is much like recovering from any other form of major surgery. A cesarean can also carry with it a feeling of failure—of guilt and anger at not being in control of your body or the birthing experience. And while you may not have experienced the perineal tears associated with a vaginal birth, once your anesthetic wears off, you may feel a throbbing pain around the incision area. Everything you do—sitting, standing, coughing, laughing, and walking—will hurt. Give yourself time to heal. Enjoy the rest.

When to Call the Doctor

Postpartum complications are rare, but they do happen. If any of the following symptoms occurs, call your practitioner or health caregiver immediately. If needed, call 911 or go to an emergency facility.

Heavy vaginal bleeding (enough to saturate a pad) for over two hours.

Bright red vaginal bleeding within four days after birth.

Foul-smelling lochia (vaginal) discharge.

Large (golf-ball-size) blood clots in lochia discharge.

Absence of a lochia discharge during first two weeks after birth.

Fever over 100 degrees Fahrenheit for more than a day twenty-four hours after birth.

Sharp chest pains.

Pain in abdomen (not after-birth cramping, which is when the muscle continues to contract as the uterus shrinks back to its original size) with swelling, within two days after birth.

Warmth, tenderness, and pain in calves or thighs.

Pain, swelling, oozing, and redness at site of cesarean incision.

Dark, pungent urine, with pain and burning during urination.

Postpartum Depression

Many women experience the "baby blues," or postpartum depression. This depression can last from one to seven days, and is caused by a temporary mental imbalance due to hormonal and brain chemical changes after birth. Symptoms include irritability, tearfulness, restlessness, and depression. How you generally deal with stress in your life will greatly influence your susceptibility to this condition, although it can affect strong, well-adjusted women as easily as nervous, neurotic women. It is nothing to be ashamed of—it's common and can be treated.

Fight postpartum depression by getting enough rest, eating body energizing foods, flushing your system out with juices and water, and using herbs as internal cleansers and healers. Get out of the house every day so that you don't feel trapped, isolated, and lonely. Go for long walks with your infant in the fresh air: walk barefoot, enjoy nature, relish the simplicity of being.

Pamper yourself every day. Browse in book or antiques shops. Let the tears roll; don't resist your sadness. Crying can be healing. Talk and laugh. Think happy thoughts.

If this period of postpartum depression lasts more than ten days, call your doctor.

DEALING WITH POSTPARTUM BLUES
THROUGH DIET

Eat simple and fresh foods, such as garden salads and seaweed broths: they will cleanse your digestive system and alkalinize your circulatory system. Let go of habitual mealtimes. Pay attention to your body: if you listen carefully, you will hear requests for the foods it needs to heal itself. Reduce the size of each meal, eat when you are hungry, and eat very slowly. Enjoy each mouthful, and stop before you feel full. While eating, think good thoughts as you sit relaxed and focused on healing yourself. Take this time to rest (let a friend or relative cook for you).

MOOD-ENHANCING POSTPARTUM DRINKS

The following drinks, full of herbs to aid the body in rebalancing its hormone levels, will help induce tension-free, restful sleep during the first few stressful days of motherhood.

Chamomile Flower Tea

A delicious, sweet-smelling tea to calm and relax.

> *1 cup spring water*
> *1 tablespoon fresh chamomile flowers*
> *½ teaspoon blossom honey*
> *1 tablespoon fresh goat's milk*

Boil the water, infuse the flowers in it for 5 minutes, and strain with a fine-mesh sieve. Add the honey and milk. Drink warm, and then rest.

MAKES I SERVING

Skullcap and Licorice Tea

Skullcap herb in tincture form will sedate and induce a restful sleep. There are no known side effects from overdoses, and it is not habit forming.

> *½ cup fresh licorice-root decoction (see basic recipe, page 26)*
> *5 drops skullcap tincture (see basic recipe, page 29)*

Strain and cool the licorice decoction. Add the skullcap tincture, and gently stir. Drink 1 cup before napping or sleeping.

MAKES 1 SERVING

Hop and Apricot Sleep-Soothing Cocktail

Drink this to calm frazzled nerves after a busy day. Hops will increase breast-milk production while nursing and soothe after-birth pains as the uterus contracts.

½ cup hop flowers
3 pinkish apricots, pitted and peeled

Make a hop-flower infusion: Immerse the hops in 1 cup of very hot water. Let steep for 1 hour.

Blend the apricots in 1 cup of spring water. Strain the hop infusion through a fine-mesh sieve and add it to the apricot purée.

MAKES 1 SERVING

Daily Affirmation for New Moms

Relax, and repeat the following affirmation as often as necessary to help you balance your new role.

My new baby helps to awaken me to the wonders in my life. By looking after myself and my needs, I am increasing the shared quality for my family. My feelings and emotions are an important part of me; when I embrace them, I embrace myself. I now recognize and establish a new awareness of success. I am as successful as I make up my mind to be. Motherhood is my nurturing direction. I now move into a fulfilling circle with opportunities everywhere for growth, understanding, and spiritual forgiveness.

All is well in my changing world. I am safe and happy. I free myself from past hurts. I willingly move into the pleasures and rewards of motherhood. Every morning I say yes to life. Life mirrors my every thought. By keeping my thoughts positive, I only experience happiness and fulfillment.

I breathe in the richness of my new life by observing with love the joy that abundantly supports me each and every day. Since it is my mind that creates my experiences, I now try to think only good and happy thoughts as I enjoy sharing my world with my new baby.

Every new opportunity offers me the chance to become more of the mother I want to be. All is well in my world. I live in limitless love and joy. Motherhood becomes me. All new experiences are opportunities for me to learn and grow.

My wonderful body and the many changes it has experienced throughout pregnancy and childbirth is perfect for me now. I rejoice and recognize the miraculous job it has accomplished, as I now hold my newborn and embrace myself with love and compassion for life. I do not have to earn love. I am a lovable person, and other people reflect the love I have for myself and my baby.

Each moment of our day is special to me. Come rain, shine, wind, snow, or humidity, we relish the simple pleasures nature provides. We watch, listen, taste, touch, and imagine the good, beneficial, and beautiful aspects of being immersed in our roles as mother and baby.

BREAST-FEEDING

I knew that I wanted to breast-feed my babies. I had been preparing for the event by massaging my nipples and drinking milk-promoting herbal teas throughout the last month of pregnancy. I was determined to be my baby's main source of nutrition for as long as it was comfortable for us both. I breast-fed my first son for over seven months, and only stopped when I discovered that breast-feeding didn't protect me from getting pregnant again!

My second son found it difficult to latch on, and we'd spend less than five minutes a feed, every hour throughout the day, and most of the night, too: I kept trying for about 10 weeks before I resorted to my homemade formula of yogurt, goat's milk, spirulina, and freshly extracted pear juice. Three times a week I made a formula of sprouted-nut-milk substitute, with roasted rice milk and pear juice. I used this formula knowing from my own research that nuts and cereal grains imitate the natural bodily processes that produced my milk from the natural foods, grains, and nuts I ate in my diet.

My third baby was also very fussy at the breast. Again I was tortured by feeding once or twice an hour, every hour. It was much harder this time because I had a two-and-a-half-year-old and a fifteen-month-old demanding my attention and needing nurturing, too. I was also unsettled emotionally, and always eating on the run. I nursed my daughter for about eight weeks after her birth before again reluctantly resorting to a homemade formula.

Even though nursing was more of a struggle for my two younger children, I still felt profoundly satisfied by the experience: nursing bonds mother and child together in a natural way bottle-feeding cannot duplicate.

Deciding to Breast-Feed (or Not)

Attitudes toward how and what mothers should feed their babies have changed tremendously throughout the past twenty years. During the 1980s, there was a surge of enthusiasm for breast-feeding in hospitals and birthing clinics.

Breast-feeding, to the surprise of many new mothers (including myself), is a learned art form. No woman is born equipped with the necessary know-how. It can be painful at first, as not all babies latch on the whole nipple and suck from deep inside the breast. Some little monsters pull on the tip, which can cause a great deal of pain and little nourishment for the baby.

The best advice I can give is go ahead and give nursing a try. If you both like it, keep going as long as possible; if you don't, stop. Don't feel guilty about your decision: it's your body. Find a support group, seek a lactation specialist, and talk to other mothers about their experiences. Once you and baby have mastered the art, it is simple and convenient—and it lets you avoid completely the nightmarish scenario of standing at the sink bleary-eyed, having just fallen out of bed for the sixth time in two hours as you fill your baby's "middle-of-the-wee-hours" bottle with cold perked coffee instead of premixed formula.

Nature's formula is always available "on tap," at the right temperature, anytime, day or night. While the baby sucks, you can grab a quick cat nap and regain your sanity in time for another challenging day.

Breast-Feeding Basics

The breasts begin to ready themselves for nursing during pregnancy. They increase in weight and volume. The nipples are sterilized by the antibacterial action of sweat and oil secreted by the nipple, and they are ready for sucking whenever the baby wants a feed.

When a baby first begins to feed from its mother, the breasts secrete a thick, yellow, creamy liquid called colostrum, which is an intermediary food supply. Biochemically, colostrum is more like blood than milk. It contains numerous lymphocytes and macrophages, which protect the body from disease-spreading organisms. It contains ample antibodies, which give the baby a natural immunity. Colostrum is especially rich in viral-disease antibodies, more so than the mother's blood. Babies who do not receive colostrum or who are nourished by unnatural formula combinations are often more susceptible to viruses and bacterial infections. Colostrum also acts as a natural laxative to cleanse your baby's intestine of meconium (the first bowel movement of a newborn). It is important to note that even though colostrum provides all the nutrition your baby needs for early growth, he (or she) will lose a few ounces in weight until he receives breast milk.

Breast milk is the perfect food for human babies: it is simply mother's blood that has risen in the body and converted in the breasts into a sweeter, less salty liquid. This process is similar to the rising and separation that occurs in fermentation.

How much should a baby feed from each breast? The most reliable guide is the behavior of your baby. In general, babies can be nursed whenever they appear hungry. Breast milk is easily and rapidly digested and will not upset the baby's fragile stomach. Feed on demand, and let your baby set a schedule.

Herbs to Aid Breast-Feeding and Weaning

The following herbs can be found in your culinary herb garden or purchased dried in health food stores or from mail-order suppliers and organic garden centers (use these outlets only if they do not spray their plants). There are herbs that aid the breast-feeding process by increasing milk production, and there are also herbs available to treat clogged ducts, engorgement, and cracked nipples that can cause pain and discomfort for the new mother.

Always consult with your physician or health caregiver before making, using, or applying any home remedy. Most medicinal herbal remedies are completely safe for both mother and baby, but always find out the facts and use the cures and treatments with knowledge and respect; then you will be able to assist Mother Nature in aiding your body's natural processes.

Make a warm or iced brew (unless otherwise stated) of the following herbs:

• *Alfalfa, dill, and fenugreek.* Will help keep your baby colic free.

• *Alfalfa and red clover.* Encourages plentiful supply of nutritious rich breast milk and relaxes a lactating mother.

• *Basil, borage, fennel, marsh mallow, and red raspberry leaf.* Promote quantity and enrich the quality of your breast milk.

• *Parsley and sage.* Will help dry up your milk while weaning.

The mineral-rich herbs also protect the mother from micro-nutrient losses during the stresses of early motherhood.

• *Aloe (gel), comfrey and marsh mallow (poultice), comfrey root (ointment), and yarrow leaf (compress).* All four remedies soothe cracked nipples and relieve pain from engorged breasts before, during, and after breast-feeding.

• *Barley (compress).* Placed inside the bra, eases swollen and painful breasts due to engorgement.

• *Barley and fennel tea.* Increases milk production, eases after-birth pains, and settles the digestion of both mother and baby.

• *Borage tea.* In addition to increasing milk flow, it acts as a mild laxative, soothes frazzled nerves, and encourages a restful sleep.

• *Comfrey (hot compress).* Soothes sore nipples, and helps to unblock ducts and tubes.

• *Grated raw potato (compress).* Placed inside the bra, frees clogged ducts and draws heat away from an inflammation.

• *Marsh mallow (breast soak).* Soothes tender breast tissue, powerfully draws out infections, and opens clogged ducts.

- *Poke root (tincture).* Clears mastitis quickly by stimulating lymph gland activity.
- *Sage tea.* Soothes sore and swollen breasts after breast-feeding has ceased.

Breast Care While Nursing and Beyond

Between feeds, gently dry brush your breasts and mist them with an herbal infusion of chamomile, comfrey, and dill. Let them air-dry in the healing sunshine. Sun drying helps to build keratin over and around the nipples, which protects them from becoming sore. Washing your breasts with your own milk also soothes and heals the delicate tissues, followed by air-drying. Always wear a supportive bra, even at night, if your breasts feel heavy (and have jumped two sizes!). If you are suffering from engorged breasts that have become hard and painful, pack your bra with grated raw potato and minced parsley leaves; then alternate with hot and cold comfrey-leaf-infused compresses. Make sure that each breast is emptied after nursing, either by pumping by hand or using a convenient suction pump. In addition, increase the feeding times to at least every 2 hours in the beginning. Continue wearing a supportive bra even after nursing has stopped, and exercise daily to increase a healthy blood flow to the breast tissue as yet another transitory role comes to a close.

Mastitis

Some lactating mothers experience a breast infection commonly known as mastitis, which results from stagnation in the breast caused by a clogged duct. The milk backs up, and the breast becomes overly full and infected. The area becomes swollen and red, and a slight fever develops.

Try hot gingerroot-infused compress or freshly grated raw-potato compress placed on the infected breast to stimulate blood circulation and relieve the stagnation. Alternatively, goldenseal and echinacea tinctures are ideal. Neither herb is harmful, although goldenseal is known to weaken the rest of the body as it debilitates the virus or bacteria.

While taking these herbs, stop nursing. Place your child on a natural-substitute formula. You can continue to pump your milk to keep up the consistent flow and demand, but discard the milk.

Mastitis can also result from an overconsumption of fatty foods (especially animal fats), sugar, fruits, spices, and caffeine. Increase your consumption of leafy green vegetables such as kale, beet greens, daikon leaves, and carrot and turnip tops. Eat them raw in salads or lightly steamed with sea vegetables, and reduce the content of salt in your foods until the condition clears up.

BABY'S FIRST FOODS

Once your baby indicates a need for more food than your breast milk or a formula can provide, it's time to start introducing light solid foods. Strained fruit juices (not citrus—don't use citrus until the baby's first year) can now be added to his diet, anywhere between the ages of five and seven months. My older son, Zak, was more than happy with breast milk until he was seven and a half months, and I only began to wean him onto a nut and grain milk substitute because I was pregnant with my second son, Josh.

Some babies require solid foods earlier than others. Be guided by your doctor, your baby's needs, and your own instincts. The first solid foods I gave my babies were banana, avocado, or freshly ground oatmeal porridge, which I prechewed and mixed with a little warmed yogurt and fresh applesauce. I gave this to the baby after the first morning feed. If you chew the solid food first, it mixes with predigesting saliva, making it easier for the baby not only to swallow but to digest as well. A quarter of a small banana, 1 scoop of a very ripe avocado, or 1 tablespoon of oatmeal will satisfy these meal requirements. Remember that babies need extra fluids, too. This is a good time to give baby a mid-morning, warmed herbal tea of catnip and fennel, or chamomile and mint.

After a few weeks on a semisolid breakfast, your baby will probably want a midday snack, too. I made all my children's weaning meals from soft fresh fruits and vegetables, which I steamed in a triple-layered pot so that I could cook a variety of foods at the same time. Suitable vegetables to start off with include squash, peas, green beans, carrots, pumpkin, spinach, lettuce, yams, potatoes, broccoli, and cauliflower. First steam, then blend or mash the fruit or vegetable with a little water. Meal sizes vary from 2 to 4 teaspoons of a puréed vegetable. Afternoon meals can consist of soft, lightly cooked fruits such as apples, seasonal berries, and pears.

Always introduce one new food at a time. If your baby doesn't like a food source, he'll let you know in no uncertain terms. In fact, you'll probably wear more of that meal yourself. Resist sweetening foods with sugar or honey; always try keeping foods as natural as possible. You can try adding a little homemade yogurt or small-curd cottage cheese, for a change of taste and texture.

It's a good idea to keep a record of these first foods, so that anything that might cause a rash or diarrhea can be identified quickly and then eliminated from the diet. After six to eight months, start adding blended sprouts like alfalfa and mung bean to porridge and steamed vegetables. Sprouts are very nutritious; their protein, vitamin, and mineral count is higher than most other natural foods, and they are easily digested. For babies ages ten to twelve months, minced raw vegetables and fruit, such as beetroot, carrots, celery, cucumber, and tomato, can be introduced. Do not be alarmed if after eating beetroot, your baby's stools and urine change to a pink color.

Lentils, peas, beans, and chickpeas are excellent first foods, but they will need to be soaked overnight, then cooked slowly and puréed with water. I like to soak my beans with a sprig of basil, dill, marjoram, or thyme, which are all natural digestive aids. Save the cooking water, and add it to the mashed vegetables or avocado. Fine nut flours, such as almond, pine, and pecan, can be mixed with ground sunflower seeds and sprinkled over fruit or cottage cheese. If you want to sweeten these first foods, use ground carob bean. Carob contains vitamins A, D, and B, riboflavin, and niacin—all important nutrients for good baby health.

Healthy Eating for Baby

Remember that a sweet tooth is cultivated, not inherited. Keep sweet foods to a minimum and get into the habit of cleansing the baby's gums with a stimulator, which can be obtained from your dentist, after each meal. Additives such as colors, stimulants, and preservatives found in most commercial infant transitional foods can cause allergic reactions. Become an observant label reader, or make your own foods using only natural, organically grown and harvested produce. Read all you can about health and natural nutrition, and give your child the best start in life using only the purest fresh, natural, and uncontaminated foods.

Teething and Finger Foods

Once your baby's first teeth are cut, he'll need chewy foods that will aid his teeth formation and soothe those sore gums. I made my babies rusks (zwieback) from whole-wheat bread.

Other great finger foods are raw vegetables like tomatoes, grated carrot, diced cucumber, grated beetroot, diced bok choy, and tiny broccoli florets. These foods are important for the baby's diet, and since he will be intrigued by different objects, smells, textures, and tastes, it is a great way to encourage healthy eating patterns at a young age. A healthy way of eating learned as a baby will chart a course for life as your child grows. It will give him pride in his body and in the way he looks. I have always encouraged my children to eat raw vegetable snack foods, and if they're still hungry after their main meal, they can have fruit, an iced herbal tea, or freshly extracted juice. There is always a selection of fresh foods in our home, and they can snack anytime on nuts, sun-dried breads, roasted seeds, and chopped raw vegetables. Healthy eating is a way of life for us, and I think this stems from their established patterns of infant nutrition.

Rusks (Zwieback)

A great, easy-to-hold first food that eases the pain on baby's first teeth.

> *10 slices of whole-wheat bread*
> *2 cups cooled vegetable or seaweed broth*
> *1 tablespoon finely ground sesame seeds*
> *1 tablespoon finely ground sunflower seeds*

Cut the bread lengthwise into 1-inch-wide slices. Mix the sesame and sunflower seeds together in a small bowl.

Brush some of the cooled broth over each slice of bread with a pastry brush. Sprinkle with a layer of the ground seeds.

Place all the slices on a wire rack, making sure there is a little space between each one.

Bake at 300°F. for about 1½ hours, or until crisp and dry.

Remove from the heat, and set aside to cool. Store, covered, in a cookie tin or large plastic container. Do not refrigerate.

MAKES APPROXIMATELY 30 RUSKS

PREGNANCY LEGACIES AND REMEDIES

The following are a list of long-lasting changes your body may exhibit after pregnancy, and some herbal remedies to lessen their effects.

Dark Nipples

During pregnancy, your nipples grow larger and darker. By twelve months postpartum they will return to normal size, but the darker color will remain. Applied daily, after you have stopped nursing your baby, the following herbal remedies will gently bleach the skin color and tone the surrounding tissue:

Nipple Bleacher

A nutrient-rich oil that will lighten the darkened skin surrounding your nipples with ten to fourteen applications.

> ½ lemon
> 1 teaspoon fresh watercress juice
> 12 large dandelion flower stalks
> ½ teaspoon rose-hip oil

Juice the lemon, set aside 2 teaspoons of the juice, and reserve the rind, which should be intact. (Save the remaining lemon juice for another use.) Mix the lemon and watercress juices in a small saucer and set aside.

Split the dandelion flower stalks. Using a pipette, suck out the milky fluid. Add it to the juices, stir, and add the rose-hip oil.

Using a small spoon, scoop half of the mixture into the lemon rind. Massage it over your nipples for about 2 minutes. Let air-dry for 10 minutes, and then rinse with warm water. Repeat daily for 2 weeks.

MAKES ENOUGH FOR 1 TREATMENT

Here's another quick remedy:

Safe Skin Bleach

A skin-kind, soothing bleach treatment.

> 1 teaspoon grated horseradish
> 2 teaspoons plain yogurt

Mix the horseradish and yogurt and apply.

Leave on for 10 minutes, then rinse with warm water.
Repeat twice daily.

MAKES ENOUGH FOR 1 TREATMENT

Excess Abdominal Skin Folds

Depending on your pre- and postpregnancy exercise regime, skin tone and elasticity will return anywhere from six weeks to six years postpregnancy. Talk to your doctor about when it is safe to start exercising again.

If you can't manage an exercise program along with all your other new daily challenges, use herbal skin remedies, brush your skin daily, and change your diet to tighten and tone.

To tone the skin from the inside, eat plenty of fresh strawberries, apricots, broccoli, dandelion, chicory, chickweed, oranges, carrots, and watercress.

Fresh sunflower, sesame, and pumpkin seeds are full of the mineral zinc and other vital nutrients that repair and regenerate your skin. Olive oil contains essential fatty acids, and should be consumed daily. Use the oil either as a dressing or to lightly sauté vegetables. Foods rich in the mineral silicon will also help you regain skin suppleness.

External application is another way to regain essential skin nutrients. Fresh apple juice is a year-round skin toning tonic. Carrot juice supplies plenty of the skin nutrient vitamin A and beta carotene. It also clears up imperfections and makes the skin feel refreshed. Tomato flesh and juice tones and firms the skin. A postpregnancy belly mask of fresh aloe, carrot juice, and egg whites will tighten and firm sagging skin folds.

Big Feet

Feet are another enlarged body part that just refuse to shrink after childbirth! Be prepared to step into a larger shoe size post-pregnancy. Slushing in cold mud, tiptoeing in snow, dancing on beach shingle (tiny pebbles or broken shells), running through morning dew, and herbal hot soaks such as sage, rosemary, and sea salt not only soothe and nourish but also tone and shrink!

Lackluster Hair

The vibrant luster and lush texture you enjoyed throughout pregnancy disappears after birth. To counteract this, eat plenty of protein-rich vegetables, especially sprouted-nut butters and milks. Sea vegetable soups and salads provide your body with essential hair nutrients that keep it strong, glossy, and thick. Drink a dietary supplement of spirulina, propolis, royal jelly, and wheat-grass juice twice daily. If your hair is dry and brittle, stop using commercial shampoos. Apply a dry-base-formula shampoo of finely ground lavender or lime flowers, thyme leaves, and cornstarch twice a week. Condition weekly with mayonnaise and molasses or make a strong infusion (see page 27) of nettle and thyme leaves.

Dry Skin

If you are nursing, you are more susceptible to dry skin, as your body fluids are being used for milk production. Make sure that you drink plenty of water! Washing with the fresh juices of carrot, lemon, apple, and tomato will refresh and tone your skin. Cucumber juice soothes and softens the skin: if you add I teaspoon of yogurt, it will protect and reduce inflammation from irritations.

A daily application of avocado supplies the nourishing oils

your dry skin craves. Avocado flesh contains substances that trigger the production of embryonic collagen, which makes baby's skin so soft and smooth. When in season, soft, ripe apricot flesh makes a fragrant skin cleanser.

Bleeding Gums

Your gums will often be inflamed after childbirth. Switch to a soft-bristle toothbrush, and swish in your mouth daily a cooled infusion of blackberry leaves, which have a toning, antiseptic, and regenerative action on the mucous membranes of the mouth and gums. Chewing fresh, young blackberry leaves also promotes gum healing.

Fresh sage leaves make excellent gum soothers. Take a young leaf and rub it over your teeth and gums daily. This will whiten your teeth and strengthen weakened gums. Red-rose vinegar makes an excellent cleansing and gum-strengthening gargle, while burdock-root decoction kills many of the destructive microorganisms responsible for mouth and gum infections. Olive-leaf infusion is also a wonderful remedy for infected and bleeding gums.

Spots, Pimples, and Blotches

Hormones, stress, poor diet, and physical exhaustion can play havoc with the appearance and texture of your skin. While a healthy raw fruit and vegetable diet, rich in absorbable skin-nutritious vitamins and minerals will rebalance some of the disruption, washing with equally nutrient-rich juices and herbal infusions will counteract free radical damage from the chemical disorganization in your changing body. Eat well, and your skin will reflect back your health and happiness. Eating red, yellow, green, and orange foods rich in carotenoid pigments are essential for healthy skin, so eat plenty of carrots, strawberries, oranges, tomatoes, sprouted seeds, peppers, spinach, and broccoli. Wild edibles such as young dandelion leaves, chickweeds, sunflower, nettles, chicory, fennel, and blood-enriching watercress are also skin-enhancing foods.

Fresh watercress-leaf juice, applied to the face, neck, and breasts, can be left on the skin overnight to cleanse and heal spots, pimples, freckles, and simple skin irritations. To encourage healthy connective tissue, make sure that you eat a good supply of silicon-rich artichokes, radishes, garlic, dandelions, seaweeds, and alfalfa sprouts.

An Aching Body

Massage is one of the best remedies for aching muscles and it invigorates skin health. Aromatherapy also provides a way for you to soothe your tired self.

Gingerroot Bath

A gingerroot bath increases circulation and decreases muscle soreness and stiffness (it will also do wonders if you are feeling feverish, chilled, or generally low).

> *1 1-inch piece gingerroot*
> *4 cups spring water*

Make a decoction with the gingerroot and water (see basic recipe, page 26). Simmer for 20 minutes. As the decoction turns yellow, pour it into a warm bath.

Immerse yourself for 10 to 15 minutes. After getting out, wrap up and stay warm.

MAKES 1 BATH

YOUR NEWBORN'S HEALTH

Newborns differ greatly in appearance: when your baby first comes home, she may not look picture-perfect. Her skin may be blotchy, pink, or red in color, or dry and flaky. If your baby's skin peels for the first few days, do not pick or pull at it: it will slough off naturally.

The soft hairs (lanugo) that cover the body fall out within the first few weeks. The eyes may be puffy and red: usually, this is due to the medication given to prevent infection after birth. Or they may be slightly cross-eyed due to the immaturity of the muscles that hold them in the frontal position. Your newborn can see, but her focus point is only about eight inches.

The umbilical stump needs to be kept clean and dry until it heals completely and falls off, as it is a potential entrance point for bacteria. Applying a little honey over the exposed stump will prevent infection. An infused comfrey-leaf poultice held over the umbilicus will soothe the cut skin, relieve pain, and promote rapid healing of the tissues.

Should an infection arise, a few drops of rosemary tincture over the stump will quickly dry up the secretions and kill any bacteria. To encourage rapid healing of the stump, place a few drops of echinacea-root tincture on the wound 3 or 4 times a day. If an infection has occurred around the wound, with redness and tenderness and/or pus, you can administer a few drops of echinacea tincture once a day, while breast-feeding your infant. The dose is usually 1 drop per pound of infant body weight. A nursing mother can also drink a warm infusion of echinacea and allow the potent botanicals to be excreted with her milk. If you are treating an infection, either through your breast milk, a tincture, or external application, make sure that you continue treatment for at least 1 week, or until the infection has completely cleared up. When diapering, make sure that the umbilicus is exposed.

The genitals of babies are usually swollen at birth. Baby girls often have a vaginal discharge, which is a normal reaction to the hormones that were in her mother's body. Sometimes there is a secretion of milk from the baby's breasts, which is influenced by the same hormones that promote and prepare the mother's breasts for nursing. This secretion ceases naturally in a few days.

The first bowel movement is usually greenish-black in color, which is the result of the substances that were in the intestines at birth. In the first few days, the color and consistency changes. All newborns go pink in the face, strain, and lift their legs up during those first bowel movements.

A newborn's extremities may be a darker color than the rest of her body due to the immaturity of her circulatory system, which is not able to carry enough warm blood to the hands and feet. If a newborn has a warm tummy and cool hands and feet, it indicates a good all-over body temperature.

Immunizations Schedule

2 months	DTP (three-in-one shot—diphtheria, tetanus, pertussis), Sabin oral live polio
4 months	DTP booster, polio booster
6 months	DTP booster
1 year	Tuberculin test
15 months	Measles-rubella vaccine, mumps vaccine
18 months	DTP booster
2 years	Polio booster, Hib (*Haemophilus influenzae*—type b) vaccine
4 to 6 years	DTP booster, polio booster

Most doctors follow the above immunization schedule, though some pediatricians are now beginning to question the wisdom of exposing a newborn to these powerful medications. If you have reservations, consult with your doctor or seek advice from other sources.

Herbal First-Aid Garden for Your Children

It is quite horrifying to realize just how many babies and small children are prescribed antibiotics for relatively minor conditions, such as fevers relating to stomachache, diarrhea, or constipation. My experience as a mother has taught me that these conditions can be treated effectively with herbal remedies made and administered in the comfort of your own home.

I don't mean to discount orthodox medical treatment: whenever treating your child with herbal remedies, consult your pediatrician. Of course, there are serious conditions beyond the reach of your first-aid garden.

Still, babies and children respond remarkably well to very small doses of herbal remedies. Even better, not all baby herbal remedies need to be given orally. Many can be applied as a warm compress, a massage, a foot soak, a chest rub, or even a healing bath.

The same principles you employed in creating your own pregnancy first-aid garden apply when planting and using a newborn first-aid garden. Read through the instructions for planting and using a pregnancy first-aid garden (pages 135–39). Begin this first-aid garden project with chamomile, lavender, elder flower, peppermint, bee balm, catnip, dandelion, aloe, calendula, eucalyptus, dill, and rosemary plants.

NOTE: WHEN USING HERBAL REMEDIES FOR BABIES AND CHILDREN, IT IS IMPORTANT TO GIVE THE CORRECT DOSE. WHILE THE ADULT DOSE

OF AN HERBAL INFUSION IS 1 CUP, A YOUNG CHILD (EIGHT TO TEN YEARS OLD) NEEDS ONLY ¼ CUP, A TODDLER (TWO TO FIVE YEARS OLD) NEEDS ONLY 1 TO 2 TABLESPOONS, AND A BABY, 1 TEASPOON, OR A FEW SIPS.

Common Ailments and Herbal Remedies

THRUSH

Most breast-fed babies will suffer from oral and diaper thrush, due to hormonal changes within the mother.

The oral form of the disease is characterized by tiny white spots on the tongue, inner cheeks, and throat, which make suckling difficult, and can be quite distressing for a newborn. Pediatricians will prescribe a sticky yellow paste, which is given to the baby orally, and painted on your breasts before nursing.

I was able to treat this condition in two of my children by painting live, homemade yogurt inside their mouths with my fingertip. For my third child, I discovered another remedy—using plantain leaves. Since these grow prolifically in my garden, I was able to put them to another good use in my children's growing pharmacy. I soaked the plantain seeds in warm water overnight and I collected and bottled the gel-like residue from the seed soak. Then I dabbed small amounts of it onto a Q-tip and applied the gel over the thrush patches.

Oral thrush is highly contagious: you must maintain the highest hygienic standards. After nursing, wash your nipples in a diluted solution of 1 part cider vinegar to 8 parts water; then air-dry. Any leftover vinegar can be stored in the refrigerator.

Yeast-infection (thrush) diaper rash, found on the genital skin folds, is another distressing condition for a newborn to suffer. As a mother, all you want to do is make the pain and discomfort go away. Start by discontinuing the use of any powder with cornstarch in it: this ingredient is known to encourage yeast growth. Cease using any antibiotics or foods that encourage loose bowels, as any upset to the intestines can cause further yeast development.

I found that applying raw egg white or slippery-elm gruel (a thick gray tea) to cleansed tender skin resulted in a remarkable improvement within a few days.

DIAPER RASH

Common diaper rash, unrelated to thrush, is very common in all newborns, especially breast-fed babies. The easiest way to cure it is to stop using diapers. Most soiling is predictable, especially when you've established a schedule for nursing.

Instead of using diapers, lay your baby on a pure sheep fleece to wick moisture and stool deposits away from the baby's delicate skin. The actual cost of the fleece is a fraction of the expense of laundering cloth diapers or buying multiple packs of disposables. The fleece is washing-machine and dryer safe, and very soft to sleep on.

If you choose to use diapers, change your baby immediately after a stool or passing of urine. Wash the skin with pure water; then dry it well. Dab some powdered arrowroot or kaolin clay over the baby's bottom, and leave uncovered for at least 30 minutes. Plantain-infused oil, cold-pressed wheat-germ, and olive oil make excellent skin-moisture barriers if rubbed on before diapering.

At nighttime or before naps, use a sweet and calming scented powder that is absorbing and healing. See Zak's Baby Powder recipe, which follows.

When I had my first son, and was seduced by the mass-marketing of baby products, I gave in and used a commercial powder to diaper him. But after he developed an allergic reaction,

I had to find an alternative. I had been using an herbal body powder for myself throughout my pregnancy, and began working
with that recipe. I created a less fragrant mixture for his delicate
skin, which I still make and use for all my active toddlers.
Kitchen arrowroot, powdered comfrey leaves and root, slippery-
elm bark, dried aloe leaves, and cornstarch are the basic ingredients, with light scents from chamomile and calendula pure
essential oils. Just 1 drop of each oil was enough to scent a mixture of herbal powders that would last for over a week of newborn diapering (twelve to fifteen diapers a day), without any
rashes or contact sores. Between diapers, my children were left
bare to air-dry.

Zak's Baby Powder

¼ cup arrowroot

4 tablespoons powdered slippery-elm bark

2 tablespoons dried aloe leaf

¼ cup pure cornstarch

¼ cup powdered comfrey leaf and root

1 drop chamomile essential oil

1 drop calendula essential oil

In a bowl, combine the dry ingredients. Add the
chamomile and calendula essential oils and mix again.
Ladle the powder into a dry shaker jar and store in a dry
place. Discard any unused powder after 8 weeks.

MAKES ENOUGH FOR 1 WEEK OR MORE OF DIAPER
CHANGES

BACTERIAL AND VIRAL INFECTIONS

There's no worse feeling in the world than standing by helplessly while your newborn suffers from a bacterial or viral infection. Colds, flu, and fever are difficult for your child's fragile, still-developing immune system to battle alone.

Echinacea-Root Infusion

Echinacea is another gentle remedy from nature's pharmacy, and one of the best fever-reducing agents: it has not been shown to cause any side effects or allergic reactions. Unlike antibiotics, herbal treatments like echinacea infusion or tincture do not actually kill bacteria: thus, there is no disruption of your baby's healthy intestinal flora, and no potential for further thrush or diaper yeast rashes.

> *1 echinacea root, chopped*
> *1 cup freshly boiled distilled water*

> Place the echinacea root in the water and let steep for 8 hours, or overnight. Strain through a fine-mesh sieve and pour into a container. The infusion can be given slightly warm or cold. My daughter refused to drink anything cold, even in sips, so I warmed it gently and she took it readily.

> The correct dose for an infant is 1 to 2 teaspoons in water for every 10 pounds of body weight.

MAKES 1 DAY'S TREATMENT

Echinacea is a valuable curative for all types of body infections. A breast-fed baby can receive the dosage required to protect it from contagious infections if the mother takes the treatment herself. A dose of 10 to 12 drops of echinacea tincture in water or juice consumed by the nursing mother 3 times a day will pass into her milk and protect the baby. A bottle-fed baby can receive a small dose of the tincture (1 to 2 drops added to 2 ounces of standard formula) as part of a regular feeding.

Goldenseal is another natural herbal antibiotic. However, although it does an admirable job of combating your child's viral or bacterial infection, it weakens the rest of the body, leaving your child vulnerable to further infections. Goldenseal is therefore not appropriate for newborns or very young children.

• *Colds.* Unless they become chilled, babies under the age of three months rarely catch cold, mainly due to the protective antibodies baby and mother pass on to each other during the last weeks of pregnancy. If your child has a cold, she will exhibit symptoms such as irritability, restlessness, sleeplessness, and a clear runny discharge from the nostrils.

If this stuffy nose causes your infant restlessness at night, administer a few drops (no more than 3) of salty water into each nostril. Wait a few seconds, then use a nasal suction bulb. If your baby develops a fever unrelated to a cold, consult with your doctor, as it could be related to an infection, or an even more serious condition.

• *Flu.* If your baby suffers from a sudden, acute fever, stomach pain with vomiting, diarrhea, and a constant runny nose and a cough, it is likely to be a form of influenza. Usually a child will be sick only for a few days. If any of the symptoms become severe, or if she is slow to recover, call your doctor.

Fever Fighters

Elder Flower Tincture

This is wonderful herbal remedy for fevers caused by the arrival of those first infant teeth, a seasonal cold, or a contact virus such as the chicken pox—which my three toddlers all had within days of each other, while on our first family vacation!

20 heads of fresh elder flowers

Pack a canning jar with fresh elder flowers. Then make a tincture, using the delicate creamy yellow elder flower head (see basic recipe, page 29). Use 1 drop for every pound of infant body weight.

Administer this remedy to bottle-fed babies by placing the tincture underneath the tongue. Give to the breast-fed baby by holding the dropper close to your nipple and squeezing out the required dosage as the baby begins to suck.

The proper dose can be given as often as required, as this herbal remedy is completely safe. After the first dose, the fever will go down in under 1 hour. Measure the dosage in a teaspoon, then transfer into an empty dropper.

MAKES ½ OUNCE

Lemon-Juice Infusion

Lemon juice is rich in infection-fighting vitamin C and will keep your newborn hydrated, even as his body temperature rises.

1 lemon
½ teaspoon molasses

Squeeze the juice from the lemon and pour through a fine-mesh strainer, filtering out the lemon pulp and seeds. Add the molasses, then I cup of hot water. Leave to cool for 10 minutes. Test, then offer it to the infant in a bottle.

MAKES I TREATMENT

Vinegar Foot Compress

This might just sound a bit weird, but it has worked wonders for my children, especially at times when we have been away from home, or staying with Grandma. This simple remedy will keep the baby's body temperature below convulsion level, until you can administer another effective herbal fever reducer or see your physician.

1 cup cider vinegar

At the first signs of a fever, pour the cider vinegar into a bowl; then soak a cotton compress, cotton diaper, or even a small towel in the vinegar for 30 seconds. Wrap around your infant's bare feet. This reduces a fever in 20 minutes.

MAKES I APPLICATION

Peppermint Infusion

This remedy is a wee bit strong for very young babies (under four months), but breast-feeding moms can pass on the botanical benefits through their own milk by drinking I cup of warm peppermint infusion 10 minutes before nursing. Older babies can be offered the cooled infusion in a bottle. I have often used a combined infusion of peppermint and spearmint, and washed it over the heated body of a very young baby. I once used this remedy to bring a temperature of over 102 degrees Fahrenheit to below 98 degrees in under 1 hour.

> *2 tablespoons peppermint leaves*
> *1 ½ cups water*

Make infusion and drink warm.

MAKES 1 TREATMENT

When to Go to the Doctor or Hospital

Here are some ailments that require professional care—you should not try herbal remedies if these symptoms develop.

SUDDEN FEVERS

When a baby has a sudden fever over 103 degrees Fahrenheit, he should be taken to the emergency room. The treatment and dosage will be determined by a physician once the cause of the condition has been determined. If the fever is prolonged, dehydration can result, which will require immediate replacement of fluids. A baby under twelve months with a fever and vomiting or very runny diarrhea will need stool and urine cultures taken on examination.

A baby in this condition will remain at the emergency facility until the fever goes down.

BRONCHITIS

If your baby has a fever, tightness and stiffness of the chest, and a wheezing, continual cough, the problem could be an inflammation of the bronchial tubes, known as bronchitis. It can follow a persistent cough or cold, or can be a complication associated with another infectious disease, such as measles, chicken pox, or whooping cough. If untreated, bronchitis could turn into pneumonia. If your infant is showing any signs of distress, consult with your doctor immediately.

PNEUMONIA

This debilitating condition results from an infection of the lungs. Symptoms include a spasmodic cough, fever, and chest pains, with a red color around the cheeks and a pale forehead and mouth. If the infection affects the lungs, it is referred to as "lobar pneumonia"; if it affects the bronchial tubes, it is referred to as "bronchopneumonia." Pneumonia is frequently a complication of other illnesses. A diagnosis can be made only by a doctor.

Since pneumonia can become serious very quickly, consult with your doctor if you suspect these symptoms.

MEASLES (RUBELLA)

High fever is a symptom of measles, but if your child's temperature rises above 103 degrees Fahrenheit, *call your doctor immediately.* Other complications of measles are encephalitis, pneumonia, and middle-ear infection. If your infant is suffering with measles, medical attention will ensure that other complications, such as meningitis and urinary tract infections, do not occur. Should your child exhibit any of these symptoms while suffering with the disease, his doctor's attention and treatment is required.

CHICKEN POX

Be aware that for infants who have an immune deficiency, suffer from leukemia (or other malignant diseases), or are being treated with antimetabolics or steroids, contracting this disease can be fatal. Complications from chicken pox rarely occur, but they include encephalitis, pneumonia, hepatitis, and nephritis.

If, while suffering with chicken pox, your infant displays any of these complications, call your doctor immediately.

MUMPS

Generally speaking, healthy children do not develop complications from this disease. On those rare occasions when complications do arise, they usually come in the form of pancreatitis, mastitis, deafness, arthritis, and meningoencephalitis (a close relative of bacterial meningitis).

Call your doctor if any of these complications arise.

WORMS

Tapeworms, hookworms, and roundworms are rare in this country. If you have recently traveled abroad and your baby returns with acute diarrhea, or has been in the presence of another person who has been to a country where parasites are common, she should be seen by a doctor. Diagnosis is made by laboratory examination of the stools (to look for eggs or adult parasites).

Roundworms are spread through contaminated food. Tapeworms are acquired by eating raw or undercooked meat or fish. Hookworms are spread through eating meat, fish, or dairy; they attach themselves to the lining of the intestines and suck blood. Treatment to eliminate these parasites usually requires drugs.

If you suspect worms, see your doctor for an immediate examination and treatment. Prolonged, this condition can debilitate the infant's system.

HEARING LOSS

Infants are screened for hearing loss or impairment at birth, especially if the mother had complications during pregnancy. If your baby seems to have difficulty recognizing your voice or turning toward you when you are talking, *consult your doctor.*

If your infant was born with good hearing that has since deteriorated, it could indicate meningitis, mumps, encephalitis, or a recurrent middle-ear infection.

EYE DAMAGE OR INFECTION

Pinkeye (conjunctivitis) is a common condition caused by an infection of the conjunctiva—the lining of the eyeball and lid. If accompanied by pus, this is highly contagious.

One of the best cures for this condition is breast milk because it contains infection-fighting antibodies (do not use this remedy if you are suffering from mastitis). Another good remedy is a chickweed or marigold infusion applied to the infected eye in drop doses. For older children an eye bath or wash can be given.

If there is no improvement in the infection within three days, consult with your pediatrician.

Babies who have experienced any trauma of the eye—a bump, puncture, or scratch—need to be taken to the doctor.

POISONING

Keep your local poison-control center telephone number accessible.

Infants are particularly vulnerable to poisoning incidents because they try to put everything into their mouths. Gardening and household-cleaning products, medications and drugs, plants, berries, etc., are all food to your curious child.

The indications that poisoning has occurred are vomiting, a red face, unusual sleepiness, rapid and deep breathing, diarrhea, mouth burns, stomach pains, and unconsciousness.

Contact your doctor or emergency facility as soon as possible. If your infant has vomited, save some and take it with you. If you know what was swallowed or eaten, tell the poison center or doctor. You will be given instructions as to what to do.

CUTS AND WOUNDS

Red, warm, swelling skin around a cut (often associated with drainage) indicates a staph infection. Most minor infected wounds will heal within a few days (especially if a strong infusion of rosemary or calendula is dabbed over the wound and left to air-dry; see basic recipe, page 27).

If the condition persists, consult with your doctor.

ANIMAL BITES

If your child is bitten by a wild animal, such as a fox, bat, skunk, raccoon, stray cat, or dog, *report to your doctor immediately.* Your child's tetanus vaccinations records will be checked (so have your card on hand) and updated. Relay as much information about the incident and animal as possible to minimize the possibility of a rabies vaccination. For an immediate treatment to a small wound, wash out any dirt and completely cover with freshly opened aloe leaves, allowing the gel to soak into the wound, which will form a false skin over it.

SEVERE BURNS

Skin burns caused by chemicals, electricity, scalding water, and fire usually require hospitalization.

Diagnosis from an expert is required to determine the severity of the burn.

Second-degree burns are shiny, red, blistered, and very painful. Third-degree burns are dark, leathery, and painless. Severe burns require immediate fluid replacement and a possible infusion of nutrient sources to increase tissue growth and heal the wound. Crawling infants are particularly at risk from burns, so child-proof your home, install smoke detectors, and make sure that your baby sleeps in flame-retardant clothing and bedding.

SEVERE ALLERGIC REACTIONS

Symptoms such as flushing of the skin, coughing, blurred vision, wheezing, vomiting, loss of consciousness, and shock are indications of a severe allergic reaction. If your child displays any of these symptoms after exposure to a known (or unknown) allergen, *call an ambulance or get your infant to an emergency facility.* Do not delay. A throat swelling can lead to suffocation. Immediate administration of epinephrine will reduce congestion and open the airways.

An Herbal Medicine Chest

Here are the herbs you can use to create first-aid treatments for less serious injuries and ailments.

BRUISES AND SPRAINS
    Dried violet leaves
    Dried comfrey leaves
    Fenugreek seeds
    Marjoram leaves

Make a poultice and apply it to the affected area (see recipe below).

Poultice

The application of a whole or partial herb plant made with fresh or hydrated leaves, seeds, or flowers.

> *1 tablespoon dried violet leaves*
> *1 tablespoon dried comfrey leaves*
> *1 tablespoon fenugreek seeds*
> *1 tablespoon dried marjoram leaves*

Combine the herbs in a pan with enough (2 cups) freshly boiled distilled water to cover. Allow to hydrate and release the healing botanicals.

Strain the herbs and mash with a fork. Cover the affected area of the skin with the warm herbal mash. Then cover with a sterile bandage. Leave the poultice on until the herbs dry naturally, about I hour. Reapply as necessary.

MAKES I TREATMERNT

SKIN CONTACT RASHES
Elder
Strawberry leaf
Hollyhock
Southernwood

Make into a combined infusion (see page 27) and bathe the affected area. Apply the tincture warm, keeping the skin wet by repeating the bathing until it cools.

TO KEEP INSECTS AWAY
½ teaspoon pennyroyal
½ teaspoon spearmint
½ teaspoon sweet basil
½ teaspoon feverfew
½ teaspoon lavender
½ teaspoon caraway

Crush and place the fresh leaves or flowers in a bowl (out of reach) in the baby's room.

WASP STINGS
>   1 teaspoon cider vinegar

Apply neat, without diluting, to the affected area of skin after the stinger has been removed.

BEE STINGS
>   ½ teaspoon loose tobacco
>   Banana skin

Tobacco: Make a moist poultice of the tobacco by either chewing it with healing saliva or mixing it with warm water and mashing it with a pestle or fork. Place the poultice directly over the affected area of skin after the stinger has been removed.

Banana skin: Remove the stinger and cover the affected area of skin with the freshly peeled banana skin.

BURNS
>   Plantain leaves (not to be confused with tropical banana's
>   leaves)
>   Fresh aloe gel

Make a live poultice (see recipe on page 262) and apply it to the burn. The plantain remedy is ideal for incidents that occur away from home, as plantain leaves carpet most public parks and campsites.

HAYFEVER
>   Raw honeycomb
>   Violet flowers
>   Mullein leaves

Eat the honeycomb or make a tea out of violet flowers or mullein leaves (see page 27).

SKIN IRRITATIONS AND RASHES
Elder flower
Stinging nettle
Strawberry leaves
Oats

Make an infusion (see basic recipe, page 27). Wash over the affected areas daily.

DIARRHEA
Gingerroot
Red-raspberry leaves
Peppermint leaves
Mullein leaves

Make infusion (see basic recipe, page 27) of one of the above herbs and give to your child to stop diarrhea.

OPEN WOUNDS
Rosemary
Periwinkle
Aloe gel

Use a rosemary and periwinkle infusion (see basic recipe, page 27) to clean the cut; then apply aloe gel to bind tissues together and form a protective scab.

EARACHE
Olbas oil
Olive oil

Mix I to 2 drops of the Olbas oil with I teaspoon of warmed

olive oil. Massage in the oil at the back of the affected ear (behind the lobe), and cover with a warmed towel.

Mom and Baby Bathing

Part of the joy of having an herbal pregnancy is being able to extend that connection with nature once your baby is born. Scents you used to establish a bond between you and your baby

Herbal Remedies Chest for Newborn Care

WITCH-HAZEL EXTRACT   A powerful astringent that heals, closes, and dries the umbilical stump.

COMFREY-LEAF POULTICE   Soothes cut and torn tissues, promoting rapid healing. Ideal for healing circumcised babies.

WARM SUNLIGHT   Excellent natural healer and infection-prevention treatment.

ROSEMARY TINCTURE   Dries the umbilical stump and destroys infections.

ECHINACEA-ROOT TINCTURE   Another umbilical healer, fever reducer, and rapid tissue healer.

BREAST MILK   Heals pinkeye (do not use if mother has mastitis), binds cracked tissues.

CATNIP INFUSION   Controls infant jaundice; breast-feeding moms can pass it through their milk; formula-fed babies can be offered it as a drink. Also soothes colic spasms.

COMFREY TEA   Colonizes beneficial bacteria in the intestines of infants, thus controlling yeast growth.

DANDELION-ROOT INFUSION   Stimulates and supports powerful liver function in newborns.

FRESH GOAT'S MILK   Helps prevent colic as a result of bottle feeding. Goat's milk has the same amount of casein as human milk, the same fat globules, and a high lactose content. If fresh goat's milk is unavailable, most health food stores carry freeze-dried goat's milk. Add acidophilus in liquid or capsule form, or plain live (homemade) yogurt.

PLANTAIN INFUSION OIL   Makes an excellent barrier oil for after baths and diapering.

POWDERED SLIPPERY-ELM BARK AND HONEY PASTE   A wonderful healing paste for very sore, bleeding patches of skin on a baby's bottom and genitals caused by untreated diaper rash and too little exposure to fresh air and sunshine.

BURDOCK ROOT TINCTURE   Balances the overproduction of sebaceous oil in the baby's scalp, preventing the reccurrence of cradle cap.

WITCH-HAZEL OR BLACK-TEA INFUSION   Slows down the overproduction of sebaceous oil secretions on the baby's scalp, preventing further incrustations of cradle cap from forming.

during pregnancy can now have a place in your active, "social mother and baby" lifestyle. The same soothing and calming herbs you used for bathing and massage can (when made less potent) be used in your baby's bath, or made into an herbal bathing mitt. Bathing with your newborn instills a sense of security and trust. I used the following recipe with all my babies. After washing and playing, I would nurse, then send my baby off to a peaceful sleep by singing a soft lullaby.

While I was still nursing, I often took an afternoon bath with my very young babies. When my children got older, I tied a bag of infused herbs under the faucet and let the active botanicals disperse into the water as the children played and calmed down from their active day. Even though my free time to be alone with my second and third babies was limited, I made sure that these special times with mom and baby continued twice or three times a week for eight weeks after birth. Now, when I snatch an hour for a long soak by myself, I can hear the patter of tiny feet, whispering, and laughter as my children peek into my sanctuary in the hope of hopping in with me.

NOTE: WHEN PREPARING BATHING OR SKIN-WASHING TREATMENTS FOR YOUR BABY USE ONLY THE FRESHEST INGREDIENTS, WHICH YOU HAVE EITHER GROWN IN YOUR OWN PREGNANCY FIRST-AID GARDEN (PAGE 135) OR KITCHEN HERBAL TEA GARDEN (PAGE 145).

Herbal Newborn Bath

A sweet-smelling, alluring bath for mom and baby to enjoy.

> ½ cup fresh chamomile flowers
> ½ cup lavender flowers
> 1 tablespoon ginseng root
> 2 tablespoons spearmint leaves
> 1 quart water

Make an infusion (see basic recipe, page 27) of the chamomile and lavender flowers, ginseng root, and spearmint leaves (save the infused herbal pulp in a bag of muslin cloth to use as a washing mitt). Let steep for 15 minutes; strain, then add to running hot water.

Leave the bathroom door closed for about 10 minutes, allowing the infusing steam to fill and warm the room. Test the temperature, and step in with baby.

MAKES ENOUGH FOR 1 BATH

Mother and Child "Reunion" Bath

This essential oil mixture blend is safe for baby's sensitive skin.

¼ cup sweet almond oil
2 drops chamomile essential oil
2 drops lavender essential oil
1 drop Mandarin essential oil
1 drop neroli essential oil
2 drops rose essential oil

Run a warm bath; then add the almond oil. Just before stepping in with your baby, add the essential oils (the remaining ingredients). Immerse yourselves and relax. Be careful getting in and out of the bath, as the oil and warm water will make the bathtub slippery.

MAKES ENOUGH FOR 1 BATH

Variation: Add some wheat-germ oil to the infused bathwater. While you're both immersed, and your bodies are lubricated with the oils, begin tactile contact massage. Use your hands and light finger pressure to glide over your baby's body and your own.

BABY BIRTH GARDENS 🌿

There are many wonderful ways to bring the benefits of herbs into your baby's room: one of my favorites is through a newborn birth garden.

A birth garden is simply a way of using nature to celebrate the life of your child. My aunt planted an apple tree to commemorate the births of each of her five children. As they all grew, they were able to reap the full benefits of the spring blossoms and summer fruits. They inscribed their names on the trunk of "their" tree.

Planting a Living Birth Garden

You can be as creative in the design of your birth garden as you wish, once you know the sex of your baby and have decided on a name. You can plant a garden of herbs and edible flowers using the letters of your child's name. A garden for "Beth" could include the herbs bay (B), echinacea (e), thyme (t), and hyssop (h). Or try planting flowers or herbs in the shape of a baby's initials. If you don't have a garden or access to a plot of land, plant a window box or a small pot in the nursery with herbs related to your baby's name.

In the ancient language of flowers, all children's names are connected with a specific flower or herb. For example:

Aaron	Fennel and sage
Abigail	Sorrel
Amanda	Sorrel and sage
Belinda	Rose
Bill	Sweet William
Cara	Iris
Charles	Fennel
Dawn	Daisy

Dennis	Wild geranium
Edward	Ivy
Elisa	Violet
Faith	Violet
Fred	Fennel
Gail	Orchid
Gary	Iris
Hope	Iris
Howard	Dame's violet
Isaac	Larkspur
Isabel	Wild geranium
Jack	Daisy
Laura	Garland of roses
Lee	Yellow violet
Marcia	Iris
Michael	Wild geranium
Nathan	Daisy
Pamela	Flax
Peter	Fennel
Rebecca	Star of Bethlehem
Roger	Apple blossom
Sara	Orchid
Sean	Daisy
Tammy	Honeysuckle
Timothy	Agrimony
Victoria	Iris
Vincent	Iris
Wendy	Sage and ivy
Winston	Ivy
Zachary	Wild geranium
Zelda	Iris

For a more complete listing of names, look to *Flora's Dictionary: The Victorian Language of Herbs and Flowers,* by Kathleen Gips.

For your daughter Amanda, you could plant the herbs sorrel and sage in the shape of an A in your garden. Or one plant could comprise the entire initial, and the other the background.

Here are a few other ways to approach your planting:

INITIAL GARDEN
Child's name: Barbara Ann Wright.

Use three different herbs or flowers, one for each name, plus one as a background. For example:

B = basil, A = anise, W = wintergreen. The background is sage.

NAME GARDEN
Child's name: Ellen Thomas.

Use five different herbs or flowers plus one as a background.

E = elder flower, L = lemon balm, L = lavender, E = echinacea, N = nasturtium. For the border, use thyme.

INITIAL GARDEN
Child's name: Joey Simon.

Use two different herbs or flowers relating to the name, and a third as a background.

J = Juniper (which will one day grow into a grand tree), S = sage. For the background, thyme.

NAME GARDEN
Child's name: Joy.

Use three different herbs, with each letter relating to a specific herb or edible flower, plus one for the border.

J = jasmine, O = orange-mint, Y = ylang-ylang. For the border, parsley.

Using Color Energies to Plan Your Baby Birth Garden

The pleasure of color is awakened by your sense of sight. Painters and writers have influenced garden design throughout history. People's color preferences vary greatly, and are influenced by their psychological, emotional, and physical responses. Beauty is in the eye of the beholder, and tastes in garden design are as individual as in home design. A garden of color choices can also become a healing garden—an outdoor room for maternal pleasure and mood enhancement.

Each day of the week relates to a specific color energy, so maybe you want to plant a garden according to the day of the week your child was born.

Monday	Violet (betony, chives, clary sage, echinacea)
Tuesday	Red (crimson clover, field poppy, red bee balm, red valarian)
Wednesday	Orange (marigolds, nasturtiums)
Thursday	Blue (borage, chicory, eyebright, hyssop, lavender)
Friday	Green (chervil, lemon balm, parsley, sage, thyme, woodworm)
Saturday	Indigo (columbine, flax, larkspur, rosemary)
Sunday	Yellow (agrimony, arnica, blessed thistle, cowslip, dandelion)

Birth Date Herbs

Certain herbs also relate to the birth of your baby. There are a variety of herbs for each month, and you can make a nursery window box or special place in your garden of herbs that come into season or bloom on each child's birthday.

Herbs for spring (March, April, May) of the pregnancy year:

March	Nasturtium, wild rose, woodbine
April	Coltsfoot, lily of the valley, myrtle blossom, violets
May	Dill, ferns, iris, parsley, snapdragons

Trees for spring (March, April, May) of the pregnancy year:

March	Chestnut
April	Apple, cherry
May	Elder, filbert

Herbs for summer (June, July, August) of the pregnancy year:

June	Poppy, privet, watercress, water lily
July	Cowslip, marigold, peony, sunflower
August	Cornflower, rosemary, valerian

Trees for summer (June, July, August) of the pregnancy year:

June	Willow
July	Oak, pine
August	Elder, witch hazel

Herbs for autumn (September, October, November) of the pregnancy year:

September	Love in the mist, white rose
October	Chrysanthemums, purple heather, sweet basil
November	Carnation, sage, wallflower

Trees for autumn (September, October, November) of the pregnancy year:

September	Almond, plum, walnut
October	Holly
November	Chestnut, mulberry

Herbs of winter (December, January, February) of the pregnancy year:

December	Snowdrop, Solomon's seal
January	Foxglove, gentian, mullein
February	Carnation, opium poppy, violets

Trees of winter (December, January, February) of the pregnancy year:

December	Cypress, spruce, yew
January	Pine
February	Elm, linden

Now, should you decide to plant a tree or herb garden on the birth of your child, you can even choose one that relates to (and has power from) its zodiac month.

Baby Crib Wreath of Herbs

You can commemorate the birth of your baby by making a wreath of herbs for her crib that corresponds to her name, and keep it in the nursery. For example:

Baby's name: Diana

D, in the language of flowers, means geranium.
Or D = dianthus, daisy, dandelion, or dill.
Or DIANA = daisy, ivy, anise, nasturtium, agrimony.

"SCENT-SATIONAL" IDEAS FOR THE NURSERY

Imbuing your child's bedroom with fragrances derived from nature is not a new concept: for centuries, mothers have sought to fill their homes with pleasant, soothing, relaxing aromas. Rooms that smell good and look good excite the senses on all levels.

Your local pharmacy is full of overpoweringly fragrant, chemically manipulated preparations that lose their scents within days. Instead of using store-bought air fresheners, I presented my newborns with herb-inspired pomanders, spice belts, potpourri blends, decorative pines, citrus wall hangers, and sleep buddies. You, too, can have tremendous fun scenting your baby's nursery: use the resources available to you from your home, garden, and mail-order suppliers (see Resources at the back of this book).

An Herbal Sleep and Play Buddy

When my children were newborns, I made each of them a personalized, herb-filled sleep and play pillow in the shape of an egghead.

One side of the "head" was a happy face, the other side a geometric pattern of stripes, blocks, and zigzags to fascinate and stimulate the baby's curiosity. For the hair, I used strips of colored satin.

You can fill the buddy with a combination of sleep-inducing and relaxing herbs, picked fresh from your garden. Add a few handfuls of fiber filling, so that it will be soft to grasp and cuddle, then seal the pillow with self-adhesive Velcro dots. Your child's new "buddy" will be washable. Simply remove the herbs; then when the buddy is clean, replace with fresh ones and reseal for another period of joyous play and peaceful sleep.

THE FRESH HERBS

Catnip leaves
Chamomile flowers
Dill flowers
Fennel seeds
Grated lemon zest
Grated orange zest
Lavender flowers
Rosemary leaves
Scented-geranium leaves
Scented rose petals
Spearmint leaves

OTHER SUPPLIES

Old pajama or pillowcase
Fabric paints (or a laundry marker and some buttons)

For the egghead, you can use recycled material from either an older sibling's pajamas, an old clean pillowcase, sheet, or shirt, or even a sock. If you don't have fabric paints, use a nontoxic black laundry marker on white material, and sew on red buttons for eyes to make up the three colors that infants can see and that stimulate their cognitive development. All told, this toy takes only about 20 minutes to sew, fill, and decorate. It will become a treasured toy throughout early childhood.

You can choose other herbs and flowers for your child's buddy, depending on what you have growing in your garden or can obtain through mail order (see Resources at the back of this book).

An Herb- and Spice-Scented Crib Belt

Spices can be as soothing as herbs. They add color, form, texture, and aroma, especially during the winter months when fresh herbs are out of season. Making a crib belt is simply a matter of gathering hulls, pods, seeds, roots, barks, and berries and stringing them together with some fine string (dental floss works well, too). Tiny seeds, berries, and flowers can be put into small self-sealing tea bags and then strung with the other herbs and spices.

Be as imaginative and decorative as you like. This gift is as much for your pleasure as it is for your baby's.

THE HERBS
   Cinnamon bark
   Coriander seeds
   Cracked cumin seeds
   Dill seeds
   Fennel seeds
   Honeysuckle blossoms
   Jasmine flowers
   Juniper berries
   Parsley seeds
   Scented rose buds

THE SPICES AND FRUIT
> Allspice
> Cardamom
> Cinnamon sticks
> Citrus peel
> Dried slices of fruit
> Elderberries
> Gingerroot
> Safflowers
> Star anise
> Vanilla bean
> Whole chili peppers
> Whole cloves
> Whole nutmeg

OTHER SUPPLIES
> 10 self-sealing tea bags or commercially prepared herbal
>   tea bags with soothing fragrances
> Strong fine string or unscented dental floss
> Hammer and nails (or darning needle), to pierce the spices

Fill the tea bags with herbs; then string the bags and spices with the string or floss. Some spices have very hard shells. The best way to get a needle through is to soak them overnight in water. If you want to be creative, when stringing the crib belt together, you can make a lovely pattern from the different textures, colors, and shapes of the spices.

NOTE: WHEN THE BELT HAS BEEN THREADED WITH THE SPICES AND HERB BAGS, MAKE SURE THAT IT IS HUNG WELL OUT OF REACH OF CURIOUS FINGERS AND MOUTHS. ALTHOUGH THESE HERBS AND

SPICES ARE NOT POISONOUS, THEY POSE A CHOKING HAZARD FOR
YOUR NEWBORN AND ANY TODDLERS IN YOUR HOME.

Herbal Nursery Pomanders

These simple nursery adornments, hung above the crib or near a
window, will give your nursery the ambience of "Old England."
Once you have collected together the basic ingredients, they take
only a few minutes to make and decorate. These pomanders will
then last for many months, releasing their aromatic potencies for
all to appreciate and benefit from.

POMANDER BALL

Memories of winter bring with them the festive aroma of cloves,
anise, citrus, and allspice. Pomander balls decorate our bedrooms
and hallways and make ideal gifts, too.

THE HERBS AND SPICES	OTHER SUPPLIES
10 whole allspice	1 large darning needle
10 balm of Gilead buds	1 small juicy orange or 1 4-inch Styrofoam ball
100 whole cloves	Thick natural fiber string or cord
5 whole rose hips	Thimble
5 star anise	

Using the darning needle, make tiny holes all over the orange
peel.

Take the fiber cord and tie a knot in one end. With the darning needle thread the cord through the orange. When it comes
out the other side, tie another knot to hold the cord in place and
leave a length from which to hang your pomander ball.

Press the herbs and spices into the orange peel, using their stems. When the whole orange has been covered, take some thin ribbon and make an attractive bow (use green, yellow, or orange—natural, earthy colors). Tie it around the cord before hanging the pomander ball.

EUCALYPTUS AND CITRUS PEEL CONES

These fragrant pinecones are another way to bring herbal decorations into your baby's nursery. The basic ingredients can be found in your home and garden: change the herbs, spices, and decorative ribbons with the seasons.

THE HERBS	OTHER SUPPLIES
Chamomile flowers	1 or 2 large pinecones
Eucalyptus pure essential oil	1 spool of thread (green or other earth color)
Eucalyptus leaves	
Ribbons of fresh orange peel (1/8-inch thick)	

Remove any loose scales from the base of the pinecone and discard.

Break off the chamomile flowers from the stem, leaving a nib next to the flower head.

Dab a drop of eucalyptus pure essential oil on about 10 of the pinecone scales: start with the big petals at the bottom, moving to the smaller ones at the top.

Twine the orange peel strips around the pine petals. Push in the eucalyptus leaves and chamomile flowers between the pinecone scales.

Once the whole cone is covered with the herbal decorations, wrap the thread around the cone, binding the herbs in place. Make a knot at the tip of the cone with enough thread left over to use as the hanger. If you want, you can bind a few small ribbon bows around the outer petals.

NOTE: INSTEAD OF EUCALYPTUS LEAVES, YOU CAN USE LAVENDER FLOWERS AND LEAVES AND SUBSTITUTE LEMON PEEL FOR THE ORANGE. OR USE OTHER AROMATIC HERB AND CITRUS PEELS. BE CREATIVE!

Using Herbal, Wild Fruit, and Vegetable Dyes

Some herbs are particularly valuable to the fashion industry because they yield rare colors. Madder *(Rubis tinctoria)* can produce some glorious golden hues of orange, terra-cotta, and yellow. Sorrel *(Rumex acetosa)* can produce fawn, bright yellow, and sage green. Woad *(Isatis tinctoria)* produces a variety of blues and grays. All these plants grow in the wild. Leaves give their best results when they are freshly picked. Some vegetables, such as onions and roots, give a rich range of colors when dried. Fruit, including berries, yield the best bright colors when they are picked ripe and juicy.

Some of the most enchanting yellows, greens, and browns to be found today come from the hardy herbs that grow on roadsides and along wild country lanes. Native Americans have been using these natural dyes for centuries. The warm, muted natural colors found in their wool, linen, and cotton fabrics are now commonly used in mechanized carpet-weaving and cloth-embroidering techniques.

Blackberry, marigold, safflower, zinnia, yarrow, rhubarb, rue, pot marjoram, and marguerite all produce natural dyes. So do a number of vegetables, such as artichokes, red cabbage, onions, parsley, and carrots. Herbs that you might have growing in your culinary or medicinal garden also have dyeing properties, including catnip, bay, St. John's wort, lady's mantle, cornflower, blueberry, mullein, sunflower, elderberry, and teasel. The marigolds used in dyeing fabric, however, are not the same as the ones you eat. Check the botanical index (page 295) and make sure that you are using the correct herb.

From your kitchen, onion skins, ripe strawberries, raspberries, currants, cherries, cranberries, rhubarb leaves and roots, tea leaves, turmeric, grapes, coffee granules, prickly pear, and citrus fruit peels all have dyeing properties well worth giving a try.

A note of caution: the only complicated part of the natural-herb dyeing process is using the mordant, which combines with the plant material to produce a fixed color. Mordants contain toxic metallic salts. These substances are irritating to the skin and lungs. For this reason, the equipment you use in the dyeing process—the saucepans and spoons—*must be used for nothing else.* You should also make sure to work in a well-ventilated room or outside while using these metallic salts. This could be a great activity for "dad" to get involved, so you won't expose yourself to these chemicals.

The Dyeing Process

Adding color to linen and wool with plant dyes is actually a very simple procedure involving only four basic ingredients: fabric (wool or cotton), water, mordant, and dye. Use unbleached, natural linen, cotton, or fine yarn (linen that has been bleached often has chemical residues within the fibers, which can have an effect on the dyeing process).

First, wash the material in warm water with a mild softening soap. Rinse off the excess suds; then leave in lukewarm water for 1 to 2 hours. When the water is completely cool, rinse the material off again with cold water. Set aside.

Next, prepare the herbal material. The plant parts used in the dyeing process are treated in different ways to produce their characteristic colors. Barks, nuts, twigs, roots and wood should be soaked overnight, then simmered for 30 minutes and boiled. Berries must be crushed, simmered for 30 minutes, and then allowed to ferment overnight to increase their color depth.

Blossoms that produce subtle purples, pinks, blues, and reds should be infused like teas (see basic recipe, page 27) and steeped for 30 minutes in boiling water. The oranges and yellows from tougher plants, such as calendula and zinnias, need to be simmered for 30 minutes. Leaves need to be simmered for 1 hour.

All dye mixtures should be strained of herbal pulp. The depth of a color depends on the amount of time it simmers, not the amount of water used in a recipe.

GENERAL GUIDELINES

Barks/roots	1 cup (soaked overnight and boiled for 1 hour) to 1 cup of water
Berries	1½ cups to 1 quart of water
Fresh blossoms	2 cups of herbs to 1 quart of water
Fresh leaves	Use 1 cup of herbs to 1 quart of water
Nuts/hulls	1 cup (soaked overnight) to 1 cup of water

Once the plant material is ready, you can begin the actual dyeing process.

In a large stainless-steel or enamel saucepan, mix together the mordant, herbs, and water in the following proportions:

Mordant (a choice of the following):
  Chrome (potassium dichromate): ½ teaspoon
  Alum: 1½ teaspoons with 1½ teaspoons of cream
    of tartar
  Copper (cupric sulfate): 2 teaspoons
  Tin (stannous chloride): 1 teaspoon with
    1½ teaspoons of cream of tartar
1 cup plant material
1 quart of pure distilled water

Add the fabric and bring the dye mixture to a boil. Let simmer for 15 minutes, adding more water as necessary. Then cool. Strain the liquid, and hang the fabric to dry.

Use the dye bath several times to make different shades of the same color. Do not expect to achieve the same exact color twice. Each time you dye fabric, the fibers will extract some of the dye from the bath. Other materials, such as yarn, basket splints, corn husks, egg shells, and reeds can be colored using natural herb dyes and metallic salts.

The following table lists some common herbs and mordants, as well as the color they produce in combination.

HERB/PLANT/FLOWER	MORDANT	RESULTANT COLOR
Black walnuts	None	Rich browns
Blackberry bark	Alum mordant	Lavender blues
Blueberries	Tin mordant	Blues
Cardinal flowers	Alum mordant	Rosy pink

Grapes	Alum mordant	Red/purple
Milkweed flowers	Alum mordant	Green/yellow tones
Milkweed flowers	Tin mordant	Rich mustard tones
Milkweed leaves	Tin mordant	Bright oranges
Mullein leaves	Alum mordant	Greens
Pokeberries	Vinegar	Reds
Ragweed	Alum mordant	Greens
Red cabbage	Tin mordant	Purples
Rhubarb leaves	Tin mordant	Orange
Wheatstraw	Alum mordant	Yellow
Yellow onion skins	Alum mordant	Pale yellow

Making a Crib Quilt

For one of my first dyeing projects, I made bed quilts using small squares of natural, unbleached cotton. I chose to use neutral earth tones—pale yellow (onion skins and alum), bright yellow (onion and rhubarb leaves and tin), rosy pink (blueberries and alum) and subtle greens (mullein leaves and alum). You can follow my example, or make a rainbow quilt, extracting the colors you need from the following flowers, leaves, roots, and barks.

Red	Bedstraw roots with alum mordant
Orange	Coreopsis flowers with chrome mordant
Yellow	Catnip (whole plant) with alum mordant
Green	Lily-of-the-valley leaves with alum mordant
Blue	Woad leaves with tin mordant
Indigo	Walnut skins and calendula with alum mordant
Violet	Calendula and wild oregano with alum mordant

You will achieve better colors if you dye small pieces of material together in each herb dye. Then dry and iron them and sew them together to make your quilt (or curtain or canopy). It will last through many washes and be a memorable keepsake for yourself and your baby.

Thyme for a
Few Last Words

When a woman takes care of her own body through self-love, self-respect, and the rituals of life's celebrations, she is changing and charting a new future for pregnancy health. Nothing can inspire more delight and wonder about human life than being part of the miracle of the birth of a healthy, fully formed baby emerging from its mother.

When I gave birth to Zak, my first son, I thought, Wow! How did I manage that? Everything that I had studied, learned, or read became void. I was completely flabbergasted by my achievement (albeit cesarean) of giving birth to this tiny reflection of my unconditional love and commitment. It made me feel very humble. Throughout my pregnancy, I had been given the honor and opportunity to bond my heart and soul with my baby through my own acts of self-nurture. The reward was this locked first glance—an unspoken celebration of our new lives. It was then that I knew my role was to love, protect, and guide this new life, my son. I knew that open to the right conditions and ambiance, we would both unfold and evolve. Twice more, I enjoyed the gathering of my deep-rooted wisdom and intuitive strength as Josh and Tamara were born.

Motherhood is much like childhood—it's governed by basic instinct, and there are a lot of new things to learn and adapt to. Motherhood and herbs date back to ancient times, and today we are all able to enjoy the true essence of their maternal, mystical, botanical, nutritional, cosmetic, healing, and nurturing excellence.

From my own evolution from womanhood to motherhood, I share my self-sufficiency experiences through avenues of self-nurture, diet, and herbal remedies. Through natural beauty, crafts, meditations, and relaxation, I hope to guide you through a beautiful herbal pregnancy, too.

I hope that your journey into motherhood is soothed by nature's tender healing and filled with time for reflection and with pleasure as you watch your infant grow. I hope that you allow yourself the full enjoyment of your growth, and I hope that you can enrich your pregnancy as you live in harmony with Mother Nature and allow your own natural rhythms to connect to the changing seasons. It's a process that will allow you to fully immerse in a celebration of prebirth bonding.

I have gained so much from my own experience of pregnancy and beyond. The pages of this book are brimming with ideas that collectively express my love and respect for Earth's healing pantry and pharmacy. It is with great pleasure that I share these nurturing and healing journeys with you, and hope that you, too, can find the same quality of unconditional love for life that I have.

Congratulations!

Please feel free to write to me and talk about the things you liked (or didn't) about *The Pregnancy Herbal,* and share your own journey. Just write to Jaqulene Harper-Roth, c/o Three Rivers Press, 299 Park Avenue, New York, NY 10171.

Or email me: rothbeauty@lycos.com.

Glossary

Analgesic—A substance within a specific herb that relieves pain.

Anhydrous—Lacking water.

Antacid—A compound that neutralizes stomach acids.

Antibiotic—A substance that inhibits the growth of or destroys microbes.

Antipyretic—A substance that counteracts fever.

Astringent—An ingredient that constricts or binds.

Colic—Cramping of the stomach or intestines.

Decant—To transfer liquid from one vessel to another.

Decoction—The liquid left after boiling an herb root or bark to extract its medical or cosmetic properties.

Diuretic—An agent that increases the secretion and expulsion of urine; can cause mineral depletion.

Edema—Abnormal accumulations in body cavities and connective tissues.

Emetic—A substance that induces vomiting.

Emollient—A substance that reduces irritations and inflammation.

Endometrium—The lining of the uterus that is retained if fertilization occurs.

Endorphin—A natural painkiller released by the body.

Gamete—A mature sex cell.

Hemolytic—A substance that destroys red blood cells.

Hemostatic—An agent that stops bleeding.

Homeopathy—A system of healing using potent yet harmless energies from plants as healing agents; treating the body as a whole functioning unit, promoting the natural healing processes within the body.

Hypotensive—Used to reduce blood pressure.

Laxative—A substance that stimulates bowel movement.

Lochia—The normal discharge from the uterus and vagina following childbirth.

Os—The opening to the uterus through the cervix.

Perineum—The area between the anal and vaginal opening.

Shock—Failure of the circulatory system to provide enough blood to all parts of the body.

Stimulant—A substance that increases the body's energy levels by increasing blood circulation.

Symbiotic—Beneficial association between parts, aiding and strengthening both.

Synergistic—The simultaneous action of two or more substances whose combined effect is greater than the sum of each working part alone.

Tonic—A substance that improves the functioning of a system.

Common and Botanical Names of Herbs

Alfalfa   *Medicago sativa*

Allspice   *Pimenta dioica*

Aloe vera   *Aloe*

Alum   *Alumen*

Anise   *Pimpirnella anisum*

Apple   *Pyrus malus*

Arnica   *Arnica montana*

Arrowroot   *Maranta arundinacea*

Asparagus   *Asparagus officinalis*

Avocado   *Persea*

Barley   *Hordeum*

Basil   *Ocimum basilicum*

Bee balm   *Monarda didyma*

Beet   *Beta vulgaris*

Betony   *Stachys officinalis*

Blackberry   *Rubus*

Black cohosh   *Cimicifuga racemosa*

Black elder   *Sambucus*

Blueberry   *Vaccinium corybosum*

Blue cohosh   *Caulophyllum thalictroides*

Borage   *Borago officinalis*

Burdock   *Arctium lappa*

Calendula   *Calendula officinalis*

Camphor   *Camphor carvi*

Caraway   *Carum carvi*

Carrot   *Daucus carota*

Cashew nut   *Anacardium occidentale*

Catnip   *Nepeta cataria*

Cayenne pepper   *Capsicum annuum*

Celery   *Apium graveolens*

Chamomile   *Matricaria chamomilla*

Cherry   *Prunus*

Chickweed   *Anagallis arvenis*

Chicory   *Cichorium intybus*

Chive   *Allium schoenoprasum*

Cinnamon   *Cinnamomum zeylanicum*

Clary sage   *Salvia sclarea*

Cleavers   *Galium aparine*

Clove   *Eugenia aromatica*

Coltsfoot   *Tussilago farfara*

Comfrey   *Symphytum officinale*

Cornflower   *Centaurea cyanus*

Cranberry   *Vaccinium macrocarpon*

Cucumber   *Cucumis sativus*

Currant   *Ribes rubrum*

Dandelion   *Taraxacum officinale*

Dill   *Anethum graveolens*

Echinacea   *Echinacea augustifolia*

Elder   *Sambucus candensis*

Elderberry   *Sambucus nigra*
Elecampane   *Inula helenium*
Eucalyptus   *Eucalyptus globulus*
Eyebright   *Euphrasia officinalis*
Fennel   *Foeniculum vulgare*
Fenugreek   *Trigonella foenumgraecum*
Feverfew   *Chrysanthemum parthenium*
Flaxseed   *Linum usitatissimum*
Garlic   *Allium sativum*
Geranium   *Geranium maculatum*
Ginger   *Zingiber officinale*
Ginseng   *Panax quinquefolius*
Goldenseal   *Hydrastis canadensis*
Henna   *Lawsonia alba, L. inermis*
Honeysuckle   *Lonicera japonica*
Hops   *Humulus lupulus*
Horseradish   *Armoracia lapathifolia*
Horsetail   *Equisetum hyemale*
Hyssop   *Hyssopus officinalis*
Ivy   *Hedera helix*
Juniper berries   *Juniperus communis*
Kelp   *Fucus vesticulosis*
Lavender   *Lavandula angustifolia*
Lemon   *Citrus limon*
Lemon balm   *Melissa officinalis*
Lettuce   *Lactuca sativa*
Licorice   *Glycyrrhiza glabra*
Linden   *Tilia europaea*
Linseed   *Linum utitatissimum*
Lobelia   *Lobelia inflata*
Luffa   *Luffa aegyptiaca*

Marigold (dye plant)   *Tagetes*

Marjoram   *Origanum majorana*

Marsh mallow   *Althaea officinalis*

Mint   *Mentha*

Motherwort   *Leonorus cardiaca*

Mugwort   *Artemisia vulgaris*

Mullein   *Verbascum thapsus*

Mustard   *Brassica*

Myrrh   *Commiphora myrrha*

Nasturtium   *Tropaeolum majus*

Nettle   *Urtica dioica*

Nutmeg   *Myristica fragrans*

Oak bark   *Quercus*

Onion   *Allium cepa*

Orange blossoms   *Citrus sinensis*

Orrisroot   *Iris florentinae*

Papaya   *Carica papaya*

Parsley   *Petroselinum crispum*

Pennyroyal   *Mentha pulegium*

Peppermint   *Mentha piperita*

Plantain   *Plantago major*

Potato   *Solanum tuberosum*

Primrose   *Primula*

Pumpkin seeds   *Cucurbita pepo*

Red clover   *Trifolium pratense*

Red raspberry   *Rubus idaeus*

Rice   *Oryza sativa*

Rose   *Rosa*

Rose hips   *Rosa gallica, Rosa canina*

Rosemary   *Rosmarinus officinalis*

Slippery elm   *Ulmus fulva*

Soapwort   *Saponaria officinalis*
Spearmint   *Mentha spicata*
St. John's wort   *Hypericum perforatum*
Strawberry   *Fragaria vesca*
Sunflower   *Helianthus annus*
Tansy   *Tanacetum vulgare*
Thyme   *Thymus vulgaris*
Tobacco   *Nicotiana tabacum*
Tomato   *Lycopersicon esculentum*
Violet   *Viola odorata*
Watercress   *Nasturtium officinale*
Watermelon   *Citrullus vulgaris*
White oak   *Quercus stellata*
Wild cherry   *Prunus serotina*
Wintergreen   *Gaultheria procumbens*
Witch hazel   *Hamamelis virginiana*
Woad   *Isatis tinctoria*
Yarrow   *Achillea millefolium*
Yucca root   *Yucca filamentosa*

Resources

HERBAL-HEALING BOOKS

All Women Are Healers by Diane Stein (The Crossing Press, 1997).

Changing Bodies, Changing Lives by Ruth Bell
(Vintage Books, 1988).

Earthmagic: Finding and Using Medicinal Herbs by Corinne Martin
(Countryman Press, 1991).

The Family Herbal by Barbara and Pete Theiss
(Healing Arts Press, 1993).

Herbal Healing for Women by Rosemary Gladstar
(Simon & Schuster, 1993).

Herbs for Common Ailments by Anne McIntyre
(Simon & Schuster, 1992).

The Herbs of Life by Lesley Tierra (The Crossing Press, 1992).

Natural Medicine for Women by Julian and Susan Scott
(Avon Books, 1991).

Witches, Midwives and Nurses by Barbara Ehrenreich and Deirdre
English (Feminist Press, 1973).

Women's Bodies, Women's Wisdom by Christine Northrup, M.D.
(Bantam, 1994).

PREGNANCY BOOKS

Healing Yourself During Pregnancy by Joy Gardener
(The Crossing Press, 1990).

Homeopathic Medicines for Pregnancy and Childbirth by Richard
Moskowitz, M.D. (North Atlantic, 1992).

Pregnancy Pure & Simple by Tracie Hotchner (Avon, 1995).

The Pregnant Woman's Comfort Book by Jennifer Louden
(HarperCollins, 1995).

The Wise Woman Herbal for the Childbearing Years by Susan Weed
(Ash Tree Publishing, 1986).

WILD FOOD AND EDIBLE FLOWERS COOKBOOKS

Edible Flowers by Cathy Wilkinson Barash (Fulcrum, 1993).

Flowers in the Kitchen by Susan Belisinger (Interweave, 1990).

The Self-Healing Cookbook by Kristina Turner (Earthtone, 1996).

Wild Food by Roger Phillips (Macmillian, London, 1983).

FOLKLORE WISDOM

Dooryard Herbs by Linda Ours Rago (Camp Hill, 1995).

Earth Magic by Claire Nahmad (Destiny Books, 1993).

Honeysuckle Sipping by Jeanne R. Chesanow (Down East, 1986).

In and Out of the Garden by Sara Midda (Workman, 1981).

The Symbology of Color by Ellen Conroy (Newcastle, 1996).

NATURAL BEAUTY

Beautiful Face, Beautiful Body by Jaqulene Harper-Roth
(Berkley, 2000).

Beauty to Die For—The Cosmetic Consequence by Judi Vance
(toExcel, 1999).

Positively Young Game Book by Julia M. Busch (Anti-Aging, 1993).

Skin Care Book—Simple Herbal Recipes by Kathlyn Quatrochl
(Interweave, 1997).

HERBAL NEWSLETTERS

The American Herb Association Newsletter
P.O. Box 1673
Nevada City, CA 95959

Herbal Gram
P.O. Box 201660
Austin, TX 78720

Herb Companion
201 East Fourth Street
Loveland, CO 80537

The Herb Quarterly
P.O. Box 548
Boiling Springs, PA 17007

Mother Earth News
P.O. Box 56302
Boulder, CO 80322
www.motherearthnews.com

Herbs for Health
P.O. Box 7708
Red Oak, IA 51591
www.discoverherbs.com

FRESH HERBS

The following suppliers sell wild crafted, or organically grown, custom-dried herbs that I have found to be of very good quality. Write or call for the latest catalogue.

Blessingway, 321 Anawan St., Rehoboth, MA 02769;
    (no telephone)
Dancing Bears Farm, P.O. Box 84, RFD 3, St. Johnsbury,
    VT 05819; (802) 633-4152

Jane Dicus, 4010 Marie Drive, Winston Salem, NC 27127;
(919) 788-1607

Earthstar Botanicals, 23485 Summit Rd., Los Gatos, CA 95030;
(408) 353-3923

Evening Star Herbs, Rt. 1, P.O. Box 314, Forestburg, TX 76239;
(817) 665-1619

Florida Herbals, Rt. 7, P.O. Box 1255-B, Tallahassee, FL 32308;
(904) 877-6210

Pippa Fog, 3901 Jocelyn St. NW, Washington, D.C. 20015;
(202) 363-3115

Hill Woman Productions, P.O. Box 317, Fineview, NY 13640;
(315) 482-2985

Meadowbrook Herb Garden, Rt. 138, Wyoming, RI 02898;
(401) 539-7603

Toni Miller, 135 St. Andrews, Edwardsville, IL 62025;
(618) 656-7024

Natural Products, Inc., 115 Meadowview Dr., Boone, NC 28607;
(704) 264-3752

Perry Botanicals, P.O. Box 158A, Owingsville, KY 40360;
(606) 674-2819

Ernestine Schrepfer, 1329 S, 51st Terrace, Kansas City, KS 66106;
(913) 287-2686

Shortgrass Farms, 6870 WCR5, Erie, CO 80516;
(303) 828-0239

Spring Valley Gardens, S6143M, Rt. 1, Loganville, WI 53943;
(608) 727-5397

Takeroot, 4 Blakes Dr., Pittsboro, NC 27312; (919) 496-7841

AROMATHERAPY

Aroma Vera, 5901 Rodeo Drive, Los Angeles, CA 90016;
(800) 669-9514

Aromatherapy for Kids, 18347 Sherman Way, Reseda, CA 91335;
   (800) 955-8253
The Essential Oil Company, P.O. Box 399, Weaverville, CA 96093;
   (800) 729-5912
Fragrant Earth, (800) 260-7401
Helios Essential Oils, (888) 327-9954; www.heliosoils.com
p.u.r.e. Aromatherapy Company, (937) 836-4352;
   www.purearomatherapy.com

OTHER ORGANIZATIONS

Breastfeeding National Network (24-hour help line) 800-835-5968
National Safe Kids Campaign, 11 Michigan Avenue NW,
   Washington, DC 20010
La Leche League International, Box 4079, Schaumburg, IL 60168
   (800) LALECHE; www.prairienet.org.III

HERBAL PRODUCTS

Frontier Co-op Herbs, 3027 78th St., P.O. Box 299, Norway,
   IA 52318
Earth Baby, 776-B North Highland Ave., Atlanta, GA 30306;
   www.mindspring.com/-ebaby/hom.htm
Herbs for Kids, 1340 Rufina Circle, Santa Fe, NM 87505;
   (800) 735-0299

HOMEOPATHY

American Botanical Council, P.O. Box 201660, Austin, TX 78720;
   (512) 331-8868
Boerick and Tafel, Inc., 1011 Arch St., Philadelphia, PA 19107;
   (215) 922-2967
Homeopathic Academy of Naturopathic Physicians, 4072 9th Ave., NE,
   Seattle, WA 98015; (206) 547-9665

CELLULAR HERBAL JUICES

Bio-Nutritional Products, 41 Burgen Line Ave., Westwood,
    NJ 07675; (201) 666-2300

NATIVE PLANTS

These organic sources do not collect plants from the wild. They grow all their herbs from wild seeds.

Niche Gardens, Rt. 1, P.O. Box 290, Dept. JW, Chapel Hill,
    NC 27516; (919) 967-0078

Wellsweep Herb Farm, 317 Mount Bethel Rd., Port Murray,
    NJ 07865; (no phone)

Woodlanders Inc., 1128 Colleton Ave., Aiken, SC 29801;
    (803) 648-7522

GREEN POWER JUICERS

Green Power International, 12020 Woodruff Ave., Suite C,
    Downey, CA 90241; (no phone)

GUMS AND RESINS

Colony Import & Export Corporation, 226 7th St., Garden City, NY
    11530; (516) 746-2560

BOTTLES

SKS Bottle and Packaging Inc., tel: (518) 899-7488;
    fax: (800) 810-0440; Web site: www.sks-bottle.com

Poya Naturals, e-mail: info@poyanaturals.com; Web site:
    http://members.tripod.com/aromaoils/bottles.htm

Carow Packaging and Dispensing, tel: (815) 455-4600;
    fax: (815) 455-7543

Index